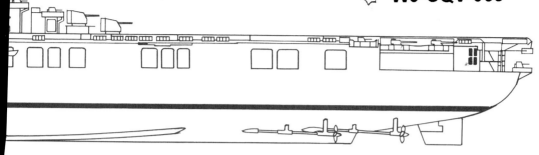

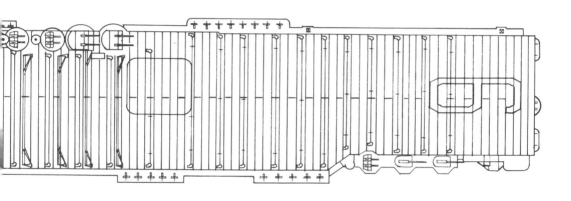

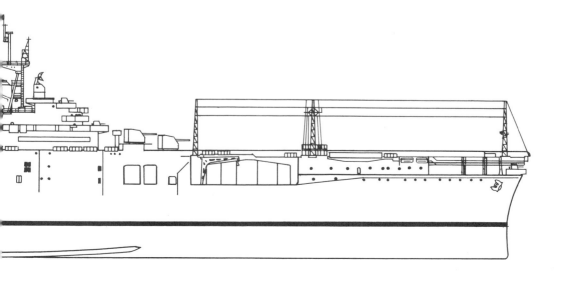

THE *ESSEX*
AIRCRAFT CARRIERS

THE *ESSEX*
AIRCRAFT CARRIERS

by ANDREW FALTUM

The Nautical & Aviation Publishing Company of America
Charleston, South Carolina

Second printing 1997

Third priniting 2000

Library of Congress Catalog Card Number 93-45533

ISBN: 1-877853-26-7

Printed in the United States of America

Library of Congress Cataloging-In-Publication Data

Faltum, Andrew, 1947-
The Essex Aircraft Carriers / by Andrew Faltum
p.   cm.
1. Aircraft Carriers—United States—History.
I. Title
V874.3.F35   1996
359.9′4835′0973—dc20
93-45533
CIP

Contents

Preface

In 1991, the *U.S.S. Lexington,* last of the *Essex* class aircraft carriers on active duty, was decommissioned. She was one of a class of twenty-four ships and her retirement marked the end of an era spanning nearly fifty years. The *Essex* class is the most significant class of warships in American naval history and it is surprising that so little has been written about them as a group. Individually, they are the subjects of some excellent books. Collectively, they deserve more attention, not only because of their numbers, but because of their role in making the aircraft carrier the backbone of the U.S. Navy. Perhaps because of their large numbers and many years of service they have been taken for granted. This book tells the story of these carriers, and is written for those interested not only in their design and structure, but in what life was like for those who served aboard them.

My own experience with the ships of the *Essex* class is rather limited, although I have been fascinated with them since I was a boy. As a teenager, I remember seeing the *Bunker Hill* in mothballs during a sightseeing boat tour of Long Beach harbor. While on active duty in the Navy, I visited the *Lexington* as an Aviation Officer Candidate at Pensacola, Florida. My only other encounter occurred in 1975 during my service aboard the carrier *Midway* as a squadron intelligence officer. While transiting the San Bernardino Straits in the Philippines, the *Hancock* used our deck to carrier qualify her air wing. It was a beautiful day and I went up to "vultures row" in the island to watch. The sight of the *Hancock* in the distance made me think of World War II and the great naval battles fought in those historic waters. I remember each of these occasions vividly because of the sense of history these ships conveyed.

I have tried to avoid technical explanations so that the average reader is not weighed down by jargon. At the same time, I feel that a description of how such a complex thing as an aircraft carrier works can be fascinating to someone who has never experienced

1

life aboard a carrier. If I am successful in conveying a little of this to the reader, I am thankful. For those with no military experience, some explanation of the conventions used in this book are in order. Dates and times are given in military fashion, that is 31 January 1942, rather than January 31, 1942, and 1300 instead of 1:00 p.m. All distances are in nautical miles unless stated otherwise. Although some sources consider the "long hull" ships as a separate *Ticonderoga* class and the surviving ships have often been referred to as the *Oriskany/Hancock* class, I have included them all under the term "*Essex* class carriers." Finally, I would like to point out that this book is a compilation from many sources, some with conflicting information. I have tried to resolve these issues whenever possible and any errors in judgment are ultimately mine.

In the course of writing this book, I have met many people who either served aboard an *Essex* class carrier or had some other experience with them. I hope they enjoy this book and perhaps find out more about these ships.

Introduction

To understand the *Essex* class carriers' design, it is necessary to first look at how the aircraft carrier evolved and how naval aviation developed in the years following World War I. The aircraft carrier evolved along with changes in the naval doctrine of the time and, as different navies came to have different views on the role aircraft would play in their naval strategies, the ships they designed came to reflect those differences in strategy and tactics. A few naval officers envisioned a role for aircraft in naval operations as early as 1909 when American, British, and French naval officers witnessed aircraft performing unheard of feats such as 112-mile non-stop flights at the international air show in Rheims, France in August of that year. Later, on 14 November 1910, civilian pilot Eugene Ely became the first to fly an airplane successfully from the deck of a ship. Using a Curtiss biplane, Ely took off from a makeshift flight deck on the *Birmingham*, a U.S. Navy cruiser at anchor in the waters of Hampton Roads, Virginia.

Two months later, Ely became the first to land an aircraft on a ship when he landed aboard another cruiser, the *Pennsylvania*, after a flight over San Francisco Bay. Using sandbags and ropes as makeshift arresting gear, Ely managed to safely land on a wooden platform erected over the *Pennsylvania*'s stern.

As a result of Ely's pioneering flights, the world's navies sought a means of taking aircraft to sea, and soon regarded the seaplane as the logical choice. In World War I, the British realized that seaplanes lacked the performance needed and began experimenting with wheeled aircraft. By the end of the war the British developed an aircraft-carrying ship with an offensive strike capability, but never got the opportunity to prove its full potential. Only after the war did Britain, the United States, and Japan develop true aircraft carriers.

The 1920s and 1930s were a dynamic time with governments swept up in a rising tide of public sentiment for disarmament. At the same time, advocates of air power struggled with conservative leaders within both the Army and the Navy. Ironically, this sentiment for disarmament would figure in the birth of the aircraft carrier. In 1920 the U.S. Senate rejected the Treaty of Versailles and the League of Nations, partly out of disagreement with President Woodrow Wilson, and partly out of a growing disillusionment with America's participation in World War I. Armaments, particularly highly visible and expensive symbols of military and naval might such as the dreadnought battleships, were now unaffordable. The time was right for change.

In 1916, on the eve of war, Congress had passed an act which would have resulted in a navy equal to any other two world navies had it been carried out. But in November 1921, the Washington Naval Arms Limitation Conference opened with an American offer to scrap tons of ships then under construction. Great Britain, the United States, Japan, France, and Italy were the major players in the conference. The treaties signed in February 1922 established the famous 5:5:3 tonnage ratio between the U.S., Great Britain, and Japan for battleships and aircraft carriers (Italy and France each getting a 1 3/4 ratio), a ten-year holiday on building capital ships, and a restriction on individual battleships of no more than 35,000 tons. The *Lexington* and *Saratoga,* originally part of a class of battle cruisers then under construction, could be completed as carriers, although at 33,000 tons, both exceeded the 27,000 ton limit. The total tonnage allowed in the U.S. for aircraft carrier construction was 135,000 tons.

While governments struggled with disarmament, the military services struggled to define the proper role of aviation. Some advocates of "air power" saw all other forms of warfare as obsolete. The Army Air Corps' chief prophet of air power, General Billy Mitchell, went so far as to declare all surface ships obsolete and felt he had demonstrated this in the famous battleship bombing tests of 1921. The battleship-dominated Navy felt the tests proved nothing since the ships were at anchor, not manned and fighting back. But the criticisms did have a positive effect. Faced with claims that all aviation should be brought under a unified air force as a separate service co-equal with the Army and Navy, the naval leadership began to pay more attention to aviation within the Navy itself, although Naval Aviation's role was seen primarily by the "battleship" navy as the "eyes of the fleet."

As a result of the Battle of Jutland in World War I, even the "battleship navy" realized the need for better reconnaissance and saw aircraft as a potential solution. This role had been filled by the cruiser, which was large enough to act independently when needed, but capable of playing a scouting role in a major fleet engagement. The "battle cruiser" concept envisioned a ship as heavily armed as a regular cruiser, but lightly armored and fast enough to stay out of harm's way in a major fleet engagement. Jutland discredited the "battle cruiser" idea as these thin-skinned ships proved unable to stand up to major caliber gunfire. The aircraft carrier was then seen as primarily a replacement for the cruiser in the scouting role. Only a few visionaries within the Navy foresaw an offensive role for the aircraft carrier, a role which the British pioneered during World War I.

In 1919, the Navy had ordered the conversion of the collier *Jupiter* to an experimental aircraft carrier. A few years later, partly in response to Mitchell's challenge and partly in response to air power advocates within the Navy itself, the Navy began to devote more efforts to expanding its aviation capabilities. The Bureau of Aeronautics was created in August 1921 followed by the addition of an Assistant Secretary of the Navy for Air.

On 7 April 1922 the *U.S.S. Langley,* named for early aviation pioneer Samuel P. Langley, received its commission as CV-1, the U.S. Navy's first "flattop." The "C" indicated a carrier and the "V" was an arbitrarily chosen letter representing heavier-than-air aircraft. While her ungainly appearance earned her the nickname "The Covered Wagon," she pioneered many aspects of carrier aviation that later became standard features of all carriers such as the arresting gear that used hooks on the tails of airplanes to engage cables strung across the flight deck and attached to a braking system. As the *Lexington* and *Saratoga* neared completion, the *Langley* and her aviators developed the methods, tactics, and doctrine that all future carriers would follow.

Beginning in 1923 with the *Langley,* aircraft carriers participated in annual fleet problems, with the *Lexington* and *Saratoga* joining in fleet exercises from 1929 onward. Commissioned late in 1927, the *Lexington* and *Saratoga* were the largest carriers in existence.[1] Their 180,000 shaft horse power (SHP) turbo-electric drive propulsion plants gave them high sustained speed (33 knots), and their size (888 feet overall length) allowed 90 aircraft to be carried. They were armed with eight 8-inch guns (the largest armament allowed under the Washington Naval Treaty) mounted in four twin turrets fore and aft of the large island structure, and 12 5-inch guns along the edge of the flight deck, three at each quarter. As the first real American aircraft carriers, the *Lexington* and *Saratoga* pioneered the use of aircraft carriers in an offensive role. During Fleet Problem IX in 1929, the *Saratoga* successfully "attacked" the Panama Canal. Three years later, the *Lexington* and *Saratoga* launched a highly successful surprise Sunday morning mock attack on Pearl Harbor—a fact not lost on the Japanese.

In 1927 President Coolidge, irritated that the second Naval Limitation Conference in Geneva could not get further cuts, urged Congress to pass legislation to bring the U.S. to parity with the British. The "cruiser bill" finally passed in 1928 and included provision for one aircraft carrier.[2] The *Ranger,* the first American ship built as an aircraft carrier from the keel up, was the result. In designing the *Ranger,* the Navy wanted the greatest aircraft carrying capacity possible for a given hull size. Based on tonnage allowed, the Navy decided to build five medium-size carriers rather than only four or fewer larger ones. With a standard displacement of 14,500 tons and a length of 769 feet overall, the *Ranger* was too small to be a really satisfactory fleet carrier. Although she could carry 86 aircraft, her lack of speed and protection limited her practical usefulness. Because of her size, she had difficulty operating in heavy seas, reducing her capability even more. The *Ranger* had features considered desirable at the time, but did not prove practical. To keep the flight deck as clear as possible, three folding funnels on each side could be swung out of the way during flight operations. Originally intended to be a flush deck design, she was given a small island instead. And though she played a role in the Atlantic during the early part of World War II, she was not suitable for fast carrier operations and was soon relegated to training duties.[3]

Coolidge was succeeded as president by Herbert Hoover, a Quaker and pacifist who trusted the Kellogg-Briand treaty which "outlawed" war to keep the peace.[4] Not one naval ship was laid down during the Hoover administration.[5] The rest of the world, however, was not so pacifistic. Aggressive dictatorships in Germany, Italy, and Japan would ultimately drag the rest of the world into war. In 1931, in the first move of a series of aggressive acts that would lead to war, the Japanese Kwantung Army moved into Manchuria. When the League of Nations commission condemned Japan, she withdrew from the League and announced that her part in the naval treaties would end in 1936.

In the late 1930s, with naval disarmament coming apart at the seams, the Japanese continued their aggression in Asia.[6] In 1937, in the midst of a full-scale attack on China itself, Japanese aircraft attacked and sank the U.S. gunboat *Panay* in the infamous "China Incident." Many in the Navy viewed Japan as the principal potential adversary and saw a war in the Pacific against Japan as inevitable.

Franklin D. Roosevelt, a former Assistant Secretary of the Navy in World War I, assumed the presidency in 1933. He was not only an advocate of sea power, but of air power as well. *Yorktown* and *Enterprise* were part of the National Industrial Recovery Act of

1933 which aimed to create employment. The Vinson-Trammel Act of 1934 provided for an eight-year replacement program which would need ten years to attain "treaty strength."[7] The *Yorktown* class applied the lessons learned by practical experience with the *Lexington* and *Saratoga* and the design proved large enough to be useful in carrier operations, with a good blend of size, speed, and aircraft carrying capacity. The *Yorktown* and *Enterprise* were laid down in 1934 and commissioned in 1937 and 1938, respectively. At 19,900 tons and 769 feet overall length, they could operate 100 aircraft. Both had eight 5-inch guns (two at each quarter along the flight deck edge), underwater protection against torpedoes, and protective decks over the machinery spaces. They were a highly successful design and formed the basis of what would become the *Essex* class.[8]

The *Wasp* was laid down in 1936 and commissioned in 1939. At 14,700 tons, she used the remaining tonnage allowed under treaty. Although similar in appearance to the *Yorktown* class, she suffered many of the same shortcomings as the *Ranger* such as lack of speed. She was the first carrier to use a deck edge aircraft elevator. The deck edge elevator allowed more flexibility in handling aircraft on the hangar deck than conventional elevators and, due to its success on the *Wasp*, was incorporated into the design for the *Essex*.[9]

In May 1938, a 20 percent expansion program of the Vinson-Trammel Act added 40,000 tons to the original treaty limit of 135,000. This allowed for the construction of two 20,000 ton carriers. Because of the urgent need for aircraft carriers, the *Hornet* was built to the *Yorktown* class design, although with some changes and slightly greater displacement. The *Hornet* was the last carrier to be finished before the outbreak of war. The other carrier, CV-9, became the *Essex*.[10]

British Aircraft Carriers

Through a series of half measures and wartime expedients, the British had invented the aircraft carrier by the end of World War I. The failure of the battle cruisers at the Battle of Jutland in 1916 stood in stark contrast to the potential shown by a lone seaplane participating in that battle. Although this incident showed the usefulness of aircraft in the scouting role, seaplanes could only land on calm water and their pontoons made them too sluggish to be capable of intercepting Zeppelins, the land-based airships that acted as the eyes of the German fleet. Early in 1916, before the Battle of Jutland, the British experimented with wheeled planes landing on 200-foot platforms roughly the width of a cruiser. About the same time came a design for a ship that could accommodate aircraft on landing as well on take off. Based on an unfinished ocean liner, the ship would eventually be finished as the *Argus*.

Meanwhile, the Royal Navy tried various improvisations. They launched land planes from platforms built on seaplane tenders or cruiser turrets, and took off from towed barges. Another interim solution was the *Furious*, which joined the fleet in 1917. The *Furious* was a 30-knot light battle cruiser which had a taking off deck built forward and later, a landing deck aft. The currents around the existing superstructure, however, made landing extremely dangerous. Even so, the *Furious* success-

fully attacked the Zeppelin base at Tondern in northern Germany in July 1917. The attack showed that aircraft carriers could fill an attack role as well as reconnaissance, although the returning aircraft had to ditch at sea or fly on to neutral Holland and internment.[11] The *Argus* was to make aerial torpedo attacks against the German fleet at its anchorage in Germany, but the war ended before she finished her trials.

With the Armistice, the Royal Navy had the only aircraft carrier in the world, with two more, the *Eagle* and *Hermes* under construction. The *Eagle* was begun as a dreadnought battleship and converted to an aircraft carrier. Completed for trials in 1920, she went into full service in 1923. The *Hermes* was the first British carrier built from the keel up. Laid down in 1918, she was launched in 1919 and completed in 1923. The *Furious*, a monstrosity that was an aircraft carrier at both ends and a cruiser in the middle, was fully converted to an aircraft carrier in 1921-25. Two more light battle cruisers, the *Courageous* and *Glorious* began conversion to aircraft carriers in 1924 and were completed in 1928 and 1930 In 1935 the keel was laid for the most famous British aircraft carrier of all, the *Ark Royal*. In a sense the first modern British aircraft carrier, the *Ark Royal* displaced 22,000 tons and carried between 60 and 72 aircraft. Launched in 1937 and completed in 1938, she had a spectacular wartime career until sunk by a German submarine in 1941.[12]

After an early lead, British carrier aviation development stagnated, partly because of the dominance of battleship proponents within the Royal Navy, and partly because of the merging of the Royal Naval Air Service with the Royal

Flying Corps in 1918 to form the Royal Air Force. The Royal Air Force gave little priority to the development of naval aviation and the Royal Navy did not regain control of its air arm until 1937. Although the Royal Navy continued to design and build aircraft carriers, the aircraft could never compete with their land-based contemporaries on anything approaching equal footing.

The *Ark Royal* was the last British aircraft carrier finished before the outbreak of war in 1939; she was also the last British aircraft carrier without an armored flight deck. The *Illustrious* class followed the *Ark Royal* and entered service in 1940. Although slightly larger than the *Yorktown* class at 23,000 tons and 753 feet overall length, they could only carry 36 aircraft. The *Formidable, Victorious,* and *Indomitable* followed the *Illustrious,* as did a modified design which was slightly longer at 766 feet, but had the same displacement. The *Implacable* and *Indefatigable,* completed in 1944, could carry up to 72 aircraft.

Despite the obsolescence of their aircraft, British aircraft carriers scored several notable successes. Perhaps the most remembered was the attack on the Italian fleet at Taranto. On 11 November 1940, a dozen Fairy Swordfish biplane torpedo bombers flew off the deck of the *Illustrious* toward the Italian mainland 170 miles away. Despite intense antiaircraft fire, the attacking aircraft pressed home their attacks, disabling three battleships, a cruiser, and two destroyers. In one stroke, the British had disabled half of the Italian fleet and caused a shift in the balance of naval power in the Mediterranean at a critical point in the war. A more convincing demonstration of the potential of carrier striking power could hardly be imagined.

Japanese Aircraft Carriers

The Japanese were the first to build an aircraft carrier from the keel up, the 7,400-ton *Hosho,* laid down in 1919.[13] The first effective Japanese carriers were the *Akagi* and *Kaga,* which like the *Lexington* and *Saratoga* were ex-capital ships converted from battle cruiser hulls as a result of the Washington Naval Treaty.[14] As built, both the *Akagi* and the *Kaga* displaced 29,600 tons. Neither of these ships was completely successful and in 1934-38 both were reconstructed, raising their capacity to 90 aircraft. Since the Washington Naval Treaty limited Japan to 80,000 tons of aircraft carriers, but did not restrict carriers under 10,000 tons, the Japanese built the smaller *Ryujo.* All the Japanese carriers displaced more than their announced tonnage, and although listed as 7,100 tons, she actually displaced 10,600 tons. The *Ryujo* underwent extensive modification to improve her stability in 1934 and two years later her forecastle was built up to improve her seaworthiness. The *Ryujo* could carry 48 aircraft. Japan rectified the mistakes of the *Ryujo* when the 15,900 ton *Soryu* was ordered in 1934. The *Soryu*'s sister, the *Hiryu,* had a slightly broader hull and displaced 17,300 tons. Like the *Akagi,* the *Hiryu* had her island on the port side. The theory was that two sister ships could operate without their aircraft traffic patterns interfering with each other. Unfortunately, the exhaust stacks on both ships were on the starboard side, forcing pilots to contend with two areas of turbulence. This proved so dangerous that the port side island design was not repeated again.

After the abrogation of the international treaties, the Japanese were free to build the carriers they wanted. The 25,000 ton *Shokaku* and *Zuikaku* were ordered in 1937-38 and finished three months before the start of the war. These ships were an excellent balance of aircraft capacity (84), speed and defensive armament, and were the most comparable of all Japanese carriers to the *Essex* class. They were the last fleet carriers finished before the outbreak of war and their availability was one of the planning factors in the decision to attack Pearl Harbor.

Like the American and British navies, the battleship had dominated Japanese naval doctrine. If the British had Jutland to ponder, the Japanese remembered how the Combined Fleet had defeated the Russians in 1905 at the Battle of Tsushima. A few individuals did realize the potential of the "koku bokan" (aircraft carriers, literally moth-er ships for aircraft). One of these was Admiral Isoroku Yamamoto, who assumed command of the Combined Fleet in 1939. Yamamoto had fought as an ensign at the Battle of Tsushima and had studied at Harvard after World War I. By the time he had served as a naval attaché in Washington, he had developed an interest in aviation. As Japan became embroiled in the conquest of China, Yamamoto believed that war with the United States should be avoided. In his view, if war were inevitable, it must begin with a quick and decisive blow at the American fleet—a blow delivered by carrier aircraft. By the time of the Pearl Harbor attack, Japanese navy fliers had several invaluable years of combat experience in China and had perfected their carrier tactics.

Chapter 1
Designing the Breed

On 31 December 1942, the *U.S.S. Essex* was commissioned at the Norfolk Navy Yard. She was the first of a class of ships that became the most significant in American naval history. Her captain, Donald B. "Wu" Duncan, an early Naval Aviator, earned his wings in 1921 at the age of 24. Duncan was both an expert aviator and a superb ship handler. Respected for his keen mind and administrative sense, he had played a significant role in planning for the daring Doolittle raid on Tokyo earlier that year. Addressing his crew, he prophesied: "It is my intention and expectation that between us, we shall make the name of *Essex* carry fear and destruction to our enemies, with praise to our friends and be an everlasting credit to our country and flag."[1] The *Essex* and her sister ships more than lived up to that prophesy. The arrival of the *Essex* class marked both the culmination of a long period in the development of the aircraft carrier, and the beginning of a new era in naval power, one based on powerful carrier task forces.

The *Essex* class began in 1939 with a plan to build a single ship. The design would absorb the remaining tonnage available under an expansion program of May 1938, which had also provided for construction of the *Hornet*. Although designed after the lifting of treaty limitations, the *Essex* class was developed from the earlier treaty-bound *Yorktown* class. As a result, the *Essex* class was a half-way design which started where the *Hornet* left off.

Designing any ship is a series of compromises; it is a metal construction that must have as strong and efficient a structure as possible, yet it must move on the sea and therefore have inherent qualities of buoyancy and stability. In a merchant vessel, power, size, and capacity are combined so the ship can be operated profitably. A warship designer faces many of the same challenges but must meet even more stringent demands, balancing the qualities of armament, protection, seaworthiness, maneuverability, speed, endurance, and habitability. While a 10,000 ton merchant ship may operate at a speed of 18-20 knots and need a 10,000 shaft horse power (SHP) propulsion plant, a cruiser of 10,000 tons would operate at a top speed of 33-34 knots and would call for a 80-100,000 SHP plant. Further, warships must be more survivable than merchantmen. While merchant ships may have large internal spaces to provide cargo holds, warships are divided into many compartments to limit flooding in case of battle damage.

Before World War II, the design process for U.S. Navy warships involved several stages that often took years to complete. After the Secretary of the Navy approved a new ship or class of ship, the General Board described the major features of the design and distributed them to the Bureaus of Construction and Repair (C&R), Engineering (BuEng), Ordnance (BuOrd), Navigation (BuNav), and Aeronautics (BuAer) through the Chief of Naval Operations.[2] Construction and Repair was responsible for ship design, but Engineering designed machinery and radios. Weapons, including bombs and torpedoes, were the responsibility of Ordnance. The Bureau of Aeronautics, unlike the other bureaus in that it had a lot of authority over operational doctrine and personnel assignments, had the responsibility for the development of aircraft- and aviation-related ship equipment such as catapults and arresting gear. The General Board was composed primarily of senior officers with varied backgrounds. Since it was the principal advisory body consulted by the Secretary of the Navy and coordinated across bureau lines, its role in long-range planning and influence on ship design were considerable.[3] Preliminary Design, a branch of C&R and later

the Bureau of Ships (BuShips), had responsibility for the initial concept of the carrier.[4] However, many changes occurred between that stage and later stages such as the detailed contract design and the subsequent development, often at the shipyard, of working drawings.

Aircraft carriers pose problems even beyond those of ordinary warship design. Orthodox warships, where the weight and location of various components, such as armament, armor, etc., are the prime considerations, are "weight critical" designs. Aircraft carriers, on the other hand, are "volume critical" since the essential components, gasoline, magazines, hangar space, and even the aircraft, are relatively light for their volume. The primary driving factor of carrier design is the number and size of the aircraft carried, driven in turn by the doctrine of the navy designing the aircraft carrier.[5] In U.S. carrier doctrine, offensive capability takes precedence over defensive qualities. The ability to operate large air groups effectively is therefore more important than passive armor protection. A carrier's aircraft are both the principal means of offense and defense and any enemy aircraft that get through still have to face the carrier's antiaircraft fire. Armor and water-tight subdivision protect the ship's vital areas to ensure survival against all except the severest attacks. In contrast to British practice, where the flight deck is the main strength deck and the sides of the ship are an integral part of the structure all the way up to the flight deck, U.S. carriers have their hangar decks as the main strength deck with the flight deck several levels above. The sides of the hangar, although capable of being closed off by light steel roller doors, are largely open so that aircraft can warm up on the hangar deck. This allows aircraft to be brought up to the flight deck and launched quickly. Armored flight decks place a great deal of weight high up in the ship's structure, resulting in greater weight of supporting structure and an increase in beam to ensure stability. For a carrier of a given displacement, this translates to less aircraft carrying capacity. The British *Illustrious* class, for example, could carry only 36 aircraft in her hangar, while U.S. prewar doctrine called for the accommodation of 72 aircraft.

Because of treaty restrictions on prewar aircraft carrier displacement, aircraft carrying capacity was limited by hull size, which determined the length and area of the flight deck. Another factor was the size and weight of the individual aircraft: newer aircraft tended to be larger and heavier, calling for larger and stronger flight deck structures. The number and location of the aircraft elevators affected flight deck operations as well as plane handling on the hangar deck, since the elevator pits became unusable space when the elevators were in the up position. The amount of aviation gasoline called for and the numbers and types of spare parts also had to be included in the design considerations.

By 1939, the *Yorktown* class, which originally carried 90 aircraft, could only carry 81 of the newer and larger aircraft then in service. It became clear that the only way to accommodate newer aircraft on a ship of the available 20,400 tons was to reduce those areas on the flight deck otherwise lost to cutouts for antiaircraft guns and to the island structure itself. In 1938, Preliminary Design had experimented with deck-mounted

5-inch guns in an aborted design for a 10,000 ton carrier, and later proposed the elimination of the starboard deck level guns in favor of enclosed mounts superimposed on the island. The new 5"/38 dual purpose gun, scheduled to replace the older 5"/25 weapons, was thought to be the best heavy weapon for aircraft carriers. The design retained the port side gallery deck level guns of the *Yorktown* because of the restriction against firing across aircraft on the flight deck when under enemy attack.[6] The new layout allowed the firing of eight weapons on either beam, since it was believed that the two superfiring twin mounts on the island could fire across the flight deck. There were two gun directors, one at each end of the island, to control the 5-inch guns. Further reduction in the island structure came from moving the aircrew ready rooms, part of the island on the *Yorktown* design, to the gallery deck immediately below the flight deck.

While the 5-inch gun was considered useful against level and torpedo bombers, automatic weapons could best counter dive bombing aircraft. The design included four 1.1-inch "Chicago piano" machine cannons, as in the *Yorktown* design, one near each pair of the twin 5-inch mounts on the island and one near each pair of single 5-inch mounts to port. Considerable discussion on the merits of the .50 caliber machine gun as an antiaircraft weapon took place, with estimates on the number of these weapons ranging anywhere from 10 to 40.

These features were characteristic of all the variants developed for the basic CV9 design. Eventually several different designs emerged, with suffix designations A through G. As requirements grew, the displacement needed to accommodate them also grew from the original 20,400 tons of 1939. Besides increased aircraft carrying capacity, the designs stressed increased efficiency and survivability of the propulsion plant. The *Hornet*'s 120,000 SHP was now considered obsolete; it did not operate at high pressure steam conditions nor did it incorporate alternating engine and boiler rooms for survivability. Unfortunately, the change meant an increase in the design displacement because of the additional machinery space needed. The ability to operate at high astern speeds was another requirement the design had to meet. This allowed aircraft to launch over the stern and recover over the bow in an emergency, so flight operations could continue despite battle damage to an unarmored flight deck. Although other carriers had arresting gear forward, the *Essex* class was the first U.S. carrier design where high astern speed was a major design consideration and early units of the class featured arresting gear on the forward flight deck.[7] Turbo-electric drive, capable of generating full power astern and superior in terms of battle damage control, was considered as an alternative to conventional geared turbines because of the great strain sustained high astern speed placed on any geared turbine system. Turbo-electric drive, however, weighed more for a given shaft horse power than a comparable geared unit. A 170,000 SHP turbo-electric drive propulsion plant was considered for design CV9-A and compared with design CV9-B, a geared turbine plant of similar power. Design CV9-C was a 120,000 SHP turbo-electric design which was compared to design CV9-D, a 120,000 SHP geared design.

These comparisons eventually led to the adoption of a geared turbine power plant based on that developed for the *Atlanta* class light antiaircraft cruisers. Two of the 75,000 SHP plants could be paired for a total of 150,000 SHP. This arrangement had the most efficient use of space and also the best watertight subdivision. Speed ahead was 34 knots and astern speed was limited to 20 knots for up to one hour. This plant was included in design CV9-E, which the General Board selected for further development. As an alternative for further discussion, design CV9-F was drawn up with a different armor arrangement. Design CV9-G incorporated an armored flight deck, but no hangar deck armor.

Armor protection for the new design required a balance among competing requirements: the protection of vital components against shellfire from attacking surface vessels, underwater threats such as mines and torpedoes, and aerial bombs dropped by attacking aircraft. Earlier carrier designs assumed that an aircraft carrier operating independently with her escorts could encounter an enemy cruiser force and, as in the *Yorktown* design, protection against the 6-inch fire of light cruisers was specified. This called for 4-inch thick side armor and 1.7-inch thick deck armor for a 60-degree target angle. This in itself was a compromise, since encounters with heavy cruisers operating independently would be more likely. Protection against 8-inch gunfire, however, would require much more armor at similar ranges. Underwater protection was somewhat improved over previous designs, with torpedo protection limited to that adequate to defeat 500 pounds of TNT. Protection against bomb damage, however, prompted the most discussion. Design CV9-E featured a 2.5-inch thick armored fourth deck, which combined with the side protection provided protection against shellfire. CV9-F featured a combination of 1.5-inch thick armor on the fourth deck and a 2.5-inch thick armored hangar deck. Numerous design problems in CV9-G, the armored flight deck variant, led to its ultimate rejection.[8] The choices boiled down to CV9-E, which protected only against shellfire and CV9-F, which protected against some bomb effects but at the expense of some protection against shells, some increase in size, and some decrease in speed.

Initially, the design was to accommodate a fifth squadron in order to increase the fighter complement, but as larger aircraft came into service, this requirement was dropped and the number of spare disassembled aircraft reduced. The new generation of aircraft required more aviation gasoline and so tanks, surrounded by voids, had to be provided for within the armored box in the hull, which included the machinery and magazines.[9]

On 31 January 1940, the General Board submitted characteristics to the Secretary of the Navy reflecting the main features of design CV9-F. These met with final approval on 21 February. The design called for a hangar deck of 2.5-inch thick Special Treatment Steel (STS), which provided not only armor protection, but had excellent structural properties as well. A 2.5-inch STS hangar deck provided protection against a 1,000-pound demolition bomb dropped from 10,000 feet. The fourth deck, protected by 1.5-inch STS, contributed to the 4-inch side protection against shellfire as well as providing an additional

barrier against any bombs which might penetrate the hangar deck. The hangar deck armor did not contribute to the protection against shellfire for the vital areas of the ship because the relatively thin side plating above the armor belt left the sides essentially open.

This increase of 6,500 tons over the *Hornet* gained a number of improvements, including a larger flight deck (at least 850 by 80 feet) equipped with two flush-deck catapults, with a third double-action type athwartships on the hangar deck. The hangar deck catapult had one track to port and one track to starboard, enabling the launch of aircraft in either direction. Ramps allowed planes to move over it, as the hangar deck was the main strength deck and could not be cut. Increased subdivision greatly increased survivability, as did the armored hangar deck, the split power plant (which would allow it to survive the effects of one hit), a triple bottom hull for protection against magnetic mines, and an effective side protection system with a 4-inch armor belt. There was also an increase in propulsive power, four more 5-inch guns, and a 25 percent increase in aviation gasoline storage. Later design changes and increased armor protection for internal components helped raise the displacement to its final contract design figure of 27,100 tons.

But one serious flaw in the design remained. In seeking to have as few openings in the armored hangar deck as possible, a large portion of the ventilation air had to be taken into the ship at the ends beyond the 2.5-inch deck. In combat, this long single trunk on the second deck acted as a conduit for asphyxiating smoke and burning gas. It had disastrous effects on the *Franklin* and was eliminated in later ships; the early units were modified during their postwar modernization. Combat experience also showed the vulnerability of the spaces on the gallery deck just below the flight deck. Ironically, this was the location of both the aircrew ready rooms and the Combat Information Center. Later design modifications moved these vital spaces under the armored fourth deck.

In August 1940, a study of the Panama Canal locks indicated that an overall width of 113 feet 2 inches could be passed over the lock walls, which allowed a maximum flight deck width of 109 feet (94 feet abeam the 5-inch gun houses). The specified flight deck length could also be exceeded to 862 feet plus 4-foot-9-inch curved ramps ("round downs") at each end. The flight deck was served by three elevators, as in the *Yorktown* design. Heavier new aircraft needed a more powerful catapult, which required the extension of the port track of the double action hangar deck catapult over the side of the ship onto a port side sponson and then onto a hinged sponson beyond. The starboard track also had a hinged sponson on the starboard side. The elimination of the port side catapult compensated for the additional weight, and the hydraulic pumping capacity of the starboard catapult doubled to provide the same rate of launch. The amidships elevator, which caused difficulties in structural design since its pit cut into the main strength deck, was eliminated at this time after favorable reports on the performance of the deck edge elevator of the *Wasp* made such an installation acceptable.[10]

Other features were proposed by BuAer based on experience gained in earlier carriers and were intended to optimize the design for the primary mission of flying and servicing aircraft. Unlike previous designs, the *Essex* flight deck had a rectangular outline. This was because of the persistence of an experienced carrier aviator, Lieutenant Commander James Russell, who was assigned as the carrier desk officer of the BuAer Ship Installations Division. When the BuShips design officer wanted to narrow the deck as it went forward because a rectangular overhang would be vulnerable to damage in very heavy seas, Russell said, "Well, we don't want that; we want to carry the maximum width of the flight deck right up to the bow, because when you're taking off the point of maximum error is right at the bow, and if you narrow the flight deck there you're giving the aviator less chance to make a successful takeoff."[11]

Particular attention was also paid to the location and layout of the aircrew ready rooms. Torpedo planes were usually spotted farthest aft, the bombers ahead of them, and the fighters forward. The ready rooms were located accordingly to allow easy access to aircraft on the flight deck. The ready rooms were air conditioned and equipped with reclining seats to keep crews comfortable during long alerts in full flight gear. Each seat had a locker beneath it with a combination lock so that confidential code books could be secured. A blackboard at the front of the room and a teletype operated from air plot provided navigation information.

Since the high-test aviation gasoline used aboard carriers presented a serious fire hazard, extraordinary safety measures were undertaken. Gasoline was carried in saddle tanks. A saddle tank was built with a central roughly cylindrical tank, surrounded by a saddle, which was surrounded by another saddle. Air and gasoline were prevented from being in the same tank together. As gasoline was used, sea water displaced it. The gasoline was pumped from the outer saddle tanks first, so that as gasoline was used the inner tanks would be surrounded by a blanket of sea water. The gasoline tanks were kept at a minimum level to prevent sea water from mixing in with the gasoline and all fuel was carefully filtered as it passed through the outlet. The entire vertical trunk, with its pumps and piping, was protected by armor. Electrical motors drove the pumps through stuffing boxes in bulkheads to prevent any electrical sparks and the whole trunk containing the aviation fuel system could be flooded with inert carbon dioxide (CO_2) gas. When aircraft refueling was completed, sea water was pumped out at the bottom so fuel would drain back down into the system. In addition, extensive fire fighting equipment was provided. There were foam, fog, and salt water fire hoses on the flight deck and other decks. Conflagration stations in each hangar bay, in cubicles with thick glass ports, controlled the overhead sprinkling system. The magazines were floodable, either by sprinkling or flooding.

All these safety features of the *Essex* design were complemented by extensive training in damage control and fire fighting and by proper ship handling techniques. In a combat zone, if a carrier was on fire, carrier skippers were advised to put their ships in a tight starboard turn. As the ship listed outboard, any flaming gasoline would be carried over the port side, away from the more valuable parts of the ship. Normally, two cruisers would be paired off with each carrier, one to go to the aid of the carrier with fire hoses and repair parties, and the other to take her under tow if needed.

Armament changes occurred as well. The original four quad 1.1-inch machine cannon mounts were increased to six by adding two more mounts to the island. A decrease to eight .50 caliber machine guns, all of them on the island, compensated for the weight. In August 1941, the 40mm Bofors and the 20mm Oerlikon replaced the 1.1-inch machine cannon and the .50 caliber machine gun throughout the fleet. On a ship the size of an aircraft carrier, a quad 40mm Bofors could be substituted for the 1.1-inch mount and by the time the first ships neared completion, a quad mount had been added to the bow under the overhang of the flight deck and another on a sponson offset slightly to port on the stern. The 20mm Oerlikon mounts had increased to 44 single mounts, with six located outboard the island on the first level above the flight deck. The rest were on walkways 4.5 feet below the flight deck on removeable platforms that allowed passage through the Panama Canal locks. Even before completion of the first ships, two more had been added.

America's entry into the war meant a need for even more antiaircraft fire power. Proposed changes included an additional quad 40mm at bow and stern in redesigned structures, a shorter flight deck to allow the bow and stern 40mm guns a greater arc of fire, and a third 5-inch gun director. Other improvements included a second flight deck catapult and relocation of the Combat Information Center (CIC) and the fighter director station under armor. Ships with the new bow mounts and the associated "clipper" bows became known as the "long hull" group, while others were completed to the earlier "short hull" design. Along with these improvements came other increases in the 40mm armament. These included three mounts on the starboard side in sponsons just below the island; two aft on the starboard quarter at the hangar deck level; two aft on the port side on the gallery deck level; and, with the removal of the hangar deck catapult, two on the port side sponson at the hangar deck level. As the "long hull" ships were completed and as earlier ships came in for overhaul, some or all of these changes were implemented. Eventually, the "short hull" ships carried up to 17 40mm mounts and the "long hull" ships

up to 18. The number of 40mm mounts in the island of nearly all ships shrank to three when the flag bridge area was expanded to provide more space.

The *Essex* class was part of the last generation of U.S. warships designed without major provision for radar. At first, the single tripod mast carried an SK radar for long-range air search, an SG radar for surface search, and various aircraft homing antennas. Experience early in the war showed the need for backup radar sets and soon the island became crowded with antennas, which led to mutual interference problems. As ships experimented with various re-arrangements, their layouts became so complex and individualistic that they could often be identified in photographs by their radars alone.

Chapter 2
Anatomy of an Aircraft Carrier

In some respects a ship is like a building; the structures are familiar, but the names are different. A ship has plating that forms the hull of the ship (outer walls), decks (floors), partitions and bulkheads (interior walls), passageways (corridors), overheads (ceilings), compartments (rooms), and ladders (stairs). Doors are openings in bulkheads; hatches are openings in decks. The forward part of the ship is the bow; the rear part of the ship is the stern. Facing forward, the left side is to port and the right is to starboard. The center-line is an imaginary line running full length down the middle of the ship; the direction from the side of the ship toward the centerline is inboard and the direction from the centerline towards the side of the ship is outboard. Athwartship means transverse to the centerline, that is, running at a right angle to the centerline.

U.S. Navy ships are laid out in a systematic fashion. The main deck is the first deck, the deck immediately below it the second deck, then the third and fourth decks. Anything above the main deck is considered superstructure and these decks are called "levels," the first deck above the main deck is the "O1" level and the next the "O2" level and so on. On an aircraft carrier, the main deck is the hangar deck; in the *Essex* class the flight deck was at the O3 level.[1] The forecastle deck was at the O1 level and the gallery deck, which was really only a partial deck fitted under the deep beams supporting the flight deck, was at the O2 level. The hull's transverse frames were four feet apart and ran from frame number 0 at the forward perpendicular to frame number 205 where the water-line met the stern. Spaces could be located by referring to deck and frame numbers, but to provide more specific information, a compartment numbering system was used. The ship was divided into three sections: A for the forward section, B for the machinery spaces amidships, and C for everything aft of the machinery spaces. A compartment designated "A-0204-L," for instance, was in the forward part of the ship, on the

O2 level, on the port side (even numbers were to port and odd numbers to starboard), and was used for crew berthing, as indicated by the suffix L for living space, which also included shops and offices. Other usage suffixes were: A—supplies and storage, C—control, E—machinery, F—fuel, M—munitions, T—trunks and passageways, V—voids, and W—water. Below the armored fourth deck, the first and second platform decks and the hold enclosed the large spaces for the engine and boiler rooms, machinery rooms, ammunition and fuel storage, stores, voids, etc.

The Island

The island of the *Essex* class, like all carrier superstructures, was cramped because of the need to keep it to the minimum size. It contained the main command and navigation positions, the sea cabins for the senior bridge officers, radar and radio rooms, and, of course, the boiler uptakes. At the flight deck level, the flight deck control office was at the forward end of the island, with the flight deck crew locker immediately behind it. This level also had the squadron lockers and the crew's head (bathroom). The first platform above the flight deck (O4 level) was the communication platform, containing the radio room, the flag office, the admiral's sea cabin, 20mm ammunition ready service rooms, and the aerological office. Above the communication platform was the flag bridge (O5 level) with flag plot, radar rooms, and a 40mm ammunition ready service room. Finally, there was the navigating bridge (O6 level), where the pilot house, captain's sea cabin, chart house, air plot and radar rooms were located. A tripod mast forward of

the funnel supported the large foremast platform on which a foretopmast pole mast was mounted.

Radar

Radar answered the problem of carrier fighter defense that existed before the war. Only radar could give sufficient warning and information to allow airborne or deck-launched fighters to intercept incoming enemy aircraft. The use of radar, however, also required some means of integrating its information with that from all other sources. The *Hornet* had a radar plot installed before the war to be "the brains of the organization which protects the fleet or ships from air attack."[2] As radar came into general use after Pearl Harbor, the Navy gained experience in how to use it and interpret the information it provided. To make the best use of the information received from radar, radio, lookouts, etc., each ship had a Combat Information Center (CIC) to sort out and keep track of the situation for the commander. The CIC predated the *Essex* class and early units had a small and cramped CIC in the island structure. Later, the CIC was relocated to the gallery deck just below the flight deck adjacent to the island.

Space had to be found on the island for the antennas and as the number of radars increased, the island became more cluttered. At first the single tripod mast had an SK radar for long-range air search, an SG radar for surface search, and YE/ZB aircraft radio homing antennas. The SK was probably the most important radar on the *Essex* class. Capable of detecting aircraft up to 100 miles away, it had a large 17-foot by 17-foot "mattress" antenna with IFF

(Identification Friend or Foe) antennas attached to the top edge. The SK-2 was an improved SK radar with a dish antenna. The SK-2 appeared late in 1944 on the "long-hull" ships and refitted earlier ships. With the addition of back-up air search radars, a second mast was sponsored outboard of the funnel, usually a lattice mast with a smaller SC-2 air search radar.[3] A second SG surface search radar added abaft the funnel made up for blind spots from the other radars. Accurate height finding was needed to control fighters efficiently and an SM height-finding radar was added, usually in the position atop the tripod mast previously occupied by the relocated large air search set.[4] Only at the end of the war did a combined air search and height-finding radar, the SX, appear. The SX displaced the secondary air search set, allowing the antenna arrangement to be simplified.

Armament
    The 5"/38 Mark 12 guns were used in both the Mark 32 twin mounts near the island and the Mark 30 single open mounts along the port side of the flight deck.[5] Although they had a maximum horizontal range of 18,000 yards and a maximum vertical range of 37,000 feet, normal slant range for antiaircraft work was about 10,000 yards, with 12,000 yards against low flying torpedo air-craft. The mounts were power operated, but still required crews to load the ammunition. The normal rate of fire was 15 rounds per minute, but a good crew could increase that rate for short periods during intense operations.
    The 5-inch guns fired semi-fixed ammunition, that is, the projectile and cartridge case containing the propellant

were loaded separately. The standard ammunition included antiaircraft (AA Common) and high explosive (High Capacity) projectiles. The AA Common weighed 55 pounds and used both impact fusing and a mechanical time fuse which had to be set before firing.[6] Unless the round actually hit an attack-ing aircraft, it was very difficult to adjust the timing to catch an aircraft within the burst radius of the projectile. Beginning in 1943, however, proximity fuses were used with 5-inch antiaircraft ammunition.
    The proximity fuse was the most important antiaircraft development of World War II and made the 5-inch gun an effective weapon against aircraft. It consisted of a miniature radio transceiv-er with its own power supply. After firing, the fuse transmitter emitted high frequency radio waves. When a target came within effective range, the trans-ceiver picked up the reflected waves and activated an electronic switch that initiated the detonation sequence. For security reasons, the proximity fuse was referred to as "variable time" (VT) and the name VT fuse stuck even after its existence was known.
    Two Mark 37 dual-purpose gun directors, one at each end of the island, provided fire control for the 5-inch guns. The Mark 37, introduced in the mid-1930s, was later fitted with a Mark 4 radar, with its distinctive twin para-bolic trough antenna mounted on the roof of the director. Because of the Mark 37's inability to fire in the blind, the Mark 12 eventually replaced the Mark 4, although it did use the same antenna. An associated height-finding radar, the Mark 22, was introduced at the same time. The Mark 22 used a small parabol-ic section antenna mounted alongside

the Mark 12 antenna. The Mark 12/22 went into the later ships and the early ships converted in 1944.

The 40mm Bofors was a Swedish design produced under license and used extensively as an antiaircraft weapon during World War II. The naval versions, water-cooled instead of the air-cooled single barrel "army" versions, were used in powered mounts. The rate of fire was 160 rounds per minute per barrel, with an effective range of 2,500 yards. Each barrel was hand fed with clips of four rounds each. As the war progressed, more Mark 2 quad mounts were added. The Mark 51 director, essentially a manually operated Mark 14 gunsight on a pedestal mount, provided fire control for the Bofors. The Mark 51 directors were located as close as possible to the quad 40mm guns they controlled. They could also act as directors for the 5-inch weapons. Later in the war, some Mark 51 directors were replaced by the generally similar Mark 57 director, equipped with a Mark 29 radar, or the Mark 63, with a Mark 28 radar dish on the quad 40mm mount itself.

The 20mm Oerlikon was a Swiss design also produced under license in large numbers. Mounted singly on a simple pedestal mount with a 60-round drum magazine, it was aimed manually and could fire at a rate of 450 rounds per minute out to a maximum effective range of 1,000 yards. Using explosive projectiles, which were more effective than the older .50 caliber machine gun rounds, it was valued as a close-in weapon against attacking aircraft that had made it through all the other defenses. The early models used a ring sight but later versions were equipped with the Mark 14 lead-computing gyroscopic sight.[7] The Oerlikon could get

into action quickly and did not require electrical or hydraulic power. The prestige it enjoyed was largely the result of its success in British use. Later in the war it proved ineffective against Kamikaze attacks and began to be replaced by twin mount versions for more fire power.[8]

The Flight Deck
The flight deck is an aircraft carrier's reason for being. In the *Essex* class, apart from the structure designed to support it, the flight deck itself was made of steel only 0.2 inch thick and covered with teak planking three inches thick. Metal aircraft securing rails were spaced at six-foot intervals in order to tie down aircraft, and where the arresting wires or barrier cables crossed the deck, metal chafing plates protected the wood. The flight deck was served by three bomb elevators on the starboard side in the vicinity of the island with a torpedo elevator located just aft of the aft 5-inch twin mount. Eight avgas (aviation gasoline) refueling stations ran around the edges of the flight deck.

Elevators
The two centerline elevators were 48 feet by 44 feet 3 inches and the deck edge elevator was 60 feet by 34 feet 6 inches. The weight capacity of the centerline elevators was 14,000 pounds and a round trip could be made in 45 seconds (10 seconds to load, 12.5 seconds moving, 10 seconds to unload, 12.5 seconds moving). When the elevators were in the down position, a safety railing encircled the flight deck opening. Elevator number one was the forward centerline elevator, elevator number two, the deck edge

elevator and elevator number three the aft centerline elevator. Number three elevator was offset to starboard to allow the maximum clearance on the hangar deck below and featured an auxiliary elevator beneath it. When the number three aircraft elevator was in the up position, this auxiliary elevator filled in nearly half the area taken up by the elevator pit and allowed more deck space for moving aircraft in the hangar bay . The centerline elevators operated by hydraulic pistons, while the deck edge elevator operated on a cable and pulley arrangement powered by a hydraulic cylinder. The deck edge elevator could fold to a raised position for passage through the Panama Canal locks.

The radio masts along the starboard edge of the flight deck were a very prominent feature on the *Essex* class.[9] To keep the flight deck clear of obstructions during flight operations, the masts could swing to a horizontal position. In the original design there were five masts, three forward of the island and two aft, but some ships had only four. Later in the war individual whip antennas replaced some of the masts. More resistant to damage, they were lighter in weight and allowed a greater number of frequencies to be used.

Catapults

The catapults for the *Essex* class were the hydraulic Type H Mark IV. The hangar deck catapult was designated H4A and the flight deck catapult H4B. Hydraulic catapults used a ram that drove a shuttle through a cable and sheave arrangement, which multiplied the speed and stroke of the ram mechanically. Pressurized air entered an accumulating tank, the pressure was

transmitted to a piston inside a hydraulic cylinder by the hydraulic fluid, and the ram was driven by the piston. At the end of the catapult stroke, fluid was pumped to the other side of the piston, returning the catapult to the starting position.

Until World War II, the catapults installed in U.S. carriers did not achieve any great operational significance, partly because rolling takeoffs were both simpler and faster. Initially, rolling takeoffs presented no problems, but as aircraft loads increased and as air groups increased in size, less deck space was available. Typically, an entire deck-load strike would be spotted on the flight deck, leaving just enough room for catapult takeoffs. As soon as enough aircraft had launched, the rest reverted to rolling takeoffs. Since aircraft did not swerve on takeoff using catapults, they were safer at night and allowed launching without lights. Moreover, catapults permitted takeoffs in a crosswind, so that the carrier did not have turn into the wind to launch. Catapults also offered flexibility in launching when the flight deck was damaged. By the end of World War II, some carriers were making 40 percent of their launches using catapults.

The hangar deck catapults were not as useful in service as intended; air currents around the ship made launching aircraft tricky and they were seldom used. Installed on only six ships, the *Yorktown, Intrepid, Hornet, Franklin, Bunker Hill,* and *Wasp,* they were later removed and a second flight deck catapult substituted.

Arresting Gear

The arresting gear operated on principles similar to the catapults. In the case of arresting gear, the cable was run through a series of pulleys attached to a ram inside a hydraulic cylinder. A valve regulated the flow of hydraulic fluid from the cylinder into an accumulating tank. As a landing aircraft's tail hook engaged an arresting wire called a "cross-deck pendant," the arresting gear cable was run out, forcing the ram to compress the hydraulic fluid in the cylinder. As the fluid was forced out of the cylinder into the accumulating tank, the resistance provided by the valve had a breaking affect, slowing the aircraft to a stop. Beyond the arresting gear wires were five Davis barriers. These barriers consisted of strands of cable that were at a height designed to snag the landing gear or propeller of any aircraft that failed to engage any of the 16 arresting gear pendants. After the plane had safely landed, the barriers could be lowered, allowing the aircraft to taxi forward out of the arresting gear. (The barriers were also connected to the arresting gear engines.) The *Essex* class carriers initially used improved versions, Mods (modifications) 5 and 6, of the Mark 4 hydraulic arresting gear used on the *Yorktown* design. One Mod had a longer run out for the after section of the arresting gear area and the other had a shorter run out for use closer to the barriers. Later carriers, beginning with the *Bennington,* used the improved Mark 5, which was fitted to all the *Essex* carriers after the war.[10]

The Gallery Deck

Immediately below the flight deck, the gallery deck contained spaces with ready access to the flight deck or the island. These included the state rooms of the senior officers and the air condi-

tioned aircrew ready rooms. Two of the ready rooms were located just aft of the amidships deck edge elevator and two were forward of the after elevator. Ready room number 1 had extra space to accommodate an enlarged fighter squadron of 27 pilots. In the early ships, the CIC had been moved from the island to larger spaces on the gallery deck generally adjacent to, but still separate from the fighter director office. Other spaces in the gallery deck served as various aviation- and communications-related shops. The areas under the flight deck open to the hangar could store items such as drop tanks and spare aircraft wings suspended from the deck head. Light metal walkways hanging from the deck beams above allowed access across these open areas.

The Hangar Deck and Forecastle Deck

The hangar occupied most of the available space between the gallery and main decks. Forward, the forecastle and the superstructure above it contained officer's staterooms while the other spaces scattered around the edge of the hangar were mostly used for maintenance shops, although some accommodation areas were located around the boiler uptakes on the starboard side. The hangar deck had two sets of sliding fire curtains which could close off the hangar deck into three sections to contain fires.

Second, Third and Fourth Decks

Below the hangar deck, the second and third decks were largely for crew accommodations and associated services. Officers' cabins were outboard and generally forward, while enlisted berthing was generally amidship and aft. The officers' wardrooms were on the second deck forward and the crew's mess was on the third deck aft, along with various offices and shops. The fourth deck was primarily used for those aviation and ship's stores not required to be under armor.

First and Second Platform Decks and Hold

Below the armored fourth deck, the first and second platform decks and the hold enclosed the ships machinery, ammunition, and fuel storage. These decks were not continuous and both the engine and boiler rooms took up large open spaces within the interior of the ship. Surrounding these vital areas was a series of voids with the outer sections loaded with fuel oil, which became part of the protection for the ship's innards along with the 4-inch armor belt and the triple bottom.

Machinery

The machinery was split into two independent units; each unit had two boiler rooms containing two boilers each and an engine room with two sets of turbines. A pair of boilers provided steam for each set of turbines, but a cross-connection in the engine room allowed boilers to be switched in case of damage or for convenience. The turbines in the forward engine room drove the outboard propeller shafts and those in the aft engine room drove the inboard shafts. Forward and aft of the boiler and engine rooms were large auxiliary machinery rooms which contained nearly all of the auxiliary equipment except for the large equipment

needed for the aircraft elevators and catapults. The Babcock and Wilcox boilers supplied steam at a pressure of 565 p.s.i. and a temperature of 850 degrees F. Because the temperature and pressure were substantially higher than in earlier designs, the machinery operated at a higher power-to-weight ratio, resulting in weight savings and lower fuel consumption. The increased efficiency also allowed the boiler uptakes to be smaller. The turbines were made by Westinghouse and consisted of a low pressure and a high pressure turbine driving the propeller shaft via a double reduction gearbox. Astern turbines were fitted at the ends of the low pressure turbines and a cruising turbine, for economy at low power, was geared to the forward end of the high pressure turbine.

Four 1,250 kW turbo-generators, located in the forward machinery room, engine room one, and boiler rooms three and four, provided the main electrical power. Two 250 kW diesel generators, one in each auxiliary machinery room, were available in case steam pressure was lost. Ship's service generators, one in the forward auxiliary machinery room and the other in the number four boiler room, supplied most of the ship's low power requirements. Three emergency 60 kW generators were located on the main deck. Four generators, two in the number three boiler room and two in the forward machinery room, supplied electrical power to an internal degaussing coil to defend against magnetic mines.

Fresh water for both the boilers and the crew came from three distillation plants which boiled sea water and condensed the vapor as fresh water. Two large triple-stage evaporators were fitted in the forward auxiliary machinery room and a smaller two-stage evaporator was fitted in the number three boiler room. High pressure and medium pressure air compressors were fitted in the two auxiliary machinery rooms and high pressure and low pressure air compressors were fitted in boiler room number three to supply air for armament, aircraft, and sundry other uses.

For fire fighting, washing the decks, and pumping out flooded compartments, nine fire pumps were fitted, one in each main machinery room, one in the after auxiliary machinery room, and two in the pump rooms forward. One bilge pump was fitted in each main machinery room for clearing the bilges and for pumping out the machinery compartments in case of flooding.

Chapter 3
Building the Fast Carriers

The *Essex* class carriers were not specifically designed for rapid production, but their moderate size and the approach taken by the designers accelerated their completion. They also benefited from the building yard expansion program, underway before the first ship was laid down, and the priority given carrier construction during the war. In 1944 Rear Admiral E.L. Cochran, chief of BuShips, reported that "the carrier program encountered fewer cases of delays resulting from material shortages than other programs owing to the high priority which [it] enjoyed."[1] Carriers had first priority until May 1942, when landing craft for North Africa moved to the top. Even then, they enjoyed a higher priority than other surface ships and by the time destroyer escorts had moved to the top priority late in 1942, most of the material required for the carriers was already in the pipeline.

The original *Essex* design was funded under the Fiscal Year 1940 (FY 40) program for construction beginning in FY 41 and completion by March 1944. By the time the first ship was ordered, however, it became clear that more would be needed. The passage of the "Two Ocean Navy" Act of June 1940, provided for three more carriers, CVs 10-12, that had already been ordered under a Chief of Naval Operations directive of 20 May 1940. After the fall of France in June, Congress voted an additional 70 percent expansion and another seven carriers, CVs 13-19, were ordered under a 16 August 1940 directive. Just after the outbreak of war, on 15 December 1941, two more, CVs 20-21, were added to the original series. Since the major shipyards were expanding when the *Essex* program began, there were enough slipways to accommodate the new construction. The first ships absorbed the available building ways for the first two years of the war. The *Essex* herself took only 17 months to complete and was commissioned on the last day of 1942, 15 months early. The *Yorktown* was more than 17 months early. The *Intrepid* and the *Hornet* were

17 and six months early, respectively, even though both had been laid down behind schedule.

Of the original 11 ships ordered, the Newport News Shipbuilding and Drydock Company completed seven in their lead shipyard at Newport News, Virginia, with the Bethlehem Steel Company of Quincy, Massachusetts completing the remaining four. Of the two ordered after Pearl Harbor, CV-20 went to the New York Naval Shipyard, Brooklyn Navy Yard, and CV-21 to Newport News. On 7 August 1942, under the second war program (FY 43 for 1943-44), 10 additional carriers were ordered from three navy yards: CVs 31-35 from New York, CVs 36-37 from Philadelphia, and CVs 38-40 from Norfolk. Later, CV-32 was reordered from Newport News to reduce congestion at the New York Naval Shipyard. Three more were ordered on 14 June 1943 under an FY 44 program intended to use up the combat tonnage authorized by Congress. One each of CVs 45-47 were ordered from Philadelphia, Newport News, and Bethlehem Quincy. In 1945, the Navy proposed that a further six *Essex* class carriers be built: CV-50 from Bethlehem Quincy, CVs 51-52 from New York, CV-53 from Philadelphia, and CVs 54-55 from Norfolk. But cancellation of the provisionally awarded contracts came one month later, in March 1945, when President Roosevelt disapproved the program. Of the 26 *Essex* class carriers ordered, all but two were completed.

The *Independence* Class

Because of the great need for fleet carriers, the Navy ordered the conversion of light cruiser hulls into light carriers in March 1942. The *Independence* class of light carriers, CVLs 21-30, supplemented the *Essex* class and allowed for a much more rapid expansion of the carrier force. Built on *Cleveland* class light cruiser hulls, these ships had the speed of fleet carriers with the limitations of escort carriers in terms of aircraft carrying capacity. As a wartime expedient, however, they were highly successful; the first ship was completed within a year and all were in commission before the end of 1943. Only one ship of the class, the *Princeton* (CVL-23), was lost in combat, in October 1944.[2] A light carrier air group normally included a fighter squadron and a torpedo bomber squadron, but no dive bombers.

Newport News

In 1940 the Navy awarded a contract to expand Newport News' slipways from two to four. Four *Essex* carriers could now be built simultaneously. In April 1941 the *Essex* (CV-9) was laid down on the same ways used to build the *Hornet;* in December the new *Yorktown* (CV-10) was laid down on the ways used by the new 35,000-ton battleship *Indiana,* launched the month before. The *Yorktown,* originally named *Bon Homme Richard,* was renamed in September 1942 to honor her predecessor lost in the Battle of Midway that June. Mrs. Roosevelt was poised and ready to christen the new ship on 21 January 1943 when the *Yorktown* began to slide down the launching ways — seven minutes ahead of schedule. Mrs. Roosevelt stepped forward and swung twice, breaking the bottle of champagne on the bow. From that moment on, the new *Yorktown* had a reputation as an eager ship.

The *Intrepid* (CV-11) was laid down at the same time as the *Yorktown* and the new *Hornet* (CV-12), originally named *Kearsarge,* in August 1942. As these ships were launched others took their places on the slipways. The *Franklin* (CV-13) was laid down in December 1942, the *Ticonderoga* (CV-14) in February 1943, the *Randolph* (CV-15) in May 1943, and the *Boxer* (CV-21) in September 1943. Of the later ships ordered from Newport News, the *Leyte* (CV-32) was laid down in February 1944, and the *Iwo Jima* (CV-46) in January 1945. The *Leyte* was completed after the war and the *Iwo Jima* was cancelled in August 1945 and broken up on the slip.[3]

Bethlehem Quincy

Bethlehem Quincy, formerly known as Fore River, had only one large slipway when it received an order for four *Essex* carriers. Two new slipways were being built, however, and two carriers were laid down on them as soon as construction had progressed far enough. The new *Lexington* (CV-16) was laid down in July 1941, followed by the *Bunker Hill* (CV-17) in September 1941 and the new *Wasp* (CV-18) in March 1942. The *Lexington* was originally laid down as the *Cabot,* although the name was later given to a light carrier of the *Independence* class. The *Wasp* began as the *Oriskany,* but was renamed in November 1942. The fourth ship, the *Hancock* (CV-19), succeeded the *Lexington* on the original slip in January 1943. The original name for CV-19 was *Ticonderoga,* while CV-14 being built in Newport News was named *Hancock.* The two ships swapped names in May 1943 when the John Hancock life insurance company of

Massachusetts offered to hold a special bond drive to raise money to build the carrier if the names were changed. The drive raised enough money not only to build the ship, but to pay for her operating expenses for a year as well. The *Philippine Sea* (CV-47), one of the later war orders, was laid down in August 1944 and completed after the war.[4]

The Naval Shipyards

The 1940 expansion program had included new building docks for the major East Coast naval shipyards, providing two new docks at both New York and Philadelphia and one new dock at Norfolk. The docks were completed in record time, well ahead of the needs of the carrier program.

The *Bennington* (CV-20) was laid down at the New York Naval Shipyard in December 1942, followed by the *Bon Homme Richard* (CV-31) in February 1943, the *Kearsarge* (CV-33) in March 1944, the *Oriskany* (CV-34) in May 1944, and the *Reprisal* (CV-35) in July 1944. The *Bon Homme Richard* was completed in time to participate in the closing operations of the war. The *Kearsarge* and *Oriskany* were completed after the war, with the *Oriskany* completing much later and in a modernized form. The *Reprisal* was cancelled in August 1945 while approximately 40 percent complete.[5]

The *Antietam* (CV-36) was laid down at the Philadelphia Navy Yard in March 1943, followed by the new *Princeton* (CV-37) in September 1943, and the *Valley Forge* (CV-45) in September 1944. The *Antietam* was completed too late to participate in active war operations, but was part of the occupation forces after the surrender of Japan in 1945. The *Princeton* and *Valley Forge* were both completed after the war.[6]

The *Shangri-La* (CV-38) was laid down at the Norfolk Navy Yard in January 1943. Her name honored the old *Hornet* (CV-8), which had launched the Doolittle raid on Tokyo in April 1942. At the time, the launch point of the Army B-25 bombers was secret. When reporters asked President Roosevelt where they had taken off from, he replied "Shangri-La," the name of a mythical place in the Himalayas described in James Hilton's novel "Lost Horizons." Later, when it became known that the bombers were launched from a carrier, a nationwide "Shangri-La" bond drive was organized. Over $900 million worth of bonds and stamps was raised and a special fund set up by the U.S. Treasury collected another $131 million. The *Shangri-La* was followed by the *Lake Champlain* (CV-39) in March 1943 and the *Tarawa* (CV-40) in January 1944, with the *Lake Champlain*'s construction funded by contributions from the citizens of New York State. She was built entirely in drydock and was "launched by floating" in November 1944, but was commissioned too late to see combat. The *Tarawa* was completed after the war.

Construction

The structure of the *Essex* class was noteworthy for its economical use of material, both in terms of reducing complexity and in saving weight. Apart from the curves required in the outer bottom plating to produce the hull form and the camber of the weather decks, practically all structures were kept

straight and flat. The types of steel section used were kept to the minimum as well. Besides flat plate, only "I" bar and angle bar, in various sizes, were used. Other sections were the "T" bar, made by cutting an "I" bar down the center to make two "T" sections, and the "l" bar, an "I" bar with one leg removed. Welding was used extensively, saving weight and time and improving the water-tightness of joints. The outer bottom (or skin) plating except at the bow and stern, the connections between the torpedo bulkheads and the fourth deck, and the keel connections were riveted. The rest of the hull was welded. More weight was saved by machining lightening holes in deck beams, vertical girders, and other structures.

Armor protection was provided by Class "B" armor and STS (Special Treatment Steel); both were nickel chrome steel alloys heat-treated to a uniform hardness and toughness. Class "B" was used for thick armor sections and the STS for thin sections. Bulkheads at stations 59 and 166 marked the ends of an armored "box" made up of 4-inch Class "B" bulkheads below the fourth deck (as a continuation of the side armor belt), and STS bulkheads continued above them up to the main deck. STS was also used for side plating. The Class "B" armor lacked the excellent structural properties of STS and constituted deadweight, but STS plating, with its excellent strength characteristics, saved weight by simultaneously providing both structural strength and armor protection. The main deck, constructed of two thicknesses of 1 1/4-inch STS was both the upper strength member of the hull and its defense against bombs. STS plating provided hull strength and protection on the ship's side, where the skin plating varied from $1 \frac{1}{8}$ inch at the sheer strake to $\frac{3}{4}$ inch behind the armor belt. Structures not related to armor protection, such as the central vertical keel, made from $\frac{5}{8}$-inch STS plate with $\frac{7}{8}$-inch STS keel riders welded to the top and bottom to form a large "I" beam, also used STS. Where STS or armor plate was not required, standard medium steel was used.

Chapter 4
The Main Battery

As important as any technical factor in the design of warships or combat aircraft, is the quality of the men who man them. A carrier's aircraft are its "main battery," and the quality of the pilots and aircrew determine its combat effectiveness. Every aspect of a carrier's existence is devoted to getting the aircraft aloft to perform their missions and to ensure their safe return. Naval aviators, always considered an elite group, have often felt that the precision and skill demanded by carrier operations placed them on a level above other military pilots. Even within the Navy itself, the aviators had their own distinctive uniforms—khakis for summer and tropical wear, aviation working greens for winter—and since brown footwear was part of the uniform, aviators became known as the "brown shoe" Navy. Aviators referred to the non-aviation community as the "black shoe" Navy, for the black uniform shoes worn with the traditional blue uniforms of the surface Navy. The enlisted aircrew members, referred to as

"airedales," also enjoyed a special status along with a flight pay bonus. As more aircraft carriers were built and as more modern aircraft entered service, the Navy expanded its aviation training to meet the growing demand for highly qualified pilots and aircrewmen.

The Naval Aviator

Before 1941, virtually all aviation training was done at Pensacola, Florida. The Pensacola Naval Air Station was known as the "Annapolis of the Air," and was both a primary and advanced air training center. In the mid-1930s the Navy adopted an Aviation Cadet training program giving college graduates an opportunity to earn their wings and receive reserve commissions in return for three years of active duty service. Many of these AvCad graduates were on active duty by the time of the Pearl Harbor attack and formed an experienced core around which the later *Essex* class air groups could be built. As training needs expanded before the war, other training bases were established at Miami and Jacksonville, Florida, and at Corpus Christi, Texas. Recruiting standards were revised to allow more applicants to qualify.[1]

During World War II, flight training was divided into phases, with various entry-level programs feeding into the training "pipeline."[2] Pre-flight stressed physical fitness, with particular emphasis on football and swimming, as well as ground school subjects such as naval orientation, seamanship, recognition, communications, and military drill. This phase was administered by several "pre-flight schools" at colleges around the country operating under contract to the Navy. Pre-flight aimed to make Navy men of the AvCads and was not required of officers in the Regular Navy, who began their aviation training during the Primary phase.

Primary flight training was provided at 16 Naval Air Stations around the country. The three months of Primary was divided between ground school and flight training. Flight training was given in brightly-colored Stearman N2S and Naval Aircraft Factory N3N open-cockpit biplanes known as "yellow perils," and consisted of four stages.

Stage A began with familiarization with the training aircraft, proceeded to dual instruction in basic maneuvers such as takeoffs and landings, and ended with the solo flight, for a total of 11 hours. Stage B was divided between 14 hours of dual instruction and 19 hours of solo practice and check flights. At this stage, greater precision in slips and S-turns to emergency landings was expected. Other maneuvers included the falling leaf, pylon 8s, and lazy 8s, and precise control in stalls and spins was required. Students passing the B

check flight went on to Stage C, 13 hours of dual instruction and 20 hours of solo practice and check flights. The main focus was on acrobatics, including the snap roll, slow roll, Immelmann turn, split S, chandelle, and loop. Stage D, the last in Primary, included 14 hours of dual instruction and 19 solo hours dedicated to formation and night flying. Students learned the old fashioned vee and stepped-up echelon formations, with night flying limited to takeoffs and landings in the traffic pattern of the main airfield.

After Primary, cadets passed on to 14 weeks of Intermediate training. Concentrated at the Pensacola and Corpus Christi Naval Air Training Centers, roughly one-third of the initial candidates did not make it through Intermediate. Intermediate was divided into Basic and Advanced, with ground training sandwiched in between the various flight training segments. During Basic, the students were introduced to the Vultee SNV Valiant, a modern all-metal, low-wing trainer known more familiarly as the "Vibrator." Students received dual familiarization in the SNV, soloed, and practiced day and night formation flying using the stepped-down echelon and vee formations. Basic consisted of about 10 hours of dual instruction and 22 hours of solo. From Basic, cadets moved on to the Instrument Squadron, where they got their first instruction in the Link Instrument Trainer. This training device resembled an aircraft cockpit with stubby wings and tail. The student "flew" the Link trainer "under the hood" to learn the rudiments of instrument flying while the operator sitting outside presented the student with various navigational problems. The students then flew about 15 actual flights "under the hood" for a total of about 20 hours. Although instructors flew with the students for safety reasons, blind flying was particularly stressful and passing an instrument check ride often gave students a greater sense of accomplishment than any other phase of flight training. After completing Instrument Squadron, students entered Advanced Training.

In Advanced, the cadets trained in aircraft typical of their future service specialization: multi-engine land-based pilots flew the Beech SNB twin-engine trainer, flying boat pilots went into the Consolidated PBY Catalina, scouting and observation pilots went to the Vought OS2U Kingfisher. Those destined for carrier assignments flew the most famous of all World War II trainers, the North American SNJ. The SNJ was the Navy version of the T-6 Texan and was a modern all-metal, low-wing aircraft with many of the characteristics of operational combat aircraft. The flight syllabus in Advanced included 76 flights with about 14 hours of dual instruction and 86 hours of solo flying. Tight vee formations gave way to the looser two- and four-plane section and division formations typical of combat, where radical maneuvering required greater spatial separation. After making practice dry runs under the eye of an instructor, the students were finally introduced to air-to-air gunnery, with live ammunition fired at a long cloth target sleeve trailed behind a tow plane. Strafing of ground targets was not practiced extensively, since it was assumed that any competent pilot could follow his own tracers to the target.

The three basic air-to-air gunnery firing patterns taught were the high

side, flat side, and low side runs. The high side run was made from a "perch" half a mile abeam the tow aircraft and on the same heading, but 5,000 feet above. The firing portion of the run was made in a descending curve. As the turn continued, the relative position of the firing plane drifted past the tow plane and toward the target sleeve. The firing plane then reversed the direction of turn toward the target. The target sleeve was in the firing plane's sights for only a few seconds before the pilot had to level his wings and pass above and astern of the target sleeve. At that point the pilot would fly on a course parallel to that of the tow plane and call "off" on the radio after passing the tow plane. The pilot then climbed up to a perch on the opposite side as other members of his flight made their runs. The flat side run was similar to the high side run, but the curve was horizontal. Low side runs were made in a slightly climbing turn. To differentiate student hits, the tips of the bullets were color coded to leave a mark on the sleeve. Out of thousands of rounds fired, only a few hits ($2\frac{1}{2}$ percent of the rounds fired was a passing score) were considered necessary to get the job done.

For divebombing practice, the SNJs carried small dummy bombs under the wings, and students often found that even small variations in speed and dive angle, and especially differences in wind velocity and direction, could cause the practice bombs to miss the 100-foot target circle. The dive bombing runs were made from an altitude of about 8,000 feet. The bombing aircraft flew over the target and executed a split-S to begin the divebombing run. The split-S is a maneuver in which the pilot half rolls the aircraft over on its back and lets the nose fall through into whatever angle of dive is desired. Once in the dive, the pilot lined up the target in his sight and released the bomb, allowing plenty of altitude to pull out of the dive safely.

After completing Intermediate flight training and earning their wings and commissions, the new "nuggets" selected for carrier duty went on to two months of Operational training in tactics, gunnery, and carrier qualification using older models of operational aircraft.[3] The focus now shifted to developing combat skills. At this point pilots assigned to dive bomber and torpedo aircraft trained together with their aircrew. After completing Operational training, aviators were assigned to squadrons.

The Air Group

The basic unit of naval aviation was the squadron, the number of aircraft and crews assigned varying with the type of aircraft and the current organizational doctrine.[4] Early on, squadrons carried designations that reflected their missions. The "V" for heavier-than-air aircraft followed by another letter—"F" for fighting, "B" for bombing, "T" for torpedo, "S" for scouting—and a number for the individual squadron.[5] Two or more squadrons assigned to a carrier formed the air group. In the early days of carrier aviation, the term was associated with the name of the ship, for example "Saratoga Air Group." Later, when the air group commander became an authorized command billet, the air group became a formal unit. In 1942 air groups were given numerical designations. The first, Carrier Air Group NINE (short title CAG-9), was commissioned in March 1942.[6] In June 1944, the introduction of new letter designations reflected the differences in the air group complements of different classes of carriers. Essex class air groups were designated CVG, while the air groups of the Independence class light carriers were designated CVLG.[7]

Before the war, a carrier air group included a fighter squadron, a dive bomber squadron, a scout bomber squadron, and a torpedo bomber squadron. The bombing and scouting squadrons were both equipped with the SBD Dauntless and performed the same missions, reflecting the importance of scouting and dive bombing in carrier tactics. As radar developed, the need for scouting aircraft lessened and led to the elimination of the scouting squadron, which was combined with the bombing squadron. The Essex was commissioned with a "double" fighter squadron of 36 Hellcats, a bombing squadron with 36 SBDs, and a torpedo squadron with 18 TBF Avengers. An extra dive bomber was assigned for liaison duties, making a total of 91 aircraft. Two other aircraft, the F4U Corsair and the SB2C Helldiver, were introduced when the Bunker Hill entered service.[8] As the war progressed, the need for more fighters led to an increase in the size of the fighter squadron and, as the number of fighters increased, the bombing squadron got smaller.

The Hellcat

The Grumman F6F Hellcat succeeded the stubby little F4F Wildcat, the only Navy fighter that held its own against the superb Japanese Zero in the first year of Pacific combat. Looking like the Wildcat's younger but bigger brother, the Hellcat was unmistakably a product of the Grumman "iron works." It was chubby and angular, but rugged and powered by a magnificent engine, the 2,000 horsepower Pratt and Whitney R-2800 Double Wasp. With a wingspan of 42 feet 10 inches and a gross weight of nearly seven tons, the Hellcat was a lot of airplane, but steady as a rock when coming aboard a carrier. The Hellcat was the first Navy fighter designed on the basis of combat experience with the Zero, and matched or exceeded the Zero's performance in nearly every category except maneuverability.[9] The Hellcat's heavy armament of six .50 caliber machine guns could easily tear apart a Zero, and its self-sealing tanks, armor plate, and sturdy structure made it more survivable than its opposition. The confidence this airplane instilled in its pilots is best be summed up in the words of Navy ace Alex Vraciu: "These Grummans are beautiful airplanes. If they could cook, I'd marry one."[10]

The Avenger

Another Grumman product, the TBF Avenger was designed as a replacement for the aging TBD Devastator torpedo bomber and became operational just before the Hellcat. A large mid-wing airplane with a crew of three, the Avenger was powered by a 1,700 horsepower Wright R-2600 Cyclone and armed with one forward firing .30 caliber machine gun in the nose cowling, synchronized to fire through the propeller arc, one .50 caliber machine gun in a power-operated dorsal turret at the end of the long greenhouse canopy and a flexible .30 caliber machine gun firing through a ventral tunnel aft of the large internal torpedo bay. Later versions of

the Avenger had two forward firing .50 caliber machine guns. With a wingspan of 54 feet 2 inches, the wings had to be folded back hydraulically. Besides carrying torpedoes, the Avenger was used as a level bomber. It was a stable airplane but, although faster than its predecessor, was too slow and heavy on the controls to be used as a dive bomber. Production was turned over to General Motors and GM built Avengers were designated TBM. The Avenger was known affectionately by its crews as the "turkey."

The Dauntless

The Douglas SBD Dauntless was the Navy's workhorse in the Pacific and the deciding factor in the Battle of Midway, the turning point in the war against Japan.[11] This two-place dive bomber was slow and vulnerable, but its ruggedness and dependability kept it in service long after its planned replacement by the Curtiss Helldiver. Considering its obsolescence, the Dauntless gave a good account of itself in tangles with Japanese fighters during the early part of the war, with its loss rate reportedly the lowest of any carrier aircraft. The SBD had a wingspan of 41 feet 6 inches and was the only carrier aircraft in an *Essex* class air group without folding wings. The later version of the Dauntless, the SBD-5, had two forward firing .50 caliber machine guns in the nose and twin .30 caliber flexible machine guns for the gunner, who sat behind the pilot under the greenhouse canopy.

The Helldiver

The Curtiss SB2C Helldiver was a mediocre dive bomber that never lived up to expectations. Its role was eventually supplanted by other types of aircraft, although many of its early faults were corrected in later versions. The Helldiver was a large aircraft whose wings and tail seemed inordinately large compared to its fuselage. Like the Avenger, the Helldiver was powered by the R-2600 Cyclone. It was armed with two 20mm cannon in the wings and twin .30 caliber machine guns for the gunner. The early Helldiver design exhibited poor stability and low-speed handling characteristics and later modifications included lengthening the fuselage and increasing the area of the tail surfaces to correct these problems. Besides being a difficult aircraft to operate from a carrier, the design of the dive flaps caused buffeting in a dive, degrading accuracy. All in all, the Helldiver performed no better than the SBD-5 except for a marginal increase in speed and a heavier forward firing armament. It was nicknamed "The Beast" by its crews, a title it fully deserved.

The Corsair

The Vought F4U Corsair combined the smallest airframe possible with the most powerful engine then available, the R-2800 Double Wasp, and resembled a "blue baseball bat with wings." Designed before the war, it was the first aircraft to exceed 400 miles per hour in level flight, but its protracted development kept it from operating from aircraft carriers until late in the war. In order to take full advantage of the R-2800's power, a large propeller was needed and, to provide the necessary ground clearance for the propeller, an inverted gull wing kept the fuselage at a reasonable ground angle and the landing gear at a manageable length. The use of the gull wing also reduced aerodynamic drag where the wing met the fuselage at a right angle. In order to make room for a large fuselage fuel tank, the cockpit in the original design was moved aft, restricting the pilot's view over the long nose. This change, combined with landing gear problems, made the Corsair difficult to bring aboard a carrier. By the time these problems were corrected, the Corsair had become the primary Marine fighter operating from shore bases and the Navy was reluctant to switch from the Hellcat, which had better carrier landing characteristics. The Corsair later won a place aboard the *Essex* class carriers when its superior speed was needed to counter the kamikaze threat. The Corsair eventually replaced the Hellcat as the Navy's primary fighter, and it continued in service into the Korean War as a fighter-bomber.

Chapter 5
Working Up

As each of the new *Essex* class carriers was commissioned, the demanding process of working up for combat began. This period is known in the Navy as the "shakedown," an apt term for the always-difficult early operations of any new ship, but particularly during war. The difficulties of learning the vagaries of a huge and complex physical plant were compounded by the need to transform a body of more than 2,500 officers and men, 95 percent of whom had never been to sea, into a cohesive crew. Many of the skills needed were taught ashore at various schools and training centers, but only constant drill and practice at sea could develop the teamwork needed to fight and win. The captain held absolute responsibility for the combat readiness of his ship and for the safety, well-being, and efficiency of the crew.[1] His ability, experience, and leadership often determined what kind of "personality" the ship would develop. As one fighter squadron commander aboard the *Bunker Hill* recalled: "In the end, the enormous responsibility for every detail of the transformation fell to the shoulders of the skipper. Possessed of the dedication of Saint Paul and the patience of Job, John Ballentine did a superb job. He was tough and uncompromising but always fair. Somehow, as we all stumbled along, he never lost his cool."[2]

In practice, the captain delegated the duties of the ship through the executive officer, often referred to as the "exec" or "XO," the department heads, and the officer of the deck (OOD). The XO was next in line of command and, by long tradition and practice, responsible for matters relating to personnel, routine, and discipline of the ship. The executive's assistants included the administrative assistant, the chaplain, the legal officer, and the chief master-at-arms. Major functions aboard ship were delegated to departments with an officer in charge responsible for the organization, training and readiness of all the men in the department. Every Navy ship has departments such as operations, navigation, gunnery, engineering, communications, and supply, but aircraft carriers also have an air department, headed by the air officer. The air department of an *Essex* class carrier was a huge organization overseeing the maintenance and operation of the arresting gear and catapults, the fueling and arming of aircraft, flight deck fire fighting, crash removal and salvage, and inspection and maintenance of aircraft and aviation equipment. Departments, in turn, were made up of divisions, ranging in size from twenty to hundreds of men.

A large portion of the ship's company on an aircraft carrier are from the "black shoe" Navy, and many of the new officers and crew members were trained in the specialties of the surface Navy. Newly commissioned Reserve officers were known by the Regular Navy officers as "ninety day wonders." The Reservists, in turn, referred to the Naval Academy graduates as "the trade school boys." Besides the traditional skills required to operate a ship, there were numerous non-flying aviation specialties in both the ship's company and the air group. Many of these ground officers were trained by the aviation community at schools set up for this purpose. The training of aeronautical engineer officers, newly commissioned from civilian life, began in February 1941 and expanded immediately after Pearl Harbor. Following the example of the British, a school for training photographic interpretation officers was established at Anacostia, District of Columbia, in January 1942. In February 1942 the Naval Training School (Indoctrination) was established at the large and relatively new Naval Air Station at Quonset Point, Rhode

Island. The Navy felt successful businessmen, lawyers, teachers, and newspapermen would make good officers if given proper indoctrination. Men between the ages of 20 and 40 from a variety of professions received two months of military drill, courses on the fundamentals of naval service, recognition, naval aviation, naval regulations, naval courts and boards, and seamanship. Upon completion of this course, graduates were sent to various units in the aeronautical establishment with many receiving further training in specialties such as photographic interpretation, fighter direction, and engineering. Many of the younger graduates attended the Air Combat Information School at Quonset Point. This two-month course trained new ACI officers on how to brief pilots before and after flight, keep them up to date on operational information, and collect intelligence data for both the pilots and higher echelons. The ACI officers, often some years older than the pilots they worked, lived and often times drank with, were a steadying influence on their squadron mates.[3]

Life Aboard

A ship the size of an aircraft carrier is like a small floating city, with all the necessities, and a few of the luxuries, of a typical city. The enlisted men ate cafeteria style on the mess deck, which was equipped with modern steam tables to keep food hot, while officers ate in the ward room. The galley prepared large quantities of food daily, including freshly baked bread, and even a soda fountain was provided. Laundry facilities handled all uniforms and bedding and other personal services included barber shops and cobblers. The providers of these services didn't enjoy the same attention aviators received, but their contributions were just as vital to the smooth functioning of the ship. During General Quarters, many of these men had battle stations that included manning antiaircraft guns or standing by in repair parties. The medical department had a completely equipped sick bay with a modern operating surgery, but during combat conditions, the mess decks could be used to treat casualties, the mess tables serving as emergency operating tables. When conditions allowed and flight operations were not in progress, various forms of recreation were available. Crewmen could sun themselves on the flight deck or play sports such as basketball or volleyball in the elevator wells. Movies were shown on the hangar deck, with crew members perched on aircraft or catwalks when no folding chairs were available.

Like most warships of World War II, the *Essex* carriers were overcrowded. The proliferation of radars and other electronics, coupled with the growing numbers of light antiaircraft weapons and larger air groups, increased space requirements for both men and equipment. The preliminary *Essex* design provided for a complement of 215 officers and 2,171 enlisted men, but by the end of the war, most *Essex* class carrier crews had increased by 50 percent.[4]

Flight Operations

The air group's most basic need was for each pilot to complete enough daytime landings and takeoffs to be able to launch and recover back aboard as safely, smoothly, and quickly as possible. At the same time, the pilots' efforts had to merge with the complex choreography of the flight deck crew. Learning the basics of aircraft launch and recovery was vital for the pilots and the flight deck crew, but it was only a small part of the teamwork required. Once the air group was aboard, the plane handlers had to learn how to position, or "spot" aircraft in a "takeoff spot" on the hangar and flight decks using tractors and human plane-pushers. Everyone working on the flight deck could be identified by the color of his jersey and helmet. Flight deck directors wore yellow jerseys, plane captains brown, plane pushers blue, fire fighters red, and the arresting gear crew green.

The flight deck and hangar deck officers used the "Ouija board," a scale diagram of the hangar or flight deck with flat cutouts representing the various aircraft aboard ship. Cutouts depicted aircraft with wings both folded and extended. The trick was for the two supervisors to arrange and rearrange the cutouts on the Ouija board so that enough open deck space remained to move other planes. Both officers needed to coordinate their efforts to ensure a smooth flow of aircraft to the flight deck using the ship's three elevators. The flight deck officer had to leave at least 415 feet of clear deck for the takeoff run of the first plane. Follow-on aircraft needed enough room to taxi forward to the takeoff position, with their wings and propeller arcs clear of any obstructions. Taxiing accidents could not only destroy aircraft, but could kill or injure crewmen, and shut down the flight deck.

With 90 or more airplanes aboard, the possible deck-spotting combinations were innumerable. In practice, however, only the most commonly used spots were worked out and committed to memory by the spotters. The flight deck was a dangerous place—strong winds and blasts of propwash could knock a man into the path of whirling propeller blades—and crewmen had to perform flawlessly whether in the dark, in the rain, or under enemy attack.

As pilots were briefed in squadron ready rooms, plane captains ran up the engines, checking them and other equipment. If satisfied, the engines were shut down. After the order "Pilots, man your planes" was sounded, flight crews strapped in and restarted the engines.

The flight deck officer would then take his position off the right wing tip of the first plane to launch, hold up his left hand with one finger extended, and slowly rotate a black and white checkered flag with his right hand. The pilot of the lead plane revved up to half power, checked his instruments, and made sure that all the control surfaces moved freely. When satisfied, the pilot would give the flight deck officer a thumbs-up sign. The flight deck officer then held up two fingers and rotated the flag more rapidly. The pilot applied full power while holding his feet on the brakes and the stick in his stomach; the brakes were held to prevent a premature rollout and the stick held back to prevent a nose-up. When the pilot nodded to signal that he was "Ready," the checkered flag was swung out and down to point at the bow of the ship. When executed properly, all this happened in a matter of seconds. As the first aircraft started its takeoff run, the flight deck officer would signal the next into takeoff position.

The flight deck officer's chief assistant, the yellow-jerseyed director, moved aircraft with hand signals: both hands held high with the knuckles toward the pilot gesturing "come on" indicated "taxi straight ahead"; one hand held so and the other hand pointing toward a wheel meant "keep moving and hold the brake indicated to turn"; hands with palms facing the pilot meant "stop temporarily"; both fists clenched meant "stop and hold the brakes locked until further orders." Using these signals the director could move the aircraft, with only a few inches of clearance, into exact position. While the director's hand signal commands were mandatory, a pilot could stop dead in his tracks if some problem was perceived. As the airplane taxied to the takeoff position, the pilot extended and locked the wings and set the wing and cooling flaps to their takeoff positions.

When the next aircraft reached takeoff position, the director would give the pilot the hold signal, pat the top of his head, and pass control by pointing with both hands at the flight deck officer. The flight deck officer, after checking that the first aircraft had cleared the flight deck, turned to begin the final run-up sequence with the next aircraft. The desired takeoff interval was 20 to 30 seconds—less time for the faster-accelerating fighters and more for the bombers. The pilot held a steady course down the center of the flight deck and as the aircraft neared the bow, the pilot eased the tail down to bring the nose up and let the airplane fly itself off the ship. As the airplane cleared the bow, the pilot executed a clearing turn 45 degrees to the right to get out of the ship's path and to keep his slipstream away from the airplane behind. Once airborne, the pilot retracted his landing gear and reduced power for a smooth, steady climb-out as the landing flaps fully retracted.

Following the clearing turn, the flight leader would resume the original launch heading while holding at 1,000 feet altitude at 150 knots. After a precise interval, he would then make a gentle "standard rate turn" to reverse course, allowing the other members of the flight to form up. As the flight headed downwind and passed abeam of the carrier, it was comfortably joined up, ready either to orbit and await following units, or to proceed with the mission. The flight leader would hold course for 30 seconds multiplied by the number of aircraft in his flight, up to a maximum of eight, before making his downwind turn.

The mission radius for carrier operations in World War II was typically less than 200 miles, with searches sometimes extended to 250 miles. A typical search pattern was laid out from the force, with sectors of 10 to 15 degrees, in the direction of the enemy. Two planes flew each sector approximately 200 to 250 miles out, followed by a cross-leg of 25 to 50 miles, and a return leg back to the carrier. Pilots received the coordinates of the location where the carrier was supposed to be when the aircraft returned shortly before launch, and pilots used dead reckoning (short for deduced reckoning) navigation to return to this point. Overwater navigation skills practiced during shakedown were critical for future combat operations. As one veteran dive bomber pilot recalled: "An aircraft carrier was not a stationary airfield, so there was relative motion to be considered in returning to a rendezvous point in the open sea. The place in the water where a carrier was to be when the scout planes returned was known as

Point Option, and believe me it could be very optional! The preplanned location could change drastically if the carrier was attacked while the search teams were away. An attack could put the entire task force into wild gyrations at speeds of over thirty knots and any concern about maintaining a Point Option position under these circumstances became moot."[5] A soft grease pencil and a metal chart board, about eighteen inches square with a clear plastic cover, were used to plot course headings and distances. Under the plastic cover was a lined compass disk which rotated around a center pin to determine compass headings between points marked on the cover's surface. The chart board's surface was boxed with lines forming squares and labelled with the latitude and longitude of the operating area. The board handled flights out to about 300 miles radius, with Point Option located as close to the center pin as possible to simplify the task of figuring out compass headings between points on the chart board's surface. Pilots also had a small computer, a metal disk about four and one-half inches in diameter marked in nautical miles (from 1 to 100), with another slightly smaller disk connected to it by a center pin. The smaller disk was marked in minutes (from 1 to 100) and was used like a circular slide rule to determine rate of speed and distance flown relative to elapsed time.

Since even with precise navigation the carrier might not be at Point Option when the aircraft returned, aircraft had receivers to help pilots home in on the YE/ZB beacon mounted on the carrier's mainmast. The YE/ZB had a range of about 30 miles and used a rotating radio signal that broadcast a different letter of the alphabet every 30 degrees as it rotated. From the letter heard through his headset, a pilot could approximate his bearing to the ship. The letters assigned to each "slice" changed daily and before launching, pilots filled in the letters on a small compass rose in the corner of their chart boards. YE/ZB was especially helpful during periods of reduced visibility and was sufficiently accurate to prevent a plane from missing the task force. "If you were returning from a 250-mile search jaunt into enemy waters, or a long strike mission," recalled one pilot, "the first faint Morse code dots and dashes in your earphones were as beautiful as a symphony."[6]

In a routine recovery aboard ship, a flight arrayed in right echelon passed abeam the carrier's starboard side at 1,000 feet of altitude, tail hooks down. After 30 seconds on this course, the flight leader broke left to take the downwind heading, with following aircraft peeling off at 30 second intervals. (A carrier always operates with her bow into the wind during takeoff and recovery operations.) The landing checklist was followed by the pilot on the downwind leg so that, when abeam of the ship's port side, he could start the 180-degree turn into the final landing approach. Once in the final "groove" approximately 200 yards astern of the ship, the airplane came under the control of the Landing Signals Officer (LSO).

The LSO, an aviator himself, passed instructions to the landing pilots using a pair of colorful paddles, correcting the speed and altitude of the approaching plane to hold it steady on course or warning a pilot of some oversight, such as an undropped tail hook. If the LSO held the paddles straight out to the side at arm's length and level with his shoulders, it meant the pilot was on glide path, on speed, and on centerline. If the paddles drooped slightly, it meant the pilot was a little low. As the pilot climbed back to the glide slope, the LSO would raise his arms slowly back to the horizontal. Similar signals were used for lateral corrections, such as dropping a wing tip. Directive signals told the pilot to do something immediately; the three most important were the "add power" signal, the "cut," and the "waveoff." The add power signal was made by holding the paddles together in front of the LSO at arm's length; the paddles were then swung open at right angles to the LSO's body. The urgency of the signals could be conveyed by how rapidly and vigorously they were repeated. The cut signal was usually given from the on-glide-slope signal; the left hand dropped to the LSO's side while the right swept down and across his body to join the left hand in a sort of waving motion. At the last instant, when the LSO gave the cut signal, the pilot cut power by pulling the throttle back to idle as the aircraft landed. If the deck was fouled or it was unsafe to land, the LSO gave the wave-off signal by waving both paddles back and forth over his head, in which case the pilot was absolutely required to apply full power and clear the area without landing.

There were exceptions to the basic pattern. For example, a plane with a critical low fuel state, damage, or mechanical trouble would get clearance for an immediate landing if the flight deck was clear and the ship not under attack. In an emergency, a pilot would set himself up to arrive in the grove by any means necessary—dive, right turn, or whatever was the quickest—and all other airplanes in the landing pattern had to fend for themselves while maintaining their required 30-second intervals.

After touchdown, the aircraft came to a rapid halt as the tail hook caught one of the arresting wires, called cross-deck pendants, stretched tautly across the after flight deck. The first wires had relatively soft arrestments since the arresting gear cables had longer run-outs, but those closer to the barriers had short run-outs and stopped aircraft abruptly within a short distance, with all the subtlety of running into a wall. As the plane came to a stop, power off, the pilot raised his tail hook while two green-shirted deck crewmen came out from the edges of the deck to clear the wire from the hook. Just beyond the arresting wires were the Davis barriers, which were raised and lowered by operators standing in the catwalk at the edge of the flight deck. Once the aircraft landed, these operators lowered the barriers to allow the pilot to taxi over them. The yellow-shirted landing area plane director would appear ahead and to the right of the airplane and signal the pilot to stop the plane's backward roll with his brakes and to start revving up to taxi forward. As a matter of course, the director would hold out his left hand with the palm down and jab into it with the upraised thumb of his right fist. This meant "hook up." As the wire dropped clear, the director signalled the pilot with a rapid "come ahead" signal to use full throttle to start rolling. Control was then passed to a second yellow jersey 100 feet forward along the flight deck. The director could signal the pilot to continue ahead fast or, by holding his hands out at waist level, palms down with a patting motion, indicate "come ahead, but slow down." As soon as the plane was out of the landing area and forward of

the Davis barriers, the throttle would be set to idle, the brakes applied lightly, and control assumed by a third yellow jersey, who guided the pilot to the "landing spot" or sent him to an elevator to be struck below to the hangar deck. Done properly, the elapsed time from "hook up" to clearing the barrier was 20 seconds or less.

Watching the yellow jerseys and responding to their commands, the pilot controlled his airplane by working the brakes and throttle. While his left hand worked the throttle, his right hand accomplished various tasks such as opening all the cooling flaps to wide, raising the landing flaps, unlocking the wings, and setting the wing control to "fold." The pilot was able to perform these tasks because the control stick was of no further use.[7]

Teamwork

Many of the new *Essex* class carriers completed their shakedown cruises in the Gulf of Paria, a 70-mile by 30-mile expanse of deep water bounded on the east by Trinidad. The only deep-water entrance is the Dragon's Mouth, at the northeast corner, while the only other pass, to the southeast, is through the shoals of the deltas of the Orinoco River. These passes were heavily mined by mid-1943 and patrolled by surface vessels and aircraft. For the new carriers, the gulf was the perfect training locale away from the danger of German submarines.[8] After becoming proficient in basic carrier operations, training moved to a higher level; the air group learned to coordinate its attacks during "group gropes." The idea was for the torpedo bombers, which made their runs at relatively low altitude and

Landing signal officer paddles signals

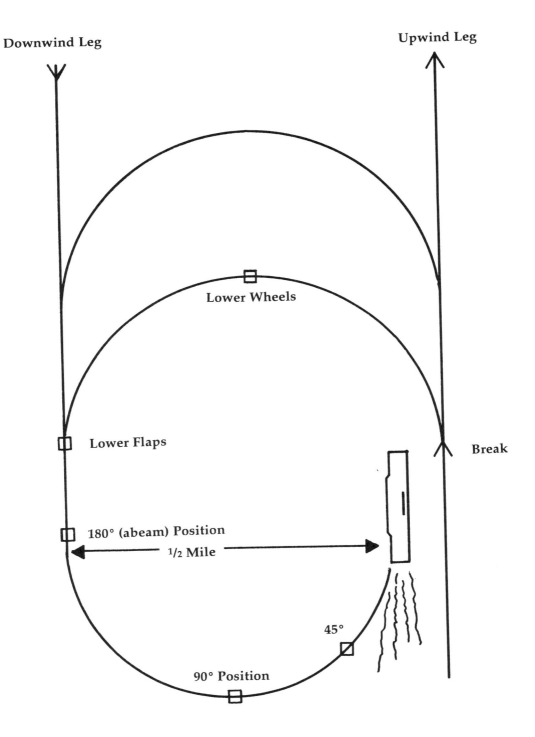

Downwind Leg

Upwind Leg

Lower Wheels

Lower Flaps

Break

180° (abeam) Position

¹/₂ Mile

45°

90° Position

Carrier landing pattern

speed, to approach the target from different angles to prevent the target ship from evading their torpedoes. At the same time, the dive bombers made their runs from above to divide the enemy antiaircraft defenses. The bombers needed fighter cover to prevent enemy aircraft from interfering with the dive bombing and torpedo runs. After the carrier and her air group completed the shakedown cruise, the ship was ready to be integrated into a larger team, a carrier task force, which, in turn was part of a still larger team.

Naval Organization— "The Big Picture"

A task force is simply a collection of military forces needed to accomplish a specific mission. Units can be drawn from several services or even different nations, placed under the operational control of a single commander, and changed as needed. During the war the Commander-in-Chief of the United States Fleet was Fleet Admiral Ernest J. King, who maintained his headquarters in Washington, D.C. As "Cominch," King represented the Navy on both the Combined and Joint Chiefs of Staff. The Joint Chiefs of Staff represented all the services; the Combined Chiefs of Staff included British and American officers and planned the global strategy of the western allies. Once a campaign had been decided upon, Cominch was responsible for the assignment of naval vessels and aircraft and overall planning of the Navy's role. The two principle subordinate fleets, the Atlantic and Pacific Fleets, had numbered fleets assigned within their areas as required, with fleet commanders establishing task

forces within their commands as they thought proper. Ships transferring into a fleet from another area were "in choppers" (from "change of operational control") and ships rotating out an area were "out choppers."

Meeting the needs of the operating forces in the "task" organization were the administrative commands of the "type" organization. These stretched all the way from the Navy Department to individual type commanders within each fleet. There were type commanders for battleships, cruisers, destroyers, etc. Each type commander was responsible for ensuring that all units under his command had proper equipment and training. Before the war, aviation was not centralized in a single type command in either the Atlantic or Pacific Fleet; carrier planes and patrol planes were in different type commands. In September 1942, Rear Admiral Aubrey W. "Jake" Fitch became Commander, Aircraft, Pacific Fleet. Among other duties, his responsibilities included the allocation and distribution of all aircraft, materiel, and aviation personnel throughout the Pacific area, aircraft maintenance, the advanced training and combat readiness of squadrons, and serving as the chief aviation advisor to the Commander-in-Chief, Pacific Fleet. The success of ComAirPac led to the formation of Commander, Aircraft, Atlantic Fleet in January 1943. Because the new carriers of the *Essex* and *Independence* classes were built on the East Coast, ComAirLant trained their air groups and gave the ships their initial shakedown. Once they were ready, they transitted to the Pacific by way of the Panama Canal and reported to the Pacific Fleet. [9]

The Lexington *in Boston Harbor, 17 February 1943. Note the five radio masts and the deck edge elevator in the folded position.*

Deck plates are put in position on the hangar deck of the Yorktown.

The skeleton of the new Yorktown *takes shape at Newport News during 1942.*

Plane handlers practice respotting aboard the Yorktown, *May 1943.*

Crewmen aboard the Yorktown *dash across the flight deck to man their battle stations during a general quarters drill, May 1943.*

A combination that spelled victory in the Pacific — F6F Hellcats and radar. This photograph was taken aboard the Lexington *during the third day of attacks on Mili Island, November 1943.*

A Yorktown *pilot describes the results of a divebombing mission over Wake Island to an Air Combat Intelligence (ACI) officer, October 1943.*

Jubilant fighter pilots lean across the tail of a Hellcat aboard the Lexington *after shooting down seventeen of twenty Japanese aircraft heading for Tarawa, November 1943.*

The air plot room of the Lexington. *The fighter director, LCDR A.F. Fleming (with pipe) and radarmen direct combat air patrols during strikes in the Marshall and Gilbert islands, November 1943.*

Japanese ships in Truk Harbor under attack by carrier aircraft, 16 January 1944, as photographed by an aircraft from the Intrepid.

An LSM loads torpedoes aboard the Essex at Ulithi, October 1944.

An aviation ordnanceman carries 20mm ammunition for SB2Cs aboard the Ticonderoga, October 1944.

A Japanese Navy B6N "Jill" torpedo bomber passes the starboard quarter of the Essex after dropping its torpedo, 14 October 1944.

Guns are manned and ready as an F6F lands aboard the Lexington during the battle off Saipan in the Marianas, 19 June 1944.

An F6F and SB2C, just returned from a mission, are spotted under the barrels of a 40mm gun mount aboard the Ticonderoga, *October 1944.*

The Franklin *swings into formation south of the Bonin Islands, August 1944. Beyond her is the light carrier* Independence CVL-22.

Ordnancemen loading rockets onto an F6F aboard the Essex *en route to strikes against Luzon, December 1944.*

Firefighters, almost hidden by smoke, turn hoses on dozens of small fires started by bombs from a kamikaze which crashed the Intrepid *off the coast of Luzon, 25 November 1944.*

Hornet *pilots manning their aircraft for strikes on Tokyo, February 1945.*

Essex *gunners at their stations as the Japanese attack, 11 April 1945.*

SB2Cs returning to the Hornet *following strikes against Japanese shipping in the China Sea, February 1945.*

The heavily damaged Franklin, *100 miles south of Shokaku, Japan, 19 March 1945. At this point the* Franklin, *with a 14-degree list to starboard, was under tow by the cruiser* Pittsburgh.

The battered Franklin *underway under her own power on the long voyage home.* Franklin *was the most heavily damaged carrier of the war to survive, although she was never restored to active service.*

The Randolph *was crashed only twice during the war; both times while at anchor. While in the Philippines in June 1945, an Army pilot, who had visited the ship, crashed his P-38 while stunting at low altitude.*

The Bunker Hill *becomes an inferno after being hit by two kamikazes, 11 May 1945.*

A kamikaze, making a bow run, is downed by antiaircraft fire before hitting the Bunker Hill, *11 April 1945.*

Columns of smoke rise from the Bunker Hill, *as seen in the distance from the* Essex.

Chapter 6
The Central Pacific

World War II began for Americans when 350 Japanese aircraft from six carriers attacked the U.S. Pacific Fleet at Pearl Harbor, Hawaii on Sunday morning, 7 December 1941. Within hours the Japanese sank four battleships, three destroyers and a minelayer, and severely damaged four battleships, two cruisers, a repair ship, and several other ships. They also destroyed 188 aircraft and damaged many more. Nearly 2,400 officers and enlisted men were killed, most of them Navymen. Japanese losses amounted to 30 aircraft and 55 aircrew—a remarkably small price to pay for the destruction wrought on their opponents.[1] Fortunately, the prime targets, the American aircraft carriers, were not at Pearl Harbor at the time of the attack. Of the three carriers assigned to the Pacific, the *Saratoga* was on the U.S. West Coast, the *Enterprise* was 200 miles west of Oahu returning from the delivery of 12 Marine F4F Wildcat fighters to Wake Island, and the *Lexington* was 420 miles southeast of Midway (700 miles west of Oahu) en route to delivering

18 Marine SB2U Vindicator scout bombers to that island outpost. The other four American fleet carriers, the *Ranger, Yorktown, Wasp,* and *Hornet,* were in the Atlantic.

The Japanese had long desired access to the resource-rich British and Dutch possessions in Southeast Asia, and expansion into this area could create a "Greater East Asia Co-Prosperity Sphere." With their forces mired in the conquest of the Chinese mainland, they sought other means to obtain these resources. The occupation of Indo-China in July 1941 caused the United States to freeze Japanese assets and to tighten existing embargoes on the export of oil and scrap metal to Japan. Realizing that any further move in this region would lead to war with the United States, the Japanese decided that an attack on Pearl Harbor would prevent American interference with their plans for conquest. Because the Americans could only fight their way through Japan's outer defenses at great cost, the Japanese expected the Americans to

The Central Pacific

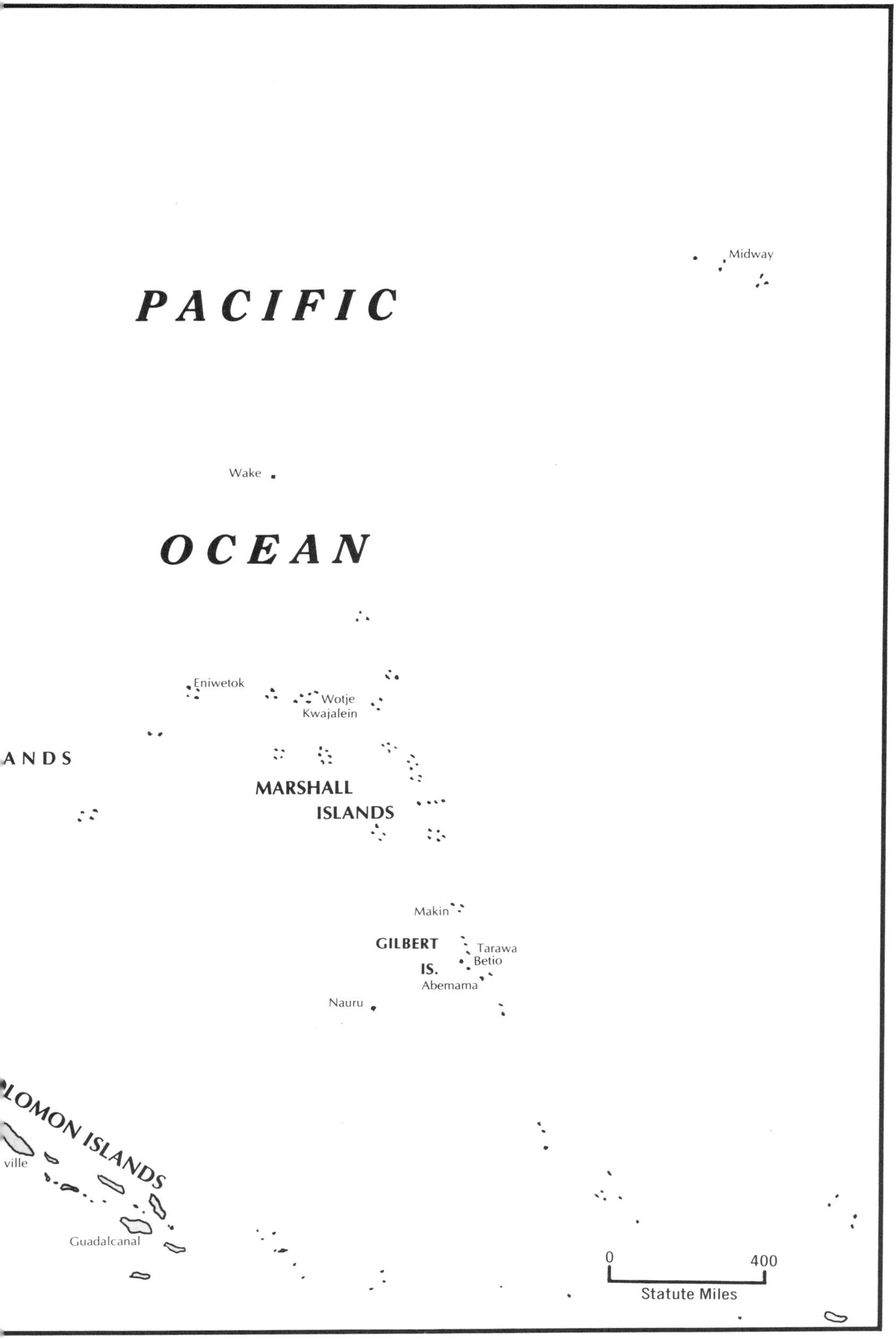

PACIFIC

OCEAN

Midway

Wake .

. :

. Eniwetok

Wotje
Kwajalein

**MARSHALL
ISLANDS**

ANDS

Makin

**GILBERT
IS.**

Tarawa
Betio

Abemama

Nauru

LOMON ISLANDS

ville

Guadalcanal

0   400

Statute Miles

negotiate a settlement that would give Japan possession of the resources she depended upon. Within the first six months of the war, the Japanese ran up an impressive string of victories, landing in the Philippines and overrunning the British in Malaya and Singapore. By the time resistance ended in the Philippines in May 1942, the British were on the retreat in Burma, the Japanese had defeated British naval forces in the Bay of Bengal, and most of the northern coast of New Guinea, plus the Bismarks, the northern Solomons, the Gilberts, Guam and Wake were under Japanese control.

Even before this outer defensive perimeter was in place, the Japanese were concerned with the buildup of Allied forces in Australia and the threat posed by the remaining naval forces of the American Pacific Fleet, in particular the aircraft carriers, which launched a series of raids on Japanese-held outposts in early 1942. The Doolittle Tokyo raid in April, which launched 16 twin-engine Army B-25 Mitchell bombers from the *Hornet* to attack Tokyo and other Japanese cities, inflicted little real damage on the Japanese homeland, but made the Japanese realize their vulnerability. Afflicted with "victory disease" after their unbroken string of conquests, the Japanese embarked on a second strategic offensive to extend the perimeter even further into the southwest, central, and northern Pacific. Seeking to gain control of the southern Solomons, southern Papua, New Guinea, Midway, and the Aleutians, the Japanese sought to force the Americans to commit their fleet to a "decisive battle" while the balance of strength was still in Japan's favor.

The first phase of the new strategic offensive was a thrust into the Solomons and southeastern New Guinea. In early May 1942, in an attempt to take Port Moresby on the southeastern side of New Guinea, the Japanese, with the light carrier *Shoho* and the fleet carriers *Shokaku* and *Zuikaku*, encountered the American carriers *Lexington* and *Yorktown* in the first naval battle in history fought entirely by carrier aircraft. The *Shoho* was sunk and the *Shokaku* damaged; the Americans lost the *Lexington*, an oiler, and a destroyer, and the *Yorktown* was damaged. But the Battle of Coral Sea was an American victory. The Japanese expedition to Port Moresby was turned back and air strikes against Australia were prevented.

The next phase of Japan's strategic offensive called for the capture of Midway and the occupation of Attu and Kiska in the western Aleutians. The assault on Midway would force the American fleet into a decisive battle. The Japanese plan called for four major sea forces which included invasion forces for Midway and the Aleutians. Unknown to the Japanese, the Americans had cracked the Japanese codes and knew of their intentions. Nimitz, in command of the Pacific Fleet since January, concentrated his three carriers, the *Enterprise, Hornet* and *Yorktown*, to defend Midway.[2] The Japanese lost all four of their fleet carriers assigned to the Carrier Striking Force, the *Akagi, Kaga, Hiryu* and *Soryu*, while the Americans lost the *Yorktown*, which had been hurriedly repaired at Pearl Harbor following the Coral Sea battle. The Battle of Midway, fought in early June 1942, was a major defeat for the Japanese and marked the turning point in the war. It shattered the myth of Japanese invincibility and dealt a blow to the Japanese carrier forces from which they never fully recovered. It also demonstrated that the aircraft carrier was now the major warship in the Pacific.

Throughout the rest of 1942, action centered on the Southwest Pacific Area.[3] With the arrival of the *Wasp* from the Atlantic and the return of the *Saratoga* from repairs on the West Coast, American carrier strength immediately after the Battle of Midway was superior to that of the Japanese. Both the Army and the Navy agreed that offensive operations were now possible and that control of the Japanese stronghold of Rabaul on New Britain should be a major objective. But the Navy was reluctant to give command to an Army general who might utilize naval forces improperly and place the precious few carriers available at risk from Japanese land-based aircraft.[4] The landing of the Marines on Guadalcanal in August marked the beginning of a desperate struggle which see-sawed back and forth for several months. A number of hard-fought naval engagements took place in and around the waters of the Eastern Solomons. The Japanese lost the light carrier *Ryujo* to American carrier aircraft in the Battle of the Eastern Solomons in August. The *Wasp* was sunk by three torpedoes from a Japanese submarine in September. The *Hornet* was sunk by Japanese carrier aircraft during the Battle of Santa Cruz Islands in October. Under the command of Admiral William F. "Bull" Halsey since mid-October, the South Pacific forces slowly turned the tide. By the end of the year, an American victory was assured.

The Central Pacific

Early in 1943, American war planners began to rethink their strategy.

With the successes of Halsey's South Pacific forces on Guadalcanal and MacArthur's Southwest Pacific forces at Papua, steps could be taken to capture or neutralize the major Japanese base at Rabaul, located on the northeastern tip of New Britain island in the western Solomons. Although overall strategic direction had called for the defeat of Germany first, long term strategic goals included the ultimate defeat of Japan. MacArthur favored a drive up through New Guinea to recapture the Philippines. The Navy favored a drive across the Central Pacific spearheaded by the new fast carriers, which included the *Essex* class and the smaller *Independence* class light carriers. In the Navy's view, Japan was most vulnerable on her eastern flank and the seizure of island bases would provide airfields from which the Japanese home islands would eventually come under attack. There was also the possibility that the Philippines could be bypassed entirely in favor of landings on Formosa or the Chinese coast. In May 1943, the Joint Chiefs of Staff resolved the dispute by approving a dual drive westward in the general direction of the Philippines. The question of whether to take or bypass the Philippines themselves was deferred for the moment and the issue of overall command of the war against Japan did not come to a head until both drives converged later in the war.

In March 1943, Vice Admiral Raymond A. Spruance, who had commanded at the Midway victory and who was currently serving as Nimitz's chief of staff, was named commander of the Fifth Fleet. The Fifth Fleet was formed from what had been the Central Pacific component of the Pacific Fleet. Spruance was a cool, calculating professional who was thoroughly "regulation." He was regarded as a "battleship man" by the aviators, but was known for meticulous planning and the careful weighing of risks. It was only by a twist of circumstance that he ended up in command of two of the three American carriers at Midway. He was serving as Halsey's cruiser screen commander when Halsey came down with a severe skin rash brought on by the stress of continuous operations. Nimitz had asked Halsey to suggest a replacement and Halsey recommended Spruance. Nimitz instructed Spruance to conduct the battle under the principle of "calculated risk," since so much was at stake at that desperate juncture of the war. Having no aviation background, Spruance had the good sense to rely heavily on the aviation expertise of his inherited chief of staff, Captain Miles R. Browning. With the victory, Spruance's star was on the rise, but the improved American position in the Central Pacific reduced the need to take risks and Spruance could now afford to be more methodical and cautious.

Rear Admiral Richmond Kelly "Terrible" Turner commanded the V Amphibious Force, which was set up in August. Turner earned his sobriquet by being a hard task master and as the war progressed, American skill in amphibious operations grew. The ground troops, which included Marine and Army troops, had Marine Major General Holland M. "Howlin' Mad" Smith as commander of the V Amphibious Corps. Smith and Turner were both strong personalities determined to have their way. The issue of who was actually in command of which invasion forces at what point in the process could only be resolved between them. "Howlin'

Mad" Smith also had to contend with command conflicts with the Army forces serving in the Central Pacific. These conflicts eventually came to a head during the Saipan invasion later in the war.

The island groups of the Pacific are arrayed in the form of a capital L. The Central Pacific Force would begin its drive westward in the Gilberts, an island group straddling the equator about 2,400 miles southwest of Hawaii. To the north and west are the Marshalls. Further west are the Carolines, strung out westward toward the Philippines. North of the central Carolines lie the Marianas, and above them, in a line aimed in the general direction of Japan, lie the Bonins. MacArthur's war, moving along New Guinea's northern coast, complemented the Central Pacific drive and, occasionally, Central Pacific forces were called in to help MacArthur's forces.

War in the Central Pacific was different from that fought in MacArthur's Southwest Pacific; the key pieces of terrain in the vast distances of the Central Pacific were coral islands. The typical Pacific coral island is a flat and sparsely vegetated platform rising only a few feet above the ocean. It is usually part of an atoll, a variously shaped ring formed by the growth of coral over the sunken remains of an extinct volcano. A large atoll may be 20 or more miles across, but the islands associated with it are usually no more than a few miles in length. Kwajalein, in the Marshall Islands, was the world's biggest atoll (65 miles in length) and Nimitz's prime target as he planned the drive across the Central Pacific in the summer of 1943. But before approaching the Marshalls, it was decided that the Gilberts, 500 miles to the southeast, must be taken. Attacking the Marshalls with the Gilberts still in Japanese hands would mean exposing American forces to danger from the rear. Another consideration was the inexperience of the forces involved, and taking the Gilberts taught many lessons, most of them costly.

The two main atolls in the Japanese-occupied Gilberts were Tarawa and Makin and it was assumed that the Japanese would not give them up easily. Before the Gilberts assault could be launched, forces needed to be gathered from the United States, Hawaii, New Zealand and the South Pacific area. Meanwhile, the fast carrier forces could learn how to use their new ships, aircraft and weapons. Their leaders and crews would also be in a learning status—"makee learn" as the old Navy expression goes.

The Marcus Strike

On 23 August 1943, Task Force 15 formed north of Hawaii. Under the command of Rear Admiral Charles A. "Baldy" Pownall, Task Force 15 included the *Essex* (commanded by Captain Donald B. "Wu" Duncan, with Rear Admiral Montgomery aboard in learning status), the *Yorktown* (Captain J.J. "Jocko" Clark), the light carrier *Independence* (Captain George R. Fairlamb), the fast battleship *Indiana*, two light cruisers, and ten destroyers. Rear Admiral Pownall flew his flag from the *Yorktown*. The task force was supported by a fleet oiler and, at Pownall's suggestion, a submarine was standing by in the target area to pick up any downed fliers. The ships cruised in a circular formation, the three carriers in the center surrounded by the battleship and cruisers, with destroyers in an outer ring. The plan

was to refuel the big ships before the strike and on retirement, with the destroyers topping off from the big ships every third or fourth day. On 27 August, after going far to the north, the task force began two days of refueling and followed a weather front all the way into the launch area. Before dawn on 31 August, task force radars picked up a returning Japanese search plane. The task force easily followed the search plane back to Marcus, since the Japanese had not changed their patrol patterns since the Halsey raids of 1942.

The sea was dead calm, the sky clear, and the planet Mars was glowing in the direction of the target. The big gun ships gave the carriers sea room while the destroyers swung out in front, marking a horizon with their lights for the pilots' reference. The carriers maneuvered at up to 30 knots, chasing any breeze, trying to give their aircraft enough wind over the deck to launch. At 0422, the first Hellcat rolled down the *Yorktown*'s deck. In the cold gray dawn the planes caught the Japanese "with their pants down" according to Pownall in his after-action report. On the first sweep, strafing fighters destroyed seven parked twin-engine Betty bombers while the bombers hit the airstrip and buildings. The TBFs carried 2,000-pound "blockbuster" bombs and the SBDs carried 1,000-pound fragmentation "daisy cutters." Five deck-load strikes were flown, two each from the *Essex* and *Yorktown* and one from the *Independence*. Flak was heavy at first and claimed three aircraft. The submarine *Snook*, acting as "lifeguard," could not locate any of the survivors and they were later captured. The task force had closed to within ten miles of the target while rearming and refueling its aircraft, but fortunately, there were no Japanese air or submarine attacks. Task Force 15 returned to Pearl Harbor on 8 September.

Following the Marcus raid, Rear Admiral Alfred E. "Monty" Montgomery, who had flown his flag aboard *Essex* during the Marcus raid, took *Essex* and *Yorktown* to San Francisco on a "logistic mission" to bring back men and vehicles. Captain Fairlamb of the *Independence* had lost his composure during the Marcus operations and was relieved when the task force returned to Pearl. Rear Admiral Pownall had shown the signs of nervousness and irritability which would eventually lead to his relief as commander of the fast carriers. Although personally affable and polite in his dealings with others, Pownall was unsuited for the command of a carrier task force. The younger aviator ship commanders and up-and-coming carrier group admirals regarded him as lacking in the aggressive spirit necessary to fully exploit the potential of the new fast carriers.

The Tarawa Raid

The plan for the Tarawa raid was similar to that for the Marcus operations, except that 25 Seventh Air Force bombers would hit Tarawa the night before (17-18 September), with photographs taken for the landings scheduled later. Task Force 15 was composed of the *Lexington* (Captain Felix B. Stump) and the light carriers *Princeton* (Captain G.R. Henderson, with Rear Admiral Arthur W. "Raddy" Radford aboard), and *Belleau Wood* (Captain A.M. Pride).[5] Pownall, who flew his flag from the *Lexington,* again displayed signs of nervousness and irrationality. He coun-

termanded the plans of his operations officer to make a key navigational turn before dawn on the day of the strike, so that the task force was almost on top of the target at first light. Although the Japanese were expected to launch strikes on the task force from Kwajalein, only three enemy aircraft appeared and these were shot down by the defending Hellcats. The carrier strikes destroyed several enemy aircraft and small boats, but camouflage spoiled the effectiveness of the bombing on the installations. Good oblique photographs were taken of the beaches, but the aircraft carrying the vertical cameras was one of two friendly aircraft shot down by flak. Pownall refused to send another photo aircraft. Unfortunately for the Marines who landed at Tarawa later in November, the obliques did not show the reefs clearly. Planning for the Gilberts invasion assumed there would be enough water under the amphibious landing craft to clear the reef, and the lack of adequate overhead photography, which might have shown otherwise, did not help. Amphibious tractors ("amphtracs") capable of crossing the reefs were only available because of the dogged insistence of "Howlin' Mad" Smith.

The Wake Raids

For the Wake raids Rear Admiral Montgomery, as commander of Task Force 14, experimented with different cruising formations, which varied between a single formation of six carriers, two groups with three carriers each, and three groups with two carriers each. Task Force 14 was divided into two "cruising groups." The First Cruising Group, under Montgomery, included the *Essex,* the *Yorktown,* and a bombardment group of four light cruisers, with the light carriers *Independence* and *Belleau Wood* under Rear Admiral V.H. Ragsdale supporting the cruisers. The Second Cruising Group, under Rear Admiral Arthur W. "Raddy" Radford, included *Lexington*, the light carrier *Cowpens*, and a bombardment group of three heavy cruisers. The task force also had 24 escorting destroyers, two oilers, and the *Skate* as lifeguard submarine.

Task Force 14 launched its first strikes in the dark predawn of 5 October. For the first time, the carrier aircraft met enemy fighters, about 30 Zeros, over the target. The Hellcats drew their first blood, shooting down most of the Zeros. Three times as many bombs hit Wake as either Marcus or Tarawa, but the Japanese responded with two flights of six bombers and six fighters each from the Marshalls. Ragsdale's Combat Air Patrol (CAP) fighters intercepted them and drove them off. The Japanese landing at Wake escaped to the Marshalls later that night. Between the flak and enemy fighters, 12 carrier aircraft were lost, although the *Skate* did pick up six survivors. The cruisers shelled Wake on both days. According to Captain Duckworth, Montgomery's chief of staff who had planned the operation, "virtually all the techniques of ship handling for a multi-carrier force which were later used successfully had their origins in this operation." The six-, two-, and three-carrier groups had all proven feasible in this operation, but it was the three-carrier task group that was adopted for the Gilberts invasion in November.

After the Marcus-Wake series of raids, the *Bunker Hill* (Captain J.J. Ballentine) arrived at Pearl that fall, along with the light carrier *Monterey* and the refurbished *Enterprise*. The *Bunker Hill* carried the only operational squadron, VB-17, equipped with the new SB2C-1 Helldiver.[6]

The Rabaul Strike

Task Force 38 under Rear Admiral Frederick C. "Ted" Sherman had struck Rabaul on 5 November 1943 with aircraft from *Saratoga* and *Princeton*, heavily damaging four heavy cruisers and damaging two light cruisers. These Japanese ships came from Truk, as had more aircraft from the Imperial Japanese Navy's Carrier Division One, to threaten Halsey's 1 November Bougainville landings. Task Force 38 supported these landings with strikes on the Buka-Bonis airfields, followed by another the next day, after which the task force withdrew to the south. After the cruiser action of the Battle of Empress Augusta Bay, search aircraft discovered the Japanese heavy cruisers at Rabaul, hence the need for the Rabaul strike by Task Force 38. In response to Halsey's request for more carrier support, Nimitz sent Task Group 50.3 under Rear Admiral Montgomery with *Essex, Bunker Hill* and *Independence* to participate in a follow on strike.

Arriving 5 November, Task Group 50.3 stayed at Espiritu Santo for three days while more escort destroyers were sought. Task Force 38 would hit Rabaul from the north while Task Group 50.3 was to strike from the south. With the attack finally set for 11 November, Halsey pointed out that "five air groups . . . ought to change the name of Rabaul to Rubble." The Task Force 38 aircraft bucked heavy weather to get a few hits, but Task Group 50.3 fared better later in the day. Two land-based F4U Corsair squadrons and a land-based F6F Hellcat squadron provided cover for the task group. One of the F4U squadrons was Lieutenant Commander Tommy Blackburn's famous VF-17 "Skull and Crossbones" squadron, which had first trained on the *Bunker Hill,* and Blackburn used the tailhooks on his Corsairs to land and refuel on that ship. The Task Group 50.3 strike aircraft torpedoed one light cruiser and a destroyer, which sank, and sank another destroyer with bombs. About 90 fighters ran into 68 Zeros and shot down six. The Japanese retaliated with strikes by about 120 aircraft. The task group had only the guns of the carriers and the destroyers for antiaircraft defense, since the cruisers had been detached to support Halsey's beachhead. The Combat Air Patrol intercepted the first enemy bombers 40 miles from the task group. As more Japanese aircraft pressed the attack, "Monty" Montgomery boomed out over the *Bunker Hill*'s loudspeaker, "Man your guns and shoot those bastards out of the sky!" The early afternoon action lasted 46 minutes, with the carriers driving off over two dozen enemy aircraft as the carrier skippers skillfully maneuvered to avoid bombs and torpedoes. Eleven aviators were lost.

This battle, known as the Battle of the Solomon Sea, marked the turning point in the aviators' opinion of the SB2C Helldiver. Even the skipper VB-9 on the *Essex,* which still flew the SBD, remarked that 90 percent of the bomber pilots were now "all for them." The Hellcats and Corsairs did well, as did the Avengers, although, because of malfunctions, the performance of the aerial torpedoes left much to be desired.

The Rabaul strikes, and those of General George Kenny's land-based Fifth Air Force, convinced the Japanese

that Rabaul was unsafe for shipping. With the landings on *Bougainville,* Rabaul now lay within range of Halsey's land-based fighters. Admiral Koga, who replaced Yamamoto as Commander in Chief of the Combined Fleet, recalled his remaining carrier planes on 13 November; of the 173 aircraft sent to Rabaul from Carrier Division One, half the fighters and almost all the attack aircraft were lost, including many experienced flyers.[7] On 11 November, Task Force 38 was redesignated Task Group 50.4 and with Task Group 50.3 proceeded north to rejoin the Central Pacific Force, while Task Group 50.1 and Task Group 50.2 rendezvoused with their oilers and escorting battleships north of the Phoenix Islands before the final approach to the targets for the Gilberts operation.

The Gilberts—Operation Galvanic

The Gilberts invasion involved three task forces: a Southern Task Force under Rear Admiral Harry W. Hill to take Tarawa, a Northern Task Force under Rear Admiral Turner to take Makin, and the Fast Carrier Force under Rear Admiral Pownall. Under Spruance, the carriers, much to the disgust of the aviators, would be limited to defensive sectors. Task Group 50.1 under Pownall made up the Carrier Interceptor Group with *Yorktown, Lexington,* and the light carrier *Cowpens.* Rear Admiral Radford commanded the Northern Carrier Group, Task Group 50.2, with the veteran *Enterprise* and the new light carriers *Belleau Wood* and *Monterey.* Rear Admiral Montgomery commanded the Southern Carrier Group, Task Group 50.3, with *Essex, Bunker Hill,* and the light carrier *Independence.* Rear Admiral

Sherman commanded the Relief Carrier Group, the newly redesignated Task Group 50.4, with the old *Saratoga* and the light carrier *Princeton.*

The softening up of the target beaches on Makin and Tarawa began several days before by Rear Admiral John H. Hoover's land-based aircraft from SoPac. Task Group 50.3 hit Tarawa 18 November and Task Group 50.1 hit airfields at Mili and Jaluit in the southern Marshalls. Task Group 50.2 bombed Makin and Task Group 50.4 destroyed Japanese air power at Nauru. While the other three task groups stayed on station, Task Group 50.4 turned east to escort garrison convoys to the objective. The surface ship bombardment of Tarawa began less than three hours before the assault, augmented by planes from the escort carriers and the fast carriers. The inexperienced *Essex* pilots thought they had destroyed Tarawa's defenses, but when Marine casualties began to mount, everyone realized the truth.

The Task Groups each sent a special radar picket destroyer 30,000 yards ahead to detect incoming enemy aircraft, but this was not enough. The only carrier with night capability was *Enterprise*.[8] On the night of 20 November, long-range Japanese Betty bombers from Kwajalein and Maloelap attacked Task Group 50.3 off Tarawa. Combat Air Patrols from *Essex, Bunker Hill,* and *Independence* brought down nine, but *Independence* was torpedoed in the dusk attack. Several men were killed on the *Independence* and she left the war zone for repairs which took six months. Because of this experience, Rear Admiral Towers, ComAirPac, recommended to Admiral Nimitz that the "defensive sector" plan of Spruance be modified and that the fast carriers be sent north to strike Japanese bases in the Marshalls. Spruance did not change plans immediately since the ground troops needed close air support, which was beginning to improve. Resistance on Betio, the principal objective in the Tarawa atoll, ended 23 November; Makin and Abemama fell the same day. But Japanese air strikes continued and two small strikes were destroyed by Task Group 50.3 on 23 and 24 November.

On the evening of 23 November, five aircraft from the *Liscome Bay* (CVE-59), one of the escort carriers providing close air support for the Army troops ashore on Makin, asked for permission to land aboard the *Yorktown* when a storm came up. The first two aircraft made it aboard safely, but the third did not; the pilot had forgotten to lower his tail hook. The aircraft bounced and the pilot tried to go around, but only succeeded in jumping the barricade. The belly tank of the aircraft ruptured and exploded, the flames setting fire to ammunition and flares stored in the aircraft parked forward. The pilot squirmed free as the flames spread. As the damage control parties rushed forward to smother the flames, the air officer ordered the other two planes to land aboard the *Lexington.* Captain Clark kept the *Yorktown* into the wind to keep the flames from spreading forward. Gasoline had spilled down to the hangar deck, and there were some anxious minutes until the fires were brought under control, some 14 minutes later. Five aircraft were destroyed and five crewmen killed, but by the next morning, *Yorktown* was again operational.

Ironically, in the predawn hours of 24 November, a Japanese submarine (I-175) torpedoed the *Liscome Bay,* which sank with the loss of 644 men, including her commander, Captain I.D. Wiltsie, and a promising carrier group commander, Rear Admiral Henry M. Mullinix. The loss of the *Liscome Bay* emphasized the danger inherent in tying carriers down to beachheads.

The major Japanese tactic was night torpedo attacks. A single Japanese aircraft, called "Tojo the Lamplighter" by the nervous carrier crews, arrived over Task Group 50.2 off Makin. On the night of 26 November, about 30 torpedo bombers flew in from the Marshalls to hit Radford's Task Group. Task Group 50.2 was ready however, with Commander Butch O'Hare's night team from the *Enterprise,* which was made up of two Hellcats and an Avenger torpedo bomber equipped with primitive radar. Two Bettys were shot down by the TBF before it rendezvoused with the Hellcats. The Japanese attack broke up in the confusion, but O'Hare's aircraft was shot down, probably by mistake by the TBF's turret gunner. A few more air actions took place, but attacks ended on 28 November, the same day organized resistance ended on the islands. Seventy-one Marshalls-based planes had been shot down, including several more staged from Truk. The last 32 Japanese carrier fighters had been sent to the Marshalls, where most were shot down. American losses totalled 47 aircraft, but the submarine *Plunger* picked up several pilots in the Gilberts.

North to the Marshalls

Spruance ordered Pownall to leave *Bunker Hill* and *Monterey* north of the Gilberts under Rear Admiral Sherman, while the rest were ordered to hit Kwajalein in the Marshalls with Pownall's

Task Group 50.1 (*Yorktown, Lexington,* and *Cowpens*) and Montgomery's Task Group 50.3 (which was reshuffled to include *Essex, Enterprise,* and *Belleau Wood*).[9] Pownall approached the area from the northeast on 4 December. The early results of the bombing and strafing attacks were poor against the installations and ships. During the 45-minute strike, Task Force 50 destroyed four merchant vessels and 55 aircraft, 28 of them in the air. As the strike returned, many Betty's were spotted on an airfield at nearby Roi, but Pownall would not launch a second strike. About noon, two flights of four Kates each attacked the task force and were shot down. As one Kate pressed its attack, *Yorktown* gunners kept lowering their fire until they were shooting into one of the escorting heavy cruisers. Pownall yelled up to Captain Clark, "Cease fire! Cease fire! You are firing at that cruiser!" Clark ignored the order and the Kate was brought down. After recovering the Wotje strike, Task Force 50 headed for friendly waters, but heavy seas slowed down the task force. Everyone in the task force knew the Japanese would make night torpedo attacks. "Jocko" Clark several times pounded the *Yorktown*'s chart desk with his fist, exclaiming "Goddammit, you can't run away from airplanes with ships!" Cruising at 18 knots, Task Force 50 prepared for a night attack. Shortly after 2000, it came. Under a bright moon, 30 to 50 Betty's, guided by snooper aircraft that had shadowed the task force, attacked. The task force broke up into two task groups as Pownall relied on independent evasive ship maneuvers and antiaircraft fire. (The task force no longer had night fighter capability following O'Hare's death.) Captain Stump of the *Lexington* later paid tribute to Pownall who, "without a doubt . . . saved us from a coordinated attack by changing course all the time." The attack was erratic, sometimes heavy, sometimes only threatening. Thirty minutes before midnight, parachute flares silhouetted the *Lexington,* and ten minutes later she was hit by a torpedo to starboard, which knocked out her steering gear. Settling five feet by the stern, she began circling to port amidst dense clouds of smoke pouring from ruptured tanks aft. She had lost steerage, but by varying the speed of her shafts, she could maneuver enough to escape. The last attack was beaten off by the ships' fire and the increasing darkness as the moon set around 0130 on 5 December. Intelligence later reported that Japanese aircraft had withdrawn to Nauru.[10] An

emergency hand-operated steering unit was quickly devised aboard the *Lex* and she made it to Pearl Harbor for emergency repairs before proceeding to Bremerton, Washington, for full repairs.

Kavieng

Rear Admiral Sherman reported back to Halsey with *Bunker Hill* and *Monterey* as Task Group 37.2. On Christmas day, Task Group 37.2 struck Kavieng, New Ireland (north of Rabaul) and eluded night torpedo attacks by rapid maneuvering and laying down a smoke screen. Strikes were repeated on New Year's Day and again on 4 January. Several enemy aircraft were shot down, while Task Group 37.2 suffered little damage. Unfortunately, targets were few.

Chapter 7
Mitscher Takes Command

Although Task Force 50 had been the first actual fast carrier force, it lacked one important ingredient—an effective commander. That situation was rectified when, on 13 January 1944, Rear Admiral Marc A. "Pete" Mitscher hoisted his flag aboard the *Yorktown* as Commander, Task Force 58. As Commander, Fast Carrier Force, Pacific Fleet, Mitscher led the fast carrier forces in the drive across the Central Pacific. An early naval aviator, Mitscher had been the captain of the old *Hornet* during the Doolittle Tokyo raid in April 1942 and at the Battle of Midway that June. After the loss of the old *Hornet* at the Battle of Santa Cruz, he took over as Halsey's land-based air commander in the Solomons.[1] Quiet and soft-spoken, Mitscher was a leader's leader who held the respect of all his carrier group commanders. Still recovering from malaria and down to 115 pounds, Mitscher was ready to give his carrier commanders their heads if they performed. "I tell them what I want done, not how," he said.

Task Force 58's sortie from Pearl Harbor late that January, marked the last time the fast carriers operated from Hawaii, which had become a rear area. Mitscher commanded 12 fast carriers (the light carriers *Langley* and *Cabot* were new), 650 aircraft, eight fast battleships, plus cruisers and destroyers. Unknown to U.S. naval intelligence, the last of Japan's best navy pilots had been lost in the Rabaul meat grinder. No carrier pilots remained. When the Japanese learned of Task Force 58's sortie, Admiral Koga withdrew most of his major units to Palau in the western end of the Carolines, leaving about 150 aircraft, including many Betty bombers, to defend the Marshalls. The carriers conducted practice exercises en route and pre-attack briefings assigned specific targets for each crew. For Operation Flintlock, the invasion of Kwajalein, Task Force 58 was given the opportunity to knock out Japanese strength before it could be used against the invasion forces. Between 29 January and 6 February, the four task groups struck daily at targets in the

Marshalls, virtually destroying Japanese sea and air power in the area.

The Marshalls

On 29 January 1944, Task Force 58 launched strikes against the Marshalls. Rear Admiral Reeves's Task Group 58.1 hit Maloelap, Rear Admiral Ginder's Task Group 58.4 bombed Wotje, Rear Admiral Montgomery's Task Group 58.2 attacked the airfield on Roi, while Task Group 58.3 under Rear Admiral Sherman hit Kwajalein Island. The few Japanese aircraft airborne over Roi were shot down by Hellcats from *Essex, Intrepid,* and *Cabot,* which then strafed parked aircraft on the airstrips. To ensure the Japanese did not stage through Eniwetok, Task Group 58.3 shifted to Eniwetok for the next three days, while Task Group 58.4 moved to Maloelap for two days and joined Task Group 58.3 at Eniwetok on the third day. Task Group 58.2 spent the next five days hitting Roi-Namur in close support. Task Group 58.1 spent the same five days on Kwajalein, while Rear Admiral Hoover's land-based air worked over Mili and Jaluit. The fast carriers lost 17 fighters and five torpedo aircraft to enemy action, and 27 other aircraft operationally.[2]

From 31 January to 3 February, the carrier aircraft took directions from the air support commanders in hitting Japanese defensive positions. Placing close air support aircraft under the direct control of specially equipped amphibious command ships (AGC) began with Operation Flintlock. The Commander Support Aircraft relieved the carriers of responsibility for control of the Target Combat Air Patrols (TAR-CAP) and selected local targets. The Support Air Control Units ashore were

also strengthened, but the tendency of pilots to ignore the signals of friendly troops continued to be a problem. Combined with the land-based strikes, the more than 4,500 sorties resulted in lower resistance than in the Gilberts. After Kwajalein fell on 4 February, Task Groups 58.1, 58.2, and 58.3 headed for the newly occupied Majuro Atoll while Rear Admiral Ginder's Task Group 58.4 continued strikes against Eniwetok.[3]

Majuro

Majuro Atoll was 2,000 miles west of Pearl Harbor and allowed commercial tankers to bypass Hawaii, cutting down on transit times to the forward area. Service squadrons provided logistic support for operational forces in the Pacific. Servron 4, which had fueled the carriers for Operation Galvanic, merged with Servron 10 when the latter, formed for Operation Flintlock, arrived at Majuro. Servron 10 supported the fast carrier forces exclusively for the rest of the war. Early in 1944 escort carriers joined the Servron to provide antiaircraft and antisubmarine protection, and to ferry replacement aircraft to the fast carriers. Administratively separate from the service squadrons of Vice Admiral William L. Calhoun's Service Force Pacific Fleet, was ComAirPac's aviation logistics. After August 1943, the shore-based Carrier Aircraft Service Units (CASU) were placed under ComAirPac. The carrier based counterpart of the CASU was the Carrier Aircraft Service Division (CASDIV), which was interchangeable with the CASU. As the large *Essex* class air groups arrived in the Pacific, the CASU/CASDIV organizations grew to 17 officers and 516 enlisted men per unit.

While most of Task Force 58 enjoyed the brief lull at Majuro, there were several command changes. Captain Clark was promoted to Rear Admiral and became Commander Carrier Division Thirteen (ComCarDiv13), while Captain Ralph Jennings took over as the new commander of the *Yorktown*. Captain J.J. Ballentine was also promoted to Rear Admiral and became Chief of Staff to ComAirPac and was replaced as skipper of the *Bunker Hill* by Captain Tom Jeter.

Four atolls where the Japanese had airbases—Jaluit, Mili, Maloelap, Wotje—and Nauru, too, were left to "wither on the vine" as the Central Pacific war moved on. They became practice targets for new carriers, or veterans returning from overhaul, on their way to the forward area. The next target for Task Force 58 was the fabled Japanese bastion of Truk, the "Gilbraltar of the Pacific," located to the west of the Marshalls in the center of the Caroline Islands chain. This strike would put an end to any Japanese attempts to interfere with the planned landings on Eniwetok, Operation Catchpole, scheduled for 17 February 1944.

The Raid on Truk

Truk had long been held by the Japanese and threatened any future American moves in the central Pacific; it would be neutralized for the invasion of Eniwetok and before the Marianas could be attacked. The task force sailed from the newly occupied anchorage at Majuro on 12 February 1944. Mitscher headed for Truk with three task groups. Rear Admiral Ginder's Task Group 58.4 remained behind to cover the Eniwetok landings, as Mitscher felt that Ginder's performance was less than satisfactory

compared to his other task group commanders.[4] When the aircrews heard that they were going to attack Truk, there were serious misgivings. Not much was really known about Truk and everything they had heard was bad. According to Commander Phil Torrey, commander of Air Group 9 aboard the *Essex*, "They didn't tell us where we were going until we were well under way. They announced our destination over the loudspeaker. It was Truk. My first instinct was to jump overboard."[5] A land-based reconnaissance mission flown from the Solomons on 3 February had shown some 20 naval vessels in Truk lagoon, but the major Japanese naval units had departed on 10 February.

Mitscher tried some new tricks for the Truk strike, including tighter task group formations and following under rain squalls on the way into the launch area. The first aircraft off would be a fighter sweep to clear the area of Japanese aircraft that might interfere with the bombers. Another tactic was to use 1,000-pound delayed action bombs on the last runway strikes to make repair during the night more difficult. Also, strikes against oil storage sites were saved for last to keep the flame and smoke from obscuring other targets.

The attack was launched at 0600 on 17 February, when the task force was a hundred miles northeast of Truk. As the fighter sweep moved in, about 50 Japanese aircraft tangled with the 74 F6Fs of the fighter sweep. In half an hour, the Americans had dealt with most of the opposition, some of whom were tough veterans of previous battles. Within an hour and a half, no more Japanese aircraft rose to challenge the attackers, and when the bombers arrived at 0930, there were no Japanese aircraft to interfere with their bombing runs. Some bombers carried fragmentation bombs in 100-pound clusters, others carried incendiary bombs and went after service installations on the air fields. Then came the dive bombers with 1,000-pound bombs, moving in to hit the shipping in the Dublon anchorage. Most of the Japanese warships had gone, but some merchantmen and a pair of cruisers remained. The bombers hit a merchantman and made a near miss on a cruiser in the first pass. With the bombers came more fighters, who strafed antiaircraft positions that were firing at the strike aircraft. The bombers attacked repeatedly, setting a tanker on fire, hitting a small carrier, and hitting the merchantman. In midafternoon a strike went after the other anchorages. One aircraft found a destroyer trying to escape and dropped four 500-pound bombs on it. The first landed astern, but the other three hit the destroyer squarely from stem to stern, leaving her dead in the water in a mass of flame and smoke. A strike later in the day dropped the delayed action 1,000-pound bombs on the bomber airfield at Moen. A still later strike, almost at the end of the day, hit the revetments on the airfields, spoiling a potential night attack. The Japanese fighters reappeared later in the day, tangling with the strike aircraft.

That night the Japanese were out looking for the task force. From around 2100 until midnight, small groups of bogies appeared on task force radars. *Yorktown* launched a night fighter to drive off the snoopers, but a small group of radar-equipped Japanese aircraft moved in on the *Intrepid,* bombed, and scored a hit with a torpedo on her starboard side aft, about 15 feet below the waterline. Five men were killed in the

explosion and her rudder was jammed hard to port. *Intrepid* fought off the remaining attackers and retired to Eniwetok at 20 knots, accompanied by the *Cabot* and other escorts. Captain Thomas L. "Tommy" Sprague was able to steer her by revving the port engine while idling the starboard screws. As he recalled later: "She was like a giant pendulum, swinging back and forth. She had a tendency to weathercock into the wind . . . turning her bow towards Tokyo, but right then I wasn't interested in going in that direction."[6] Later, a makeshift sail of hatch covers was rigged on the forecastle at the hangar deck level to help reduce the strain on the screws, and wind resistance was created by spotting all aircraft forward and all cargo aft, to keep the stern low in the water. Keeping anything like a straight course was out of the question and the *Intrepid* made up her own zig-zag pattern as she worked her way erratically back to Pearl. After temporary repairs, she proceeded on to Hunters Point Naval Shipyard in Bremerton, Washington.

On the same night the *Intrepid* was torpedoed, the *Enterprise* launched the first night carrier strike of the war with radar-equipped Avengers, sinking two tankers and five freighters and damaging five others.[7] The smoke was still rising over the lagoon when the morning fighter sweep arrived the following day. Not a single Japanese fighter rose to challenge the fighters and they resorted to strafing the already burning ships and airfields. There were three more strikes which hit other ships and sank two destroyers. The total score was two light cruisers, four destroyers, three auxiliaries, two sub tenders, two sub chasers, an armed trawler, a plane ferry, 24 merchant ships (five of them tankers), and 250 Japanese aircraft destroyed. The carriers lost 25 aircraft, but most of the crews had been picked up by submarines and seaplanes. The Truk strike had ensured that the Japanese would not interfere with the capture of Eniwetok, which later became a fleet anchorage.[8]

Task Force 58 Strikes Against the Marianas

Following the Truk strike, the task force stayed at sea, replenishing underway on 19 February before moving on to strike the Marianas. Spruance and Servron 10 returned to Majuro. With the departure of *Intrepid* and *Cabot,* and the later departure of the *Enterprise,* which bombed bypassed Jaluit on 21 February, Task Group 58.2 was reshuffled to include the *Essex, Yorktown,* and *Belleau Wood,* while Task Group 58.3 was now made up of *Bunker Hill, Monterey,* and *Cowpens.*

The Marianas stretch for some 425 miles in a rough arc beginning about 335 miles southeast of Iwo Jima down to Guam, 250 miles north of the Carolines. The four biggest of the islands—Saipan, Tinian, Rota and Guam—are all at the southern end of the chain. On the night of 21-22 February, a Japanese Betty bomber spotted Task Force 58, but Mitscher was undeterred, saying, "We'll fight our way in." The task force fought off night attacks on the run in to the launch point. The strikes were launched from a hundred miles west of Saipan and Tinian before dawn. Most of the 74 intercepting aircraft were shot down. A new airfield discovered on Guam was attacked; 168 Japanese aircraft were destroyed and several transports

sunk against six American aircraft lost. Task Force 58 retired to Majuro on 22 February.

In March 1944, Mitscher was officially made Commander, Fast Carrier Forces Pacific Fleet and promoted to Vice Admiral. The *Lexington,* returning from her repairs on the West Coast, had launched practice strikes against bypassed Mili on the 18th, and Mitscher hoisted his flag aboard *Lexington* two days later. Spruance became a full Admiral and both Rear Admiral Hoover and Rear Admiral Lee became Vice Admirals.[9] In line with a new policy that non-aviator commanders would have aviators as chiefs of staff, and vice versa, Captain Arleigh Burke was assigned as Mitscher's new chief of staff. Burke was a destroyer man known for his aggressive leadership of Desron 23, the "Little Beavers," in the Solomons. Relations were frosty at first, but Mitscher eventually came to respect Burke and the two made an excellent team. There were also changes in the task group commanders. Rear Admiral Sherman went home on leave and was replaced as ComCarDiv 1 by Rear Admiral Keen Harrill. Also new was Rear Admiral Frank D. Wagner as ComCarDiv 5, while Rear Admiral Montgomery relieved Mitscher as ComCarDiv 3.

Also in March, the new *Hornet* reported to Majuro under the command of Captain Miles R. Browning. Browning, regarded as a hero for his service as Spruance's chief of staff during the battle of Midway, was unfortunately not successful as captain of a fast carrier. The *Hornet* was not a happy ship. One pilot remembered Browning as "a scowling, chain-smoking martinet who prowled the bridge of the *Hornet* like a caged animal. Every order was a snarl, and his subordinates reacted to him with fear and hatred. His use of profanity was well-known, and he was not above dressing down an officer or enlisted man on the flight deck from the bridge, without using, or needing, a bullhorn. Pilots kept a discreet distance from the captain at all times."[10] Rear Admiral Clark, who joined as ComCarDiv 13 in learning status, flew his flag aboard the *Hornet*. After several incidents, including some near collisions caused by the captain's unwillingness to listen to anyone else, he became concerned that the *Hornet* was not ready for combat. But Clark could not relive Captain Browning until he committed some overt act. It finally came while the *Hornet* was anchored at Eniwetok. During the screening of a movie on the hangar deck, someone accidentally actuated a carbon dioxide fire extinguisher. Hearing the unusual hissing noise, someone called out, "It's a bomb!" In the ensuing panic, several were injured and one man who had fallen through an opening in the hangar had to be pulled out of the water. Even though the man thought he heard another man fall in, Captain Browning countermanded the duty officer when he ordered a small boat search around the ship. Admiral Clark recommended both a boat search and a crew muster, but these instructions were ignored. Once the injured were taken to sick bay, the chairs were set up again and the movie resumed. The body of the second man who had fallen overboard was found floating in the harbor two days later. In the court of inquiry that followed, Browning was found guilty of negligence and Mitscher ordered him to be relieved. He was ordered to a naval

air station in Kansas, and served the rest of his career in virtual oblivion. His relief was Captain William D. Sample, a strong yet gentle officer who soon had the ship's company operating at top efficiency.[11]

Palau

Task Force 58 sortied from Majuro 22 March 1944, heading for Palau in the western Carolines. Swinging south to avoid Truk-based search aircraft, the task force was spotted on 25 March. Thus alerted, the Japanese withdrew their fleet units to Singapore, Borneo, and Japanese waters. On the night of 29 March the Japanese made their usual night torpedo attacks, which were driven off by antiaircraft fire. At dawn on 30 March, Task Force 58 launched a fighter sweep from 90 miles south of the target, eliminating 30 airborne Zeros. The fighters then joined the bombers in attacking the large amount of merchant shipping. A Japanese destroyer was sunk by torpedoes and TBMs mined Palau waters. This turned out to be the first and only time mines were dropped by planes from the fast carriers during the war. It proved too dangerous for the low and slow TBMs, and was left to long-range land-based bombers thereafter. That night, another 60 enemy aircraft flew into Palau, and on 31 March, Task Groups 58.2 and 58.3 hit Palau again while Task Group 58.1 hit Yap to the northeast. All three task groups hit Wolei on 1 April. A few aircraft visited Ulithi, northeast of Yap, but most of the targets were on Palau. Along with the dozens of aircraft shot down, about 130,000 tons of Japanese shipping was lost to bombing and delayed action mines. Of 44 aircrew ditching at sea, 26 were picked up by submarines, seaplanes, and destroyers.

During the Palau operations, Rear Admiral Ginder worried to the point of becoming ineffective and Captain Truman Hedding, Mitscher's former chief of staff (temporarily attached to the Task Group 58.3 staff), had to take charge. Ginder was relieved and replaced by Rear Admiral Clark upon Task Force 58's return to Majuro.

When the fighting in the South Pacific ended in March 1944, there was no longer any reason for Nimitz to split his operations. The title of Central Pacific Force was abolished in April in favor of Fifth Fleet, which had been the administrative title of the Central Pacific Force. Simultaneously, all the forces under Halsey became Third Fleet. Spruance shifted his flag to Pearl Harbor to begin planning the invasion of the Marianas, leaving Mitscher on his own until June.

Hollandia

The Hollandia operations briefly brought together the Central and Southwest Pacific forces. Following the neutralization of Japanese air forces in the Palaus, Task Force 58 provided close air support for MacArthur's Hollandia landings on 22 April. General Kenny's massive land-based air attacks on 30 March and 3, 5, and 12 April largely eliminated Hollandia as a Japanese air base and the carrier strikes of 21 April turned out to be anticlimactic. Task Force 58 had sortied from Majuro 13 April under Mitscher's direct command, with three task groups under Reeves, Montgomery, and Clark. The task force feinted toward Palau, then hit New Guinea 21 April. Only snooper

aircraft from the west harassed Clark's Task Group 58.1. The operation went smoothly as the Japanese offered only token resistance. Mitscher used his night fighters to watch for enemy night torpedo attacks and to keep the Japanese troops awake. On 24 April, the task force withdrew to the new fleet anchorage at Manus in the Admiralties, at the northwestern end of the Bismark Archipelago. Later landings at Wakde, Biak, Noemfoor, and Sansapor carried MacArthur's forces to the northwestern point of the New Guinea Vogelkop, 550 miles west of Hollandia, in a little more than three months.

The Second Truk Strike

Meanwhile, a daylight land-based B-24 raid on Truk from SoPac was surprised on 29 March by a force of 90 Japanese fighters. The bombers shot down 21 and lost two. Truk was back in business. Nimitz passed the word to Mitscher at Manus and Task Force 58 sortied to hit Truk again. A predawn fighter sweep on 29 April began the second carrier battle over Truk, followed immediately by a Japanese torpedo plane attack on Task Force 58. Antiaircraft and Combat Air Patrols drove off the attackers, while Japanese antiaircraft fire over Truk was equally intense. Although 60 Zeros challenged the Hellcats, the quality of Japanese pilots had deteriorated and by midmorning Task Force 58 controlled the air over Truk. The next day, more were destroyed on the ground, bringing the total to 90 aircraft. The Americans lost 26 aircraft, but over half of the 46 aircrew were picked up, 22 by the submarine *Tang* alone. The Japanese could no longer maintain Truk as a major airbase, even though heavy antiaircraft and a few aircraft remained. Mitscher detached heavy surface ships for shelling; cruisers shelled Satawan on 30 April, while Vice Admiral Lee formed the battle line to shell Ponape on 1 May. Mitscher headed for Majuro with Task Groups 58.2 and 58.3 and assigned Clark's Task Group 58.1 to give the battleships air cover. During this period Rear Admiral Clark initiated visual fighter directors on the carriers because of the Mark 4 radar's problems with detecting targets close to the horizon. The visual fighter directors spotted incoming aircraft looking for the carriers and vectored the Hellcats to intercept them. Lee and Clark then headed for Eniwetok, which was being used as an auxiliary anchorage to relieve the load on Majuro.

In May 1944, some air groups were changed during the breather before the next series of operations. In January 1944, ComAirPac had scheduled rotations for six to nine months, but with the tempo of operations, this was shortened to six months in April. Altogether, six air groups were rotated home. Also, more carriers reported for duty—*Essex* returned from overhaul and *Wasp* (Captain Clifton A.F. "Ziggy" Sprague) and *San Jacinto* (Captain Harold M. Martin) were new. A new task group Task Group 58.6 was formed for training. Of the two new Rear Admirals available, Keen Harrill as ComCarDiv1 and Frank Wagner as ComCarDiv 5, Wagner would not last long. Boastful and irritating, he was shipped out to the Southwest Pacific for the duration in June. Also reporting later that month was Rear Admiral Ralph Davison, the first of the escort carrier group admirals to "fleet up" to command of a fast carrier task group. He flew his flag aboard

Yorktown in training status. Task Group 58.6, under Rear Admiral Montgomery, included *Essex, Wasp,* and *San Jacinto,* the last of the *Independence* class light carriers. The task group departed Majuro 14 May and divided as it approached Marcus. *San Jacinto* steamed north and west searching for enemy picket boats while *Essex* and *Wasp* attacked Marcus on 20 May. Heavy antiaircraft fire made accurate bombing difficult and negated the use of rockets, which required a long gliding approach. Weather interfered the next day, so Montgomery broke off the attack. *San Jacinto* rejoined and on 24 May all three carriers hit Wake.

Operation Forager—Capture of the Marianas

Although most of Japan's carrier aircraft and their experienced crews had been lost in the defense of Rabaul, enough new aircraft and crews had become available by spring of 1944 to encourage Japanese hopes of luring the Americans into one big decisive battle. In May Admiral Toyoda, the new Commander in Chief of the Combined Fleet, issued orders to launch Operation A-Go in an attempt to lure Spruance into the waters between the Palaus, Yap, and Woleai, where Japanese land-based and carrier aircraft would annihilate the American fleet.[12] The Japanese First Mobile Fleet comprised the bulk of the surface forces left in the Combined Fleet. Despite the losses of the previous months, it was still a formidable force of 73 surface ships, including 9 carriers (6 fleet carriers and 3 light carriers), 5 battleships, 7 heavy cruisers, 34 destroyers and 6 oilers. Admiral Jisaburo Ozawa had commanded the First

Mobile Fleet since relieving Admiral Nagumo in November 1943, and was a formidable opponent for Mitscher. Carrier Division 1 included the *Shokaku, Zuikaku,* and the new 33,000-ton *Taiho.* Carrier Division 2 had the *Hiyo, Junyo,* and *Ryuho.* Carrier Division 3 had the *Chitose, Chiyoda,* and *Zuiho.* Ozawa could muster over 400 aircraft aboard the carriers and was counting on land-based aircraft from other Japanese bases to take part in the coming battle.[13]

Ozawa's forces rendezvoused at Tawi Tawi, the westernmost island of the Sulu Archipelago off the northeast coast of Borneo, on 16 May, but were spotted by the submarines *Bonefish* and *Puffer.*[14] Admiral Toyoda had intended to send a powerful naval force, including the super battleships *Yamato* and *Musashi,* to repulse MacArthur's forces at Biak off the northwest tip of New Guinea, but by mid-June it was apparent that the Central Pacific forces under Spruance would strike in the Marianas. On 13 June the Japanese fleet sortied from Tawi Tawi and headed for the Marianas.

Operation Forager, the capture of the southern Marianas, would provide bases 3,000 miles farther west than Pearl Harbor, and enable the Army Air Force's new long-range B-29 bombers to reach Japan. The strikes of February had provided photographic coverage of the islands, but the Joint Chiefs of Staff had not made the decision to invade the Marianas until March. The target date for the invasion of Saipan was 15 June. While Guam, the southernmost island in the chain had been an American possession for nearly 40 years before the war, Japan considered Saipan home territory. Its loss would be regarded as a breach of Japan's inner lines of defense.

Saipan, Tinian, Rota and Guam

Task Force 58 departed Majuro 6 June 1944 and refueled from Servron 10 two days later. At Mitscher's disposal were six *Essex* class carriers, the *Enterprise,* and eight *Independence* class light carriers. Together these carriers operated a total of 483 Hellcats, 222 Helldivers, and 199 Avengers (plus 27 night Hellcats and three night Corsairs). The targets were scheduled to be hit 12 June, but Mitscher decided to change the pattern of strikes launched at dawn and moved the fighter sweep up to the afternoon of 11 June. The task force launched from 192 miles east of Guam. The first strike by 208 Hellcats and eight Avengers hit the airfields on Saipan and Tinian, destroying 36 Japanese aircraft. After strafing Guam and Rota, aircraft from Clark's Task Group 58.1 met about 30 Japanese fighters and shot them down. Antiaircraft fire was thick. Over Tinian, VF-28 Hellcats from the light carrier *Monterey* entered a landing circle of Betty's, which they quickly shot down. Aircraft from Task Groups 58.3 and 58.4 faced smoke pots at Saipan. The Hellcats strafed and bombed the airfields, claiming 150 aircraft destroyed, mostly on the ground. Eleven Hellcats were shot down and three of the pilots rescued. On the three days before the Saipan landings, the task force worked over the Marianas; antiaircraft fire continued to be heavy. The TBMs used rockets again, since Mitscher wanted to save bombs for a possible naval battle. On 13 June, VT-16 from *Lexington* lost its popular skipper, Lieutenant Commander Robert H. Isly during a rocket attack. The rockets were later shifted to the fighters.[15] Lieutenant Commander William I. Martin, commander of VT-10 from the *Enterprise* who was shot down during a bombing mission, bailed out and his parachute opened just before he hit the water. However, he made valuable observations of the landing beaches before swimming out to sea to be picked up.

The pre-landing strikes also hit some shipping. While strafing Pagan, aircraft from Harrill's Task Group 58.4 found a convoy to the north and attacked it on 12 and 13 June, sinking 10 transports and four small escorts. A *Hornet* fighter located another convoy to the east of Guam on the 12th, and on 13 June Clark's Task Group 58.1 sent 20 Hellcats with bombs escorted by two radar-equipped night fighters to attack it at long range. The night fighters located the ships, but the fighter pilots had so little bombing experience that they damaged only one vessel. *Hornet* aircraft also dropped warning leaflets to the Chamorro natives on Guam on 12 June. On the night of 15 June, Montgomery's Task Group 58.2 beat off a small torpedo plane attack from Yap with a combination of antiaircraft fire, maneuvering, and night fighters.

The fast battleships of the task force shelled Saipan on 13 June with poor results. The old battleships and escort carriers under Turner arrived the next day to join the fast carriers in hitting the island. Resistance on Saipan, despite all the pre-landing strikes, was tenacious. Lieutenant General Holland M. Smith was forced to commit his floating reserve, the Army's 27th Infantry Division, on 15 June and the landings on Guam, originally scheduled for 18 June, were postponed.

The Iwo Strikes

Spruance knew, through decoded intercepts of Japanese message traffic, that the Japanese were staging aircraft through the Bonins and Volcanos to the north, principally Iwo Jima and Chichi Jima. He directed Mitscher to send two task groups north to neutralize the threat. Mitscher sent Clark's Task Group 58.1 and Harrill's Task Group 58.4, but gave neither carrier group commander tactical command. Clark was junior to Harrill, but was all fighter; Harrill would prove to be too timid. By instructing them to cooperate as independent commanders, but to remain "tactically concentrated," Mitscher could ensure that the job would get done. The two task groups rendezvoused north of the Marianas and Clark tried to persuade Harrill to carry out his orders. Harrill excused his reluctance on the grounds of low fuel and the possibility of missing out on the expected battle with the Japanese fleet. Spruance had received word that night that the Japanese fleet had sortied, and decided that the strikes should be cut to one day, 16 June, to allow both task groups time to rejoin Task Force 58 before the Japanese struck. Clark, however, raced north to get in an attack on 15 June to allow the two days of strikes that he felt were needed. About 135 miles from Iwo Jima on the afternoon of 15 June, Clark launched his aircraft, which cleared the air over Iwo of the two dozen Zeros sent up to challenge them. Clark's aircraft then successfully bombed shipping and installations at Iwo, Chichi, and Haha Jima. Harrill lagged behind, unwilling to launch in the heavy weather, although he did manage to get off his Combat Air Patrol. By putting two night fighters over the target area, Clark prevented the Japanese night aircraft from taking off, keeping them grounded the next day. The weather prevented air operations on the morning of 16 June, but cleared enough that afternoon for Clark to get in three more strikes against Iwo. Harrill did not launch. The task groups turned south that evening to rejoin the rest of the task force. Task Force 58 broke off support of the beachhead on 17 June, leaving the escort carriers to provide close air support to the Marines, while Spruance ordered the amphibious shipping to a position east of the landing area in anticipation of the arrival of the Japanese fleet. The stage was set for the coming battle.

Chapter 8
Philippine Sea

When Admiral Toyoda learned of the Saipan landings on 15 June, he activated A-Go, but there was no hope of luring the American's south—the Americans would have to be destroyed in the Marianas. Spruance, however, was alerted on the evening of 15 June by a report from the submarine *Flying Fish* that a Japanese carrier force was heading in his direction from the San Bernardino Straits. An hour later, the submarine *Sea Horse* reported a battleship force heading northeast of the Surigao Strait. To Spruance, the possibility of two separate forces seemed likely and raised concerns about the possibility of an "end run" by the Japanese if his forces were pulled too far away to cover the Saipan landings, his primary mission. Between 15 and 18 June, the two forces searched each other out. On the morning of the 16th, Spruance seemed ready to take the initiative and ordered his flagship, the cruiser *Indianapolis*, out to join the carriers. On the afternoon of 17 June he issued a battle plan calling for the carriers to first knock out the

Japanese carriers and then attack the battleships and cruisers, after which the battle line could come up and finish off any stragglers and cripples or to engage the Japanese fleet if they decided to fight it out. He would leave the tactical operational details to Mitscher and Lee.

That evening a position report of "15 or so large combatant ships" heading east came in from the submarine *Cavalla*. The Japanese appeared to be about 800 miles away, but, based on Mitscher's calculations, the opposing forces would close on each other enough to allow the Americans to strike if the task force headed west. Since Spruance had left tactical matters up to Mitscher and Lee, subject to his overall direction, Mitscher sent a message to Lee: "Do you desire a night engagement? It may be we can make air contact this afternoon and attack tonight. Otherwise we should retire eastward." Lee, who had never trained with his battle line commanders as a unit and who was well aware of Japanese skill in night combat from the Guadalcanal

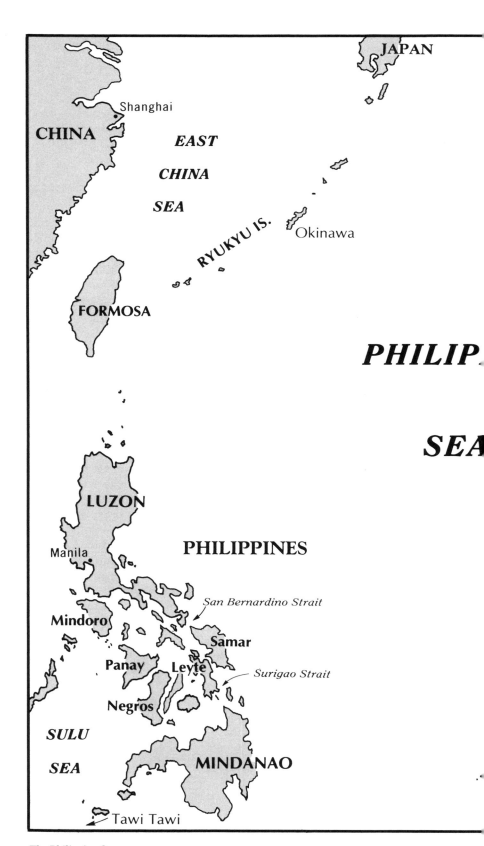

The Philippine Sea

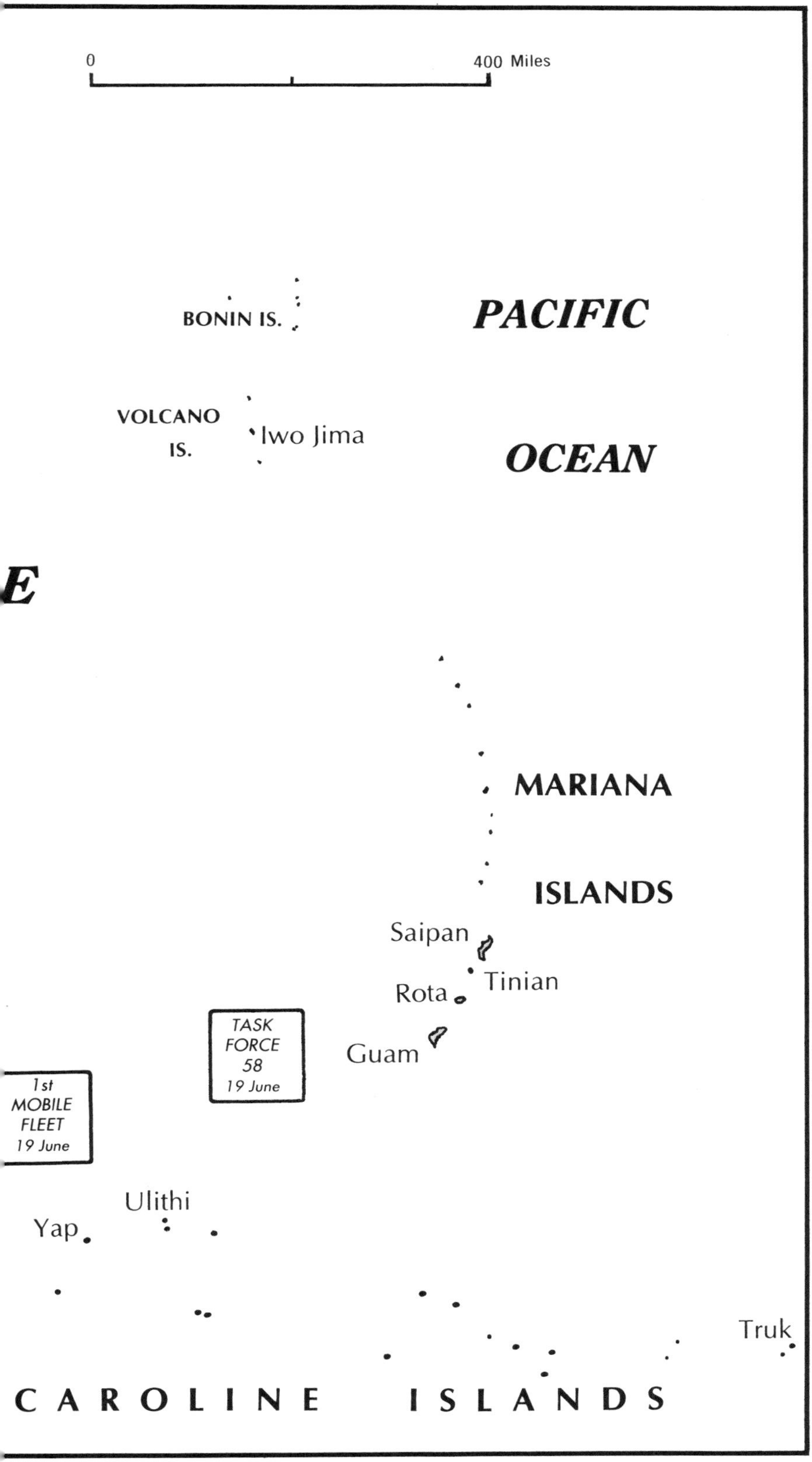

0   400 Miles

BONIN IS.

PACIFIC

VOLCANO
IS.   Iwo Jima

OCEAN

E

MARIANA

ISLANDS

Saipan
Tinian
Rota
TASK
FORCE
58
19 June
Guam

1st
MOBILE
FLEET
19 June

Ulithi
Yap

Truk

C A R O L I N E   I S L A N D S

days, responded, "Do not, repeat NOT believe we should seek night engagement. Possible advantages of radar more than offset by individual difficulties of communications and lack of training in fleet tactics at night. . . ." While willing to take on a damaged or fleeing enemy, even at night, Lee was not ready to take on the Japanese in night combat if they were undamaged and attacking. Instead of heading west toward Ozawa, the task force turned south and then east toward Saipan.

On the morning of the 18th, Spruance issued an order intended to prevent the task force from being drawn too far away to cover the landings. The task force would advance westward during the day and retire eastward at night to cut down on the odds of being "flanked" during the night. Because of air operations and the need to conserve fuel, an advance of only about a hundred miles was made to the west during the day of 18 June. Ozawa, however, after finding the task force that afternoon, turned south and maintained a distance of about 400 miles between his carriers and the Americans. He intended to launch his attacks on the American fleet at dawn the next day. In order to coordinate his attacks with land-based aircraft and to prepare the airfields in the Marianas to receive his strike aircraft on their shuttle missions, Ozawa sent Admiral Kakuta, commander of the Japanese land-based air forces in the Marianas, a coded message on the evening of 18 June.

Although the American land- and carrier-based air searches had not found the Japanese fleet, high frequency radio direction finding (HF/DF or "huff-duff") stations in the Aleutians, at Pearl Harbor, and in the South Pacific picked up the transmission. Nimitz' intelligence officers at CincPac headquarters triangulated Ozawa's position and relayed it to Spruance. Mitscher estimated that if the fleet turned westward at 0130, Task Force 58 would be in a position to strike the enemy at 0500. Unfortunately, Spruance also received a late message from ComSubPac stating that a dispatch from the submarine *Stingray* had been garbled in transmission. The last known position of the *Stingray* was considerably different from that given by the CincPac intercept and it was not known if the Japanese were jamming the *Stingray*'s message. When Mitscher requested permission to turn westward that night, Spruance chose to place more credence in the garbled transmission, responding: "Change proposed does not appear advisable. Believe indications given by *Stingray* more accurate than that determined by direction finder. If that is so, continuation at present seems preferable. End run by other carrier groups remains possibility and must not be overlooked."

Although Ozawa's force was inferior to Spruance's in every ship category except heavy cruisers, he did have some tactical advantages. He had nearly 100 land-based aircraft at Guam, Rota, and Yap, and the Japanese carrier aircraft could search out to 560 miles, allowing Ozawa to find Task Force 58 while remaining out of range. Mitscher's search aircraft could reach out to a maximum of 350 miles. Vice Admiral Hoover's land-based air searches covered out to 600 miles, but Ozawa was careful to remain out of their search areas. Using the Japanese held islands, Ozawa could launch strikes on shuttle missions while remaining out of reach of the American carrier strikes. Ozawa also had the "weather gauge," meaning that the prevailing easterly winds allowed the Japanese carriers to close the distance to their targets while launching into the wind, whereas Mitscher had to turn eastward away from the Japanese to launch and recover aircraft.

The American forces facing them included 15 fast carriers and 11 escort carriers in a fleet that totaled more than 800 surface ships and 28 submarines. Spruance was aware of the Japanese advance, but search planes had not sighted the Japanese on 18 June or on the morning of 19 June. At dawn on the 19th, the *Lexington,* flagship of Task Force 58, was about 90 miles northwest of Guam and about 100 miles southwest of Saipan. Task Force 58 was arrayed in the shape of a giant backward letter "F." In a line from north to south about 12 nautical miles apart were Clark's Task Group 58.1 with *Belleau Wood, Bataan, Hornet,* and *Yorktown;* then Reeves's Task Group 58.3 with *Princeton, Enterprise, Lexington,* and *San Jacinto,* and Montgomery's Task Group 58.2 with *Cabot, Wasp, Monterey,* and *Bunker Hill.* Harrill's Task Group 58.4 with *Cowpens, Langley,* and *Essex* was 12 nautical miles west of Clark. Vice Admiral "Ching" Lee's Battle Line, Task Group 58.7, with the fast battleships *Washington, North Carolina, Iowa, New Jersey, South Dakota,* and *Alabama,* was 15 nautical miles west of the middle task group, Reeves's Task Group 58.3. Radar picket destroyers were stationed to the west of the battleships.

Although expecting the Japanese from the west, the first attack came from two Judy dive bombers and six Zero fighter bombers flown from Guam, which had been reinforced during the night. On Tinian, Admiral Kakuta had received Ozawa's message and had brought up aircraft from Truk and other areas to Guam and Tinian and launched a strike at dawn. A Zero appeared suddenly out of a cloud and dropped a bomb on the picket destroyer *Stockham.* The bomb missed and the Zero was shot down by the destroyer *Yarnell.* Either that fighter or a Judy shot down by a Hellcat warned the Japanese on Guam of the American fleet's location, for thirty minutes later, task force radars picked up several blips. The *Belleau Wood's* Combat Air Patrol was vectored 90 miles out and arrived over Guam's Orote airfield about 0630 to discover considerable air activity. The Japanese opened up with their antiaircraft fire, but at 15,500 feet, the aircraft were too high and the bursts exploded 2,000 feet below them. Planes from the *Cabot, Hornet,* and *Yorktown* arrived and the sky was soon full of vapor trails, an unusual occurrence in the Pacific war. The action continued as another group of reinforcing enemy aircraft heading toward Guam from the southwest was picked up on task force radars just after 0800. Mitscher ordered three task groups to send fighters, and about three dozen Hellcats were soon heading for Guam, arriving about one hour later. Planes from the *Bunker Hill* arrived to find many Japanese aircraft landing and taking off. Some of the Hellcats went down to strafe while others provided top cover. The strafing Hellcats ran into some experienced Japanese fliers and, while downing 15 aircraft in the air and several more on the ground, lost one of their own. To prevent further shuttle attacks through Guam, Mitscher ordered bombers and fighters to hit the airfields again.

"The Marianas Turkey Shoot"

Meanwhile, Ozawa had not been idle. At dawn the First Mobile Fleet started an intensive search for the American carriers with 43 planes, launched in three groups at half-hour intervals. A sighting was made around 0730, followed by a strike made by 16 Zero fighters, 45 Zero fighter-bombers (older models fitted to carry bombs), and 8 Jill torpedo bombers of Carrier Division 3. This was followed by a strike of 48 Zero fighters, 53 Judy dive bombers and 29 Jill torpedo bombers of Carrier Division 1.[1] During the two-and-one-half hour flying time to reach the American fleet, Task Force 58 had been busy with aircraft staging through Guam, but just after 1000, radar detected Ozawa's first strike 150 miles away. Mitscher recalled all fighters out on search and combat missions and ordered the carriers to begin launching all available fighters. At 1020 they were launching as the Japanese arrived. The Japanese, as they came within sight of the carriers, circled and regrouped. The delay proved fatal. Of 69 attacking aircraft in the first wave, 42 were destroyed for the loss of one Hellcat. The battleships *South Dakota* and *Indiana* were hit and slightly damaged, but no Japanese planes got through to the carriers. The second strike of 109 planes was detected around 1100 at 115 miles, and was again met by Hellcats, although six Judy's got through to attack the *Wasp* and *Bunker Hill,* which were only slightly damaged. The Japanese lost 94 aircraft. "Hell," exclaimed one excited pilot, "this is like an old time turkey shoot!" The name stuck. A third strike included 15 Zero fighters, 25 Zero fighter-bombers and 7 Jills from Carrier Division 2. There was some confusion among the Japanese and only about 20 aircraft found the American carriers. This strike was also intercepted and seven Japanese aircraft were shot down. The fourth strike was launched from Carrier Division 2 plus the *Zuikaku* and included 82 planes. This strike did not find the carriers and headed for Guam where they were set upon by Hellcats from the *Cowpens, Essex,* and *Hornet.* Altogether, the Japanese lost 73 of the 82 strike aircraft. By that afternoon, the Japanese had lost a total of 253 carrier planes against a loss of 29 from Task Force 58.

The Japanese also lost the *Shokaku* and the *Taiho.* The *Shokaku* had been hit by three torpedoes from the submarine *Cavalla* just before noon. By the time stragglers from Ozawa's first strike had returned, *Shokaku* was ablaze, forcing her aircraft to land on other carriers. The veteran of the Pearl Harbor attack blew up later that afternoon. The *Taiho,* torpedoed earlier, had a ruptured gasoline storage tank and fumes spread throughout the ship. The damage control officer decided that the best way to clear up the fumes was to open all the ventilation ducts and blow them away, but this only served to spread them throughout the ship. Eventually the vapors reached a spark that ignited an explosion. One explosion followed another and the *Taiho* was lost late in the afternoon with heavy loss of life. Ozawa had to transfer his flag to the cruiser *Haguro.* With only about a hundred planes left, Ozawa withdrew to the northwest to regroup.

When it became clear that the Turkey Shoot had stripped the Japanese carriers of much of their offensive capability, Spruance released Mitscher to finish Ozawa. But the Japanese were too far out of range and American air searches could not locate them. Although the aviators must have felt that they had destroyed or damaged every Japanese aircraft in the Marianas, the Japanese had already brought up replacement aircraft. Spruance ordered night sweeps over the Marianas and Harrill's Task Group 58.4 was detached to cover them while Mitscher went after Ozawa. Four night fighters from the *Essex* worked over Guam and Rota that night, shooting down three aircraft at dawn the next day, 20 June. The task group hit Guam at daylight and destroyed another 40 planes on the ground, effectively eliminating the last Japanese air strength in the Marianas. The other three task groups recovered their aircraft that evening and Mitscher headed west at 2000 on the 19th. Although searches went out to 325 miles the next morning, they found nothing. Neither did Vice Admiral Hoover's land-based air searches or the submarines. At noon, a search by Hellcats equipped with drop tanks went out to 475 miles, the longest American carrier search of the war, but again found nothing. An afternoon search from the *Enterprise* had detected the Japanese near the limit of its range and radioed a report back to the task force around 1530. The radio transmissions alerted the Japanese, but because the original transmission was garbled, Mitscher did not receive a corrected report until 1800. The *Enterprise* had launched 12 fighters, 12 dive bombers, and 6 torpedo bombers at 1630, heading westward in the general direction of the enemy. It would be close. The Japanese were near the extreme limits of striking range and the returning aircraft would be coming back in darkness with little fuel remaining. Only a handful of the pilots had any significant night training.

Mitscher did not hesitate. He informed Spruance he was going ahead and launched 77 Helldivers and Dauntlesses, 54 Avengers, and 85 Hellcats.

The sun was just touching the horizon as the strike aircraft reached the Japanese fleet. There was no time to coordinate and no margin for error. Ozawa, who had shifted his flag to the carrier *Zuikaku*, sent up his remaining aircraft, many of which were promptly shot down by the escorting Hellcats. The torpedo bombers scored a hit on the light carrier *Hiyo* about 1820, jamming her steering. That made her an easy target for another torpedo and she blew up at 1930. *Junyo*, another of the light carriers, took two bombs and six near misses which buckled her plates, but she survived. The light carriers *Ryujo* and *Chiyoda* were damaged by near misses and a battleship and a cruiser were hit. Two of the supply ships were sunk. Now the long trip back began. As the striking aircraft headed for home about 20 of the remaining Japanese aircraft followed them for a time, but were kept at bay by the escorting Hellcats.

"Turn on the Lights"

Straggling back to the carriers in the dark, damaged aircraft dropped behind, many to be lost. Others ran out of fuel before they reached the carriers. Darkness had fallen before 2000 and the sky was overcast, further hampering the pilots. When the strike aircraft were about 70 miles out, Mitscher increased the speed of the task force to close the distance. As the first planes returned around 2030, there was mass confusion. With more and more aircraft running out of gas, Mitscher weighed the possibility of a Japanese submarine attack against the loss of more of his aviators. "Turn on the lights," he said, and the task force lit up, sending searchlight beams and star shells into the overcast sky. "Tell 'em to land on any carrier." Pilots headed for any carrier they could find. There were many deck crashes. Other aircraft ditched alongside ships of the task force. By 2230 that night, the last of the strike aircraft were recovered. Of the 216 attacking aircraft only 100 landed that night. Only about 20 were casualties of the battle, the rest were lost into the sea or in deck accidents. Mitscher recommended heading the task force toward the last location of the Japanese fleet at 16 knots. The next morning at 0600, Mitscher launched another strike toward a position reported by Saipan-based night patrol planes, in addition to search planes carrying only extra fuel tanks. The strike aircraft did not find the enemy, but the search aircraft did. They found a force of battleships and destroyers, and farther ahead, three small carriers. The Japanese were heading toward Okinawa at 20 knots. Spruance, aboard the *Indianapolis*, steamed out to join the battleships, which were out ahead of the task force under the cover of the *Bunker Hill* and *Wasp*.[2] The task force did not find any cripples and Spruance called off any further pursuit later that day. The task force retired toward Saipan, picking up floating aviators en route. In the end, all but 16 pilots and 22 crewmen were saved. The overall results of the two day Battle of the Philippine Sea included American losses of 130 aircraft and 76 aviators against Japanese losses of three carriers, 480 planes and nearly the last of their trained carrier pilots.

Most of the task force retired to Eniwetok, while Task Group 58.4 remained off Guam. Clark's Task Group 58.1, ordered to bomb Pagan en route, received permission to detour north to hit the Bonins. On 24 June, Task Group 58.1 aircraft took off in heavy seas to strike the Jimas. The Japanese sent three strikes against the task group, all of which were intercepted and repulsed. The last two strikes managed to reach the task group, but antiaircraft fire helped drive them off. The Japanese lost 66 aircraft and, for the time being, were unable to attack the Americans off Saipan and Guam. Task Group 58.1 reached Eniwetok on 27 June, the last of the three task groups to arrive.

The Summer of 1944

As the last days of June wore on, Task Group 58.4 remained off Guam and Rota to soften them up for the upcoming landings. The composition of the task group changed as carriers rotated to Eniwetok for rest, command changes, and air group transfers. On 30 June, Clark's Task Group 58.1 and Task Group 58.2, now under the command of Rear Admiral Ralph E. "Dave" Davison, were sent to hit the Bonins again, which they did on 3-4 July. After hitting the Bonins, the task groups followed Task Group 58.4 to Eniwetok, which had retired the day before. On the way south, Task Group 58.1 and Task Group 58.2 hit Guam and Rota and rotated between the islands for a week of strikes. On 9 July organized resistance on Saipan ended. Guam and Tinian would be next. Task Group 58.3 and Task Group 58.4, now commanded by Rear Admiral Gerald W. "Gerry" Bogan, joined in the pre-landing bombardments on the 13th. On 21 July the Marines landed on Guam and the next day, Mitscher left Bogan's Task Group 58.4 behind to cover the beaches while he headed for the Palaus with Task Group 58.1, Task Group 58.2, and Task Group 58.3.[3] Between 25 and 28 July, Task Group 58.2 and Task Group 58.3 worked over the Palaus, while Task Group 58.1 hit Yap, Ulithi, Fais Ngulu and Sorol, which were also photographed for possible use as fleet anchorages. On 4 and 5 August, Task Groups 58.1 and 58.3 hit the Bonins yet again, with the cruisers shelling the islands the following day. On 9 August, Task Force 58 anchored at Eniwetok for a two week rest period. It had been a long grind and there was more to come.

On 12 August organized resistance on Guam ended. Rear Admiral Frederick C. "Fightin' Freddie" Sherman returned to relieve Montgomery as commander of Task Group 58.3 that same day. There were other changes and additions as the fast carrier forces prepared for the next phase of the Pacific war. The carriers themselves were getting improvements as the new Mark 22 radar, which operated with the older Mark 4 and Mark 12 radars to give better position data on incoming enemy aircraft, was installed on more carriers. The new *Franklin, Ticonderoga,* and *Hancock* reported to the Pacific and there were changes in the organization of the air groups. At the end of July, the air groups had been authorized to change from 18 torpedo, 36 bomber and 36 fighter aircraft to 18 torpedo bomber (TBM), 24 dive bomber (SB2C) and fighter (F6F) aircraft "to capacity," i.e., about 54. The venerable SBD Dauntless had operated from the fast carriers for the last time in the Marianas campaign. During August, each of the *Essex* class carriers traded 12 SB2C Helldivers for 12 F6F Hellcats and all the bomber pilots were checked out in fighters. Although the F4U Corsair had finally been approved for carrier operations in April 1944, it had become the standard Marine fighter and could not be spared. Some of the night Corsairs, assigned to the fast carriers in early 1944, were taken off the fast carriers.[4]

All fighter aircraft could serve as fighter bombers, and new weapons included 20mm cannon, napalm, and 5-inch and 11.75-inch rockets. Napalm was a special mixture of gasoline and a jelling agent. Though used in the Marianas with some success, it was difficult to mix and store aboard ship. The warhead on the 5-inch rocket slowed it down on the early model, but in spring 1944, production of an improved version with a more powerful motor began, giving it more velocity than the earlier 3.5-inch rockets. The High Velocity Aircraft Rocket (HVAR), nicknamed the "Holy Moses" by the aircrews, went into combat in August. It gave one aircraft the equivalent firepower of a destroyer salvo and was so popular among pilots in Europe and the Pacific that it had to be rationed. The 11.75-inch rocket, nicknamed the "Tiny Tim," was ten feet long and designed for use by carrier aircraft. It was rushed aboard the carriers on an emergency basis beginning in June.

Another result of the Battle of the Philippine Sea was a directive from ComAirPac requiring that all carrier pilots to be night qualified. In addition, the recently repaired light carrier *Independence* was designated as a night carrier and departed Pearl Harbor for Eniwetok on 17 August. Until the Saipan operations, each carrier returned to Pearl

Harbor to pick up a new air group and engage in a 10-day training period. Beginning that summer, all new air groups trained aboard available aircraft carriers at San Diego or Hawaii and were ferried to their ships at advanced anchorages just before going into combat.[5]

Of all the changes occurring late in August, the most profound would be the change in fleet commanders. On 26 August Vice Admiral William F. Halsey, Jr. relieved Vice Admiral Raymond A. Spruance as commander of the Central Pacific forces. The Fifth Fleet became the Third Fleet and Task Force 58 became Task Force 38 as part of the "two platoon" system of rotating fleet command.

Chapter 9

Halsey and the Third Fleet

Bill Halsey was the opposite of Ray Spruance. Where Spruance was cautious and methodical, Halsey was bold and brash. Halsey was the first carrier admiral to follow the doctrine of risk. Early in the Pacific war, while other carrier admirals avoided confrontation with the Japanese to preserve precious carriers, Halsey went looking for trouble, beginning with his raid in the Marshalls in February 1942. It was Halsey who had commanded the naval task force that launched the Doolittle Tokyo raid in April 1942 and it was his leadership of the South Pacific forces that culminated in the successful drive up the Solomons chain. When Halsey effectively worked himself out of a job in the South Pacific, which had become a backwater area, he was ready to take on the Japanese wherever he could find them.

Halsey was a late comer to naval aviation, having earned his wings in 1934 at the age of 52. At the time, senior captains were given a rudimentary aviation orientation and issued wings as "naval aviation observers," thus quali-fying them for future command of carrier units. Halsey, however, was not satisfied with observer's wings and insisted on being reclassified as a student pilot. He won his wings and even went on to qualify in fighters and torpedo bombers, although he was probably the worst pilot the Navy ever produced. Halsey was known as "Bill" to his friends and "Bull" to the correspondents. He was like a bull in both senses of the term. He was the aggressive commander charging into the enemy like a raging bull, but also the "bull in the china shop" who could be his own worst enemy. Unlike Spruance, Halsey would be the real commander of the fast carriers and for many, the terms "Third Fleet" and "Task Force 38" were synonymous.

Vice Admiral John S. "Slew" Mc-Cain, also known as "Jock," was sent from Washington to the Central Pacific a few months earlier to "learn the ropes." Fearless and aggressive, McCain had many colorful traits, such as wearing an old "lucky" cap during operations. He was generally well liked, but sometimes sloppy, both in his personal appearance, spilling tobacco while rolling his own cigarettes, for instance, and in the way he conducted operations. Like Halsey, McCain was one of the older aviators, earning his wings in 1936 at the age of 52. His last assignment in Washington as Deputy Chief of Naval Operations (Air) convinced Admiral King that he had done a good enough job to rate command of the fast carrier task force. For the time being, he was in "makee learn" status and commanded one of the fast carrier task groups.[1] This lasted longer than he wanted, since Mitscher would stay in command of the fast carriers for several more months.[2]

On 28 August Task Force 38 departed Eniwetok. Davison's Task Group 38.4 with *Franklin, Enterprise,* and *San Jacinto* hit Iwo and Chichi Jima 31 August-2 September before moving on to hit Yap in the western Carolines on 6 September. Meanwhile, the other three task groups, McCain's Task Group 38.1 with *Hornet, Wasp, Belleau Wood,* and *Cowpens,* Bogan's Task Group 38.2 with *Intrepid, Bunker Hill, Cabot,* and *Independence,* and Sherman's Task Group 38.3 with *Essex, Lexington, Princeton,* and *Langley,* hit the Palaus 6-8 September. On 9 September, Task Group 38.4 refueled and assumed a supporting role until the 18th, while the others hit Mindanao on the 9th and 10th. The Task force encountered almost no enemy resistance and went on to hit the Visayas in the central Philippines 12-13 September, destroying almost 200 enemy aircraft and many ground targets and ships. Mindanao and the Visayas were hit again on the 14th, and Manila and the Visayas on 21, 22, and 24 September for a total of 893 enemy aircraft

destroyed and 67 ships sunk. Ensign Thomas C. Tillar of *Hornet*'s Air Group 2 was shot down over Leyte and sheltered by the natives there. Upon his return, he relayed native reports of weak Japanese defenses. Halsey recommended that MacArthur's Mindanao landings scheduled for 15 September be cancelled in favor of immediate landings on Leyte. His recommendations were passed up the chain.

Return to the Philippines— The Invasion of Leyte

At the Pearl Harbor conference in late July 1944, MacArthur had convinced president Roosevelt and Nimitz that the Philippines were a necessary stepping stone to further operations and that the idea of "Leyte then Luzon" was sound. Once the United States was committed to the liberation of the Philippines, the Leyte and later Luzon operations became crucial to the destruction of the Japanese empire. From Leyte, the Americans could deploy ships, aircraft and amphibious forces to the north and to the west, cutting off Japan from its resources in the East Indies. The Japanese shipping lifeline could be "corked" at the Luzon bottleneck. During the September 1944 Quebec conference, a timetable had been drawn up. In September, MacArthur was to take Morotai and Nimitz Pelelieu. In October Nimitz would take Yap in the Carolines, Ulithi a few days later, then Talaud. In November, MacArthur would occupy Sarangani Bay on Mindanao, and in December, MacArthur and Nimitz would invade Leyte in concert. Discussions regarding further landings, whether on Luzon or Formosa, were left open. Halsey's operations, however, had shown just how weak the Japanese were on Leyte. He recommended cancelling the Pelelieu, Morotai, Yap, and Mindanao operations in order to move the invasion of Leyte up by two whole months. Within hours of MacArthur's acceptance of this proposal, the Joint Chiefs of Staff ordered MacArthur and Nimitz to invade Leyte on 20 October, with Vice Admiral Wilkinson's amphibious forces, the III Amphibious Force, joining them after taking Pelelieu. Anguar, a two-mile-long island south of Pelelieu, would be seized and used as a bomber base.[3] Kossol Passage, about 60 miles north of Anguar, became a temporary fleet anchorage and a base for PBM Mariner flying boats. The real prize, however, was Ulithi Atoll.

Ulithi

Ulithi Atoll, occupied 23 September, became the major fleet anchorage in the Pacific, but the various task groups went to other anchorages while it was being readied. Task Group 38.1 anchored in Seadler Harbor at Manus in the Admiralties on 29 September; Task Group 38.2 arrived at Saipan 28 September; and Task Group 38.3 went to Kossol Passage on 27 September. Task Group 38.4 stayed off the Palaus until early October. On 1-2 October, Task Group 38.2 and Task Group 38.3 went to Ulithi, which was hit for the next three days by a typhoon.[4] Because the fast carrier force could not even retire to Ulithi when the tempo of operations picked up, an At Sea Logistics Service Group was formed with 34 fleet oilers, 11 escort carriers, 19 destroyers and 26 destroyer escorts. Fueling at Ulithi, each replenishment group would sortie with

a dozen oilers for a rendezvous with the fast carriers. The escort carriers provided air cover for the replenishment group and ferried replacement aircraft and pilots to the fast carriers. Halsey set each refueling rendezvous at the extreme range of Japanese land-based aircraft and the Japanese never succeeded in disrupting replenishment operations. The Service Group allowed the Third Fleet a strategic mobility unprecedented in naval warfare. It would be needed, for the Third Fleet would face another fleet battle, many weeks of close support operations for ground forces, heavy weather, and a storm of another kind—the kamikazes. As a June 1944 ComAirPac Analysis distributed in late July warned: "Losses will be heavier. Overconfidence is not justified."

Task Force 38

On 7 October, Task Force 38 rendezvoused 375 miles west of the Marianas to begin a series of pre-landing attacks on Japanese airfields. It was a most formidable force. With eight *Essex* class carriers, the old *Enterprise,* and seven *Independence* class light carriers, the fast carrier force carried more than 1,000 aircraft. Halsey's first task was to neutralize Japanese air strength north of the Philippines, primarily at Kyushu, Okinawa, and Formosa, then to shift southward to hit the Luzon and Visayan airfields.[5] Despite poor visibility caused by overcast skies, Task Force 38 successfully attacked Okinawa shipping and airfields on 10 October, sinking 19 small warships and destroying over 100 enemy aircraft, for a loss of 21 carrier aircraft. Most of the crews were picked up by the lifeguard submarine. The next day, a less-successful strike was launched against Aparri at the northern end of Luzon. On the 12th, Halsey began a three-day series of heavy air attacks on Formosa.

The Air Battle at Formosa

The carriers of Task Force 38 arrived at their launch positions before dawn. At 0544 the first strike, a fighter sweep to clear the air over Formosa and the Pescadores, was launched. In perfect flying weather, no fewer than 1,378 sorties were flown from all four carrier groups on the first day, followed by 934 the next morning. On the afternoon of the 13th, the Japanese struck back, hitting the *Franklin* and the heavy cruiser *Canberra.* Four torpedoes were aimed at *Franklin,* but all missed. One of her Hellcats, on final approach, noticed another attacking aircraft and took a waveoff to shoot the enemy down. Another enemy aircraft took a direct hit and skidded out of control across the flight deck. "Too close for comfort," one officer recalled later—it was so close that its wingtip ripped the seat of his trousers before falling into the sea.[6]

Aboard the *Essex,* the supply officer was given the job of battle announcer so men below deck could visualize the action: "Four raids coming in . . . near on port quarter . . . it's heavy! Oh, there is a Betty burning . . . tremendous fire. Raid over 38.2, port quarter. AA fire port quarter very heavy. Another Betty down . . . they burn beautifully, thirty seconds and then fade out . . . three of them . . . another raid on starboard bow 14 miles. AA astern of us straight up in the air. They're all over the place now . . . *Essex* is about to open fire . . . it's getting darker by the minute now . . . Be very dark soon, we hope . . . It's very low.

Babies closing in now. This is the sixth performance for the *Essex* on these night shows with these little monsters and it's the darkest night yet . . . and getting darker by the minute . . . so don't get excited about it. There are night fighters in the air . . . trying to break off this raid. So far, night fighters from the *Independence* have splashed five Bettys! This is Columbus Day and Task Force 58 is giving them a wonderful fireworks demonstration. This is also National Fire Prevention Week, so don't drop any matches in the dry grass. They're dropping flares now . . . just dropped two off the port quarter . . . ."[7] And so it went until the attackers had been splashed or driven off.

On the third day the task force launched only 146 sorties, but B-29s from the 20th Air Force's XX Bomber Command based in China took up the slack. Japanese counterattacks crippled the light cruiser *Houston,* which was taken under tow. For a time, the air battle was titanic, and Halsey's fliers turned it into another turkey shoot. On the first day, 101 Japanese aircraft sorties, combined with intense antiaircraft fire, brought down 48 carrier aircraft, but at tremendous loss to themselves in aircraft destroyed, both in the air and on the ground. Overly optimistic reports by inexperienced Japanese pilots, however, led Admiral Toyoda to change his air defense plans. Instead of making his last stand in the Philippines, he committed his land-based aircraft to the destruction of the American fleet at this seemingly opportune time and place.

Japanese plans for a decisive naval battle in November had been upset when the Third Fleet sortied in October. On 10 October, Vice Admiral Kusaka, Admiral Toyoda's chief of staff in

Tokyo, ordered Vice Admiral Fukudome to commit his land-based Second Air Fleet, operating primarily from Kyushu, Okinawa, and Formosa, to the destruction of the American fleet and ordered Admiral Ozawa to transfer his 300 under-trained carrier pilots ashore. On the 12th, Admiral Toyoda himself flew to Formosa to direct the air attacks on the enemy naval forces. Later that day, he ordered Rear Admirals Obayashi and Matsuda to send their carrier planes (CarDiv 3 and CarDiv 4) to Formosa to join in the attack. It was to be all or nothing at Formosa. Unfortunately for the Japanese, over 500 Japanese aircraft were destroyed along with some light shipping and installations. Toyoda had prematurely sacrificed his air strength for the defense of the Philippines.

The damaged *Canberra* and *Houston,* covered by the light carriers *Cabot* and *Cowpens* with cruisers and destroyers as escort, slowly withdrew toward Ulithi. Halsey used "CripDivOne" as bait, hoping to lure out the Japanese fleet. The three cruisers under Vice Admiral Shima sailed out from Japan, but Shima soon learned that Task Force 38, contrary to Japanese claims, was not sunk and wisely decided to turn around.

With Formosa neutralized, Task Force 38 turned its attention to the isolation of the Leyte beachhead. On 15 October, Task Group 38.4 began five days of strikes against Luzon, and was joined by Task Group 38.1 and Task Group 38.2 on the 18th. On 15 October three enemy planes attacked the *Franklin*. One managed to get through "Big Ben's" antiaircraft fire and scored a hit on the after outboard corner of the deck edge elevator, killing three men and wounding 22.

The next day, the aircraft of the fast carriers paid their first visit to Manila. Suspecting that the Japanese would wait for the Mindoro or Luzon landings before challenging the Americans in a fleet engagement, Halsey made plans to rotate his carrier groups through Ulithi for rest and replenishment. What he did not know was that Toyoda, having lost most of his air strength at Formosa, was forced to revise his plans.

The vanguard of the American invasion forces had been sighted off Suluan on 17 October. That same day, Ozawa, left with carriers without carrier aircraft, recommended to Toyoda that his force be used as a sacrificial decoy to allow Vice Admiral Kurita's battleship-cruiser force based at Singapore to attack and destroy the landing force off Leyte. Ozawa's carrier decoy force would have just enough aircraft, 116, to launch a shuttle strike to Luzon and convince Halsey that this "northern force" was heading for Leyte. The real blow would come from Kurita's "center force" passing through the central Philippines via the Sibuyan Sea and the San Bernardino Strait to descend upon Leyte Gulf from the north and east of Samar Island. This force would include the super battleships Yamato and Musashi, two older battleships, six heavy cruisers, a light cruiser, and several destroyers. Another "southern force" of two old battleships, one heavy cruiser, and destroyers commanded by Vice Admiral Nishimura, would transit the Sulu and Mindanao Seas and approach the landing area from the south via the Surigao Strait. The "southern force" would be supported by Vice Admiral Shima and his three cruisers from Japan.[8] In every respect, the plan was suicidal. The Japanese navy was laying down its life as a blue water navy to protect the Philippine lifeline, now part of the interior defenses of Japan itself.

As these plans were put into action, Vice Admiral Onishi, commander of the land-based First Air Fleet in the Philippines, took desperate measures of his own. On 19 October, he activated the Kamikaze Corps of suicide planes.

Chapter 10

Leyte Gulf

American operations in the Philippine Islands fell under the command of General Douglas MacArthur, who relied primarily on Lieutenant General George Kenney's land-based Army air forces for air support. "MacArthur's Navy," the light surface naval forces of the Seventh Fleet, was commanded by Vice Admiral Thomas C. Kinkaid. Kinkaid, as the last non-aviator to command a carrier force, had lost the old *Hornet* in 1942. Since that time, he had little to do with aircraft carriers and would not have been at Leyte if plans had not changed. Under the revised timetable, Halsey was to support the Leyte operation, but remained under the overall command of Admiral Nimitz's Central Pacific theater. This divided command arrangement was the root cause of the problems at Leyte Gulf, especially in communications and coordination between the two fleets. Halsey acted as a free agent as Nimitz's fleet commander, and assumed virtual tactical command of Task Force 38, leaving Mitscher in the lurch. It was not uncommon to hear

Task Force 38 referred to as the Third Fleet, since the Central Pacific amphibious units were under the Southwest Pacific forces for the invasion.

The Sixth Army landed on Leyte Island on 20 October under air cover provided by 18 escort carriers under the control of Rear Admiral Tommy Sprague. The escort carriers operated Hellcats, Wildcats, and Avengers and were organized into three task units known by their call sign "Taffy." "Taffy One" was commanded directly by Tommy Sprague, "Taffy Two" by Rear Admiral Felix B. Stump, and "Taffy Three" by Rear Admiral Clifton A.F. "Ziggy" Sprague. All four of the fast carrier task groups, joined by Fifth Air Force bombers, patrolled or attacked airfields. From the 20th through the 23rd, American aircraft met little resistance in the air and destroyed over 100 enemy aircraft on the ground. The Sixth Army, moving steadily inland under this cover, hoped to gain as much ground as possible before the Japanese launched their expected air, naval and

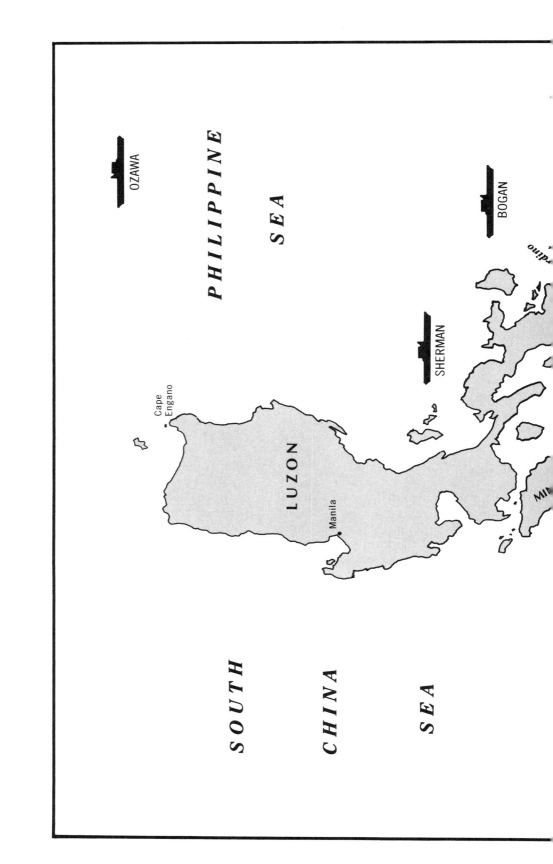

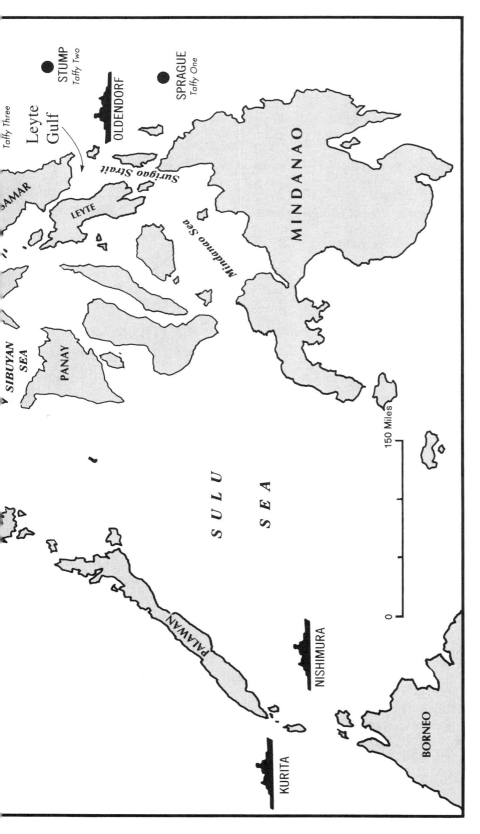

The Battle of Leyte Gulf

ground counterattacks. Meanwhile, equipment and supplies piled up on the beachhead as the transports raced to unload their cargoes and clear the area before the Japanese struck back. For protection, Kinkaid counted on Rear Admiral Jesse B. Oldendorf's battle line of six old battleships, the escort carriers and their aircraft, and the aircraft of the fast carriers, which could range out to 250 miles and still be within striking distance if necessary.

Halsey began to rotate his task groups to Ulithi for rest and replenishment and McCain's Task Group 38.1 was 600 miles to the east when Halsey learned after daybreak on the 24th that two submarines had sighted Kurita's center force west of the Philippines in the Palawan passage.[1] McCain had five carriers with him: *Wasp, Hornet, Hancock, Monterey,* and *Cowpens,* while the *Bunker Hill* had retired to Ulithi on the 23rd for more fighters. This left Halsey with 11 carriers. After carrier search planes had sighted both Kurita's center force and Nishimura's southern force, he ordered his three available task groups to cover the approaches to Leyte Gulf. Sherman's Task Group 38.3 with *Essex, Lexington, Princeton,* and *Langley* would cover the northern approach and was to stay off the Polillo Islands east of Luzon. Bogan's weakened Task Group 38.2 with *Intrepid, Cabot,* and the night carrier *Independence* was off the San Bernardino Strait. Davison's Task Group 38.4 with *Franklin, Enterprise, San Jacinto,* and *Belleau Wood* was to the south covering the Surigao Strait. Halsey recalled McCain's Task Group 38.1, arranging an at-sea refueling for the task group for the next morning. Halsey also ordered air strikes to begin, with Sherman and Davison to close on Bogan, who was

closest to the enemy. During the morning all three task groups were heavily engaged. To the south Davison's aircraft made ineffective attacks on Nishimura's southern force, after which Halsey ordered him to assist Bogan, whose planes were attacking Kurita's center force in the Sibuyan Sea. Meanwhile, Sherman's task group came under heavy air attack by Japanese aircraft from Luzon and he had to break off his air strikes and concentrate on defending his task group. Although over 50 Japanese aircraft were shot down or turned away, one got through to hit the light carrier *Princeton* with a bomb that went through several decks before exploding. Her crew struggled to save their ship, but she was rocked by a tremendous explosion when torpedoes stowed below were set off. The cruiser *Birmingham,* which came alongside to help fight fires, was also severely damaged by the explosion. The *Princeton* was abandoned and sunk later that day by a torpedo from the cruiser *Reno.* She was the first carrier lost by the Fast Carrier Task Force.

While Sherman continued to beat off fresh attacks, Halsey turned his full attention to the center force, concluding that Kinkaid could deal with the oncoming southern force, which would be within gun range of Oldendorf's old battleships around midnight. The battle in the Sibuyan Sea lasted from around 1030 to 1400. The striking aircraft met almost no air opposition, since Japanese commanders considered the attack on Sherman's task group to be more important than air cover for Kurita. The 72,000 ton super battleship *Musashi,* repeatedly hit by bombs and torpedoes, fell behind, sinking. She retired and, later in the early evening, rolled over and sank.

Kurita's other ships sustained damage as well, but he still had four battleships, six heavy cruisers, and other escort ships. At around 1400 he turned westward in apparent retreat. The returning aviators were jubilant and their exaggerated claims led Halsey to believe that the center force no longer represented a serious threat to the Leyte beachhead. Still, Halsey did not discount the possibility that the center force would turn eastward again and he sent a preparatory battle plan to his task commanders to cover the possibility. Four of his six battleships, two heavy and three light cruisers, and 14 destroyers would form Task Force 34 under Vice Admiral Lee as Commander Battle Line. He later amended the plan by voice radio message to his subordinate commanders: "If the enemy sorties, TF 34 will be formed when directed by me." By accident, Kinkaid had received the first message, but had no way of intercepting the clarification message. He therefore assumed that the Task Force 34 battle line was formed and guarding the San Bernardino Strait. Admiral King in Washington and Nimitz at CincPac headquarters had also received the first message and assumed that Task Force 34 had been formed and was guarding the San Bernardino Strait.

With the Surigao and San Bernardino Straits supposedly covered, the next question on Halsey's mind was the location of the Japanese carriers. Sherman had permission from Mitscher to search to the northeast, and at 1405 launched a search in that direction. Ozawa, for his part, did everything he could think of to get noticed, including sending fake radio messages, sending out air searches, and launching a 76 plane strike against Sherman's task group. The strike was set upon by Sherman's Hellcats and the task group antiaircraft fire, but the Americans thought this was another land-based attack like the one that had bombed the *Princeton.* Sherman's searching Helldivers finally located the northern force at 1640, only 190 miles away. After weighing various factors with his advisors, Halsey reasoned that the center force might turn eastward again if he went north to get the Japanese carriers, but felt it unlikely that the center force would enter Leyte Gulf until late in the morning. He could run north to knock off the carriers, then turn south to help drive off Kurita. Besides, Oldendorf should have finished with the southern force by then and be available to assist if needed. Putting his finger on the plot of the northern force, he declared, "We will run north at top speed and put those carriers out for keeps." At 1950 he radioed Kinkaid at Leyte: "Central force heavily damaged according to strike reports. Am proceeding north with three groups to attack carrier forces at dawn." Sixteen minutes later, Halsey received a report from an *Independence* night Hellcat that the center force had been sighted in the Sibuyan Sea heading for the San Bernardino Strait at 12 knots. This still did not stop Halsey. After passing on the contact report to Kinkaid, Halsey ordered Bogan's and Davison's task groups to join Sherman and ordered McCain to stop refueling and return. Kinkaid still thought Task Force 34 was guarding the San Bernardino Strait, but did not question that Halsey was leaving it apparently without air cover. Mitscher, also left in the dark, had assumed that the battle line would be formed when Task Force 38 headed north and did not learn that all the battleships were to accompany the carriers north until midnight, when all the task groups rendezvoused off Luzon. Commodore Burke and Commander Jimmy Flately, Mitscher's new operations officer, both urged Mitscher to recommend to Halsey that he send the battleships back to the San Bernardino Strait with Bogan's task group to provide air support. Mitscher, still smarting from the rebuff given by Spruance at his suggestions off Saipan, told Flately: "If he wants my advice he'll ask for it." "Ching" Lee also told Halsey that the northern force was a decoy, but was ignored. The run north was not really a run. As soon as Bogan and Davison, moving at 25 knots, had joined on Sherman, the task force slowed down to 16 knots. At midnight, Halsey turned over tactical command to Mitscher, who promptly increased the speed to 20 knots. Halsey ordered a 0100 night search from *Independence*, over Mitscher's protest that it would only alert the Japanese. At 0205, the radar-equipped Hellcats sighted Japanese ships only 80 miles north of the task force. That meant that a night surface action would take place around 0430. Halsey ordered Lee to form the battle line and more time was lost as Lee slowly and carefully pulled his battleships out of the formation. Halsey again slowed down the task force when he learned that Oldendorf was engaging the southern force in the Surigao Strait. As it turned out, the Japanese ships only 80 miles away were the hermaphrodite battleships *Ise* and *Hyuga* under the command of Rear Admiral Matsuda.[2] Matsuda's battleships formed the detached van of Ozawa's force and he was indeed seeking a night surface engagement to attract Halsey north. Ironically, Matsuda,

seeing lightning flashes to the south, mistook these for land-based air attacks on Halsey's forces. On the strength of Matsuda's erroneous report, Ozawa ordered the battleships to rejoin the carriers. When no surface battle materialized at 0430, Mitscher assumed incorrectly that the search aircraft had scared the Japanese off. He could only arm his bombers and launch long-range search-strikes at first light.

Meanwhile, Kinkaid was awaiting two night battles. The one in the Surigao Strait began at 2230 on 24 October as PT boats engaged Nishimura's force and reached its peak around 0400 the next day, with the almost complete annihilation of Nishimura's ships by Oldendorf's battle line "capping the T." This was a classic surface engagement maneuver of the type studied by every battleship sailor since Japanese Admiral Togo used it to crush the Imperial Russian navy at Tsushima Strait in 1905. Shima, following behind Nishimura, took one look at the destruction and wisely turned around. At the recommendation of Captain Dick Whitehead, the air support coordinator assigned to Kinkaid on loan from the Central Pacific forces, the escort carriers prepared two fighter-torpedo strikes for the dawn mop up. One was for the Surigao Strait, the other for any stray ships that might have slipped past Lee's battle line in the expected second night battle, although Kinkaid had heard nothing further about the northern or center forces. PBY Catalina seaplanes would conduct night searches to the north. As the southern force was being pounded to pieces, Kinkaid held a staff meeting to "check for errors of commission or of omission," but no one could think of anything. After the meeting adjourned around 0400, Kinkaid's operations officer, Captain Richard H. Cruzen, returned and said, "Admiral, I can think of only one other thing. We have never directly asked Halsey if Task Force 34 is guarding San Bernardino." Kinkaid agreed and at 0412 sent off a message to Halsey asking for confirmation of that fact. Halsey received the message at 0648 and replied in the negative at 0705, too late for Kinkaid to do anything about it. After the old battleships had mauled Nishimura's ships, Oldendorf had entered the Surigao Strait looking for cripples. By dawn, Oldendorf's battle force was 65 miles from the Leyte beachhead.

At daybreak on 25 October, the battle for Leyte Gulf was about to heat up. The PBY searches had turned up nothing of interest and the search flight for the northern sector was just being launched at 0645, when without any warning, the center force was sighted visually by the escort carriers off Samar. Within 15 minutes, 18.1-inch shells from the super battleship *Yamato* were dropping in among the hapless escort carriers of "Ziggy" Sprague's Taffy Three. Taffy Three turned away from the advancing Japanese, laying smoke and calling for help. At 0707 Kinkaid radioed in plain language to Halsey that his ships were under heavy attack by major Japanese surface units. This message, like others in the divided communications setup, took over an hour to be delivered.

Meanwhile, Mitscher had launched his searches north and then swung them eastward followed by deckload strikes. Ozawa was 190 miles northeast of Task Force 38 and steaming south when his radar picked up Mitscher's search aircraft. He turned away and managed to open the distance by another 40 miles

before being spotted at 0710. The attack by Task Force 38 began with ten deck-load strikes of Mitscher's orbiting planes, which had been waiting for the search aircraft to make contact. First on the scene was Air Group 15 from *Essex* and Commander David McCampbell, the air group commander, became target coordinator.[3] Ozawa launched his last 29 planes. The four Japanese carriers were sitting ducks. Unlike the hurried twilight attack of the Battle of the Philippine Sea, the morning attack was well executed and systematic. The light carrier *Chitose* went down under a heavy bombing attack at 0937. A torpedo struck Ozawa's flagship, *Zuikaku*, forcing him to shift his flag to a cruiser. A second bombing strike set the *Chiyoda* afire, and she was eventually abandoned. Afternoon strikes by Lexington's Air Group 19 and Langley's Air Group 44 finished off two of the carriers. The *Zuikaku*, veteran of the Pearl Harbor attack, was repeatedly bombed and torpedoed until she sank at 1414. The light carrier *Zuiho* was continually hit until she sank at 1526. Cruiser fire sank the abandoned *Chiyoda* at 1655. The old hermaphrodite battleships *Ise* and *Hyuga* managed to survive by skillful maneuvering and intense antiaircraft fire.

Meanwhile, the escort carriers battled for their lives and pleaded for help. Although Halsey had received Kinkaid's plea at 0822, he felt that Kinkaid could handle the situation with the forces at his disposal. As he stated later, "I figured that the 18 little carriers had enough planes to protect themselves until Oldendorf could bring up his heavy ships."[4] The little carriers tried their best. Dick Whitehead recalled the strike planes going after the southern force cripples, and these attacked Kurita, but the other aircraft were armed for combat air patrol, antisubmarine patrol, and ground support operations. Without torpedoes and heavy bombs, these planes could only use what they had and many continued to make dummy runs to divert Japanese fire away from the escort carriers. The destroyers and destroyer escorts valiantly attacked the Japanese with torpedoes and 5-inch gunfire. Oldendorf was still three hours away and the Army bombers over the Visayas could not be contacted. Kinkaid and Ziggy Sprague pleaded by radio with Halsey to send the fast carriers and the fast battleships to save them from the continual pounding.

Halsey had all this information by 0930, but was not deterred. He did, however, order McCain's Task Group 38.1 to the rescue, although McCain's ships were over 300 miles from Leyte—a long flight for the carrier aircraft. Halsey needed several more hours to finish the northern force with his carriers and battleships. In desperation, Kinkaid called for Lee's Task Force 34 in plain language, but Halsey didn't turn around. Kinkaid realized at last that Task Force 34 was not guarding the San Bernardino Strait, but neither Admiral King in Washington nor Admiral Nimitz at CincPac headquarters knew its whereabouts. Nimitz fired off a coded message to Halsey asking for the location of Task Force 34. Not all of the normal cryptographer's "padding" was removed and Halsey received the message as: "From CINCPAC. Where is, rpt, where is TF 34. The world wonders."[5] Kinkaid's communicators correctly removed the padding at both ends of the message, but Halsey's signalman did not, removing only the first phrase. Halsey received this message at 1000

and his first response was immediate. Losing his temper at this obvious criticism from Nimitz, he threw his cap to the deck and began swearing until he could be calmed down by his chief of staff, Mick Carney. The Nimitz message prodded Halsey into taking action, but not before another hour had been lost while he thought things over. At 1055 he ordered the entire battle line south. Two battleships under Rear Admiral Oscar Badger and covered by Bogan's Task Group 38.2 were to charge ahead at 28 knots, but Bogan's destroyers needed refueling first. Halsey then informed Nimitz of his decision: "Task Force 34 with me engaging carrier force. Am now proceeding with Task Group 38.2 and all fast BB to reinforce Kinkaid. . . ." Halsey wanted all or nothing. He took all the battleships with him, leaving nothing behind to finish off the *Ise* and *Hyuga.* In the end, by not dividing his battleships, Halsey allowed *Ise* and *Hyuga* to escape, and by waiting until 1055 to turn south, he allowed Kurita to escape as well.

Although Ozawa had succeeded in luring Halsey away, Kurita did not capitalize on the opportunity. The fierce air and destroyer attacks had cost him three heavy cruisers and at 0911 he ordered his ships to break off their pursuit of the escort carriers, intending to regroup his scattered forces before continuing into Leyte Gulf. He believed he had engaged and sunk several carriers from Task Force 38, although he had sunk one escort carrier, the *Gambier Bay,* and damaged others. After receiving a false contact report that had enemy carriers closing in from the sea, and fearing land-based American air strikes, Kurita decided at 1230 to clear Leyte Gulf.[6] The action off Samar had ended.

No American carriers appeared and Kurita, low on fuel, turned for the San Bernardino Strait and home. Just after 1300, as the center force retired, McCain's carriers attacked from far to the east, but did little damage. At around 2000 that night, Halsey ordered six night Avengers launched from the *Independence.* One of these spotted 15 ships passing along the coast off Samar and into the San Bernardino Strait. The night carrier men convinced Halsey to let them have a crack at Kurita, and Halsey agreed at 0300 on the 26th, but not before a severe thunderstorm had caused the aircraft shadowing the center force to lose contact. A strike of four night Avengers and five night Hellcats was launched, but did not locate Kurita. McCain and Bogan launched strikes over the Sibuyan Sea at dawn, with disappointing results: one light cruiser sunk and one heavy cruiser damaged.

The Americans had won the largest naval battle in history. Against American losses of the light carrier *Princeton,* two escort carriers, two destroyers and one destroyer escort, the Japanese lost 45 percent of all ships engaged, a total of three battleships, one heavy carrier, three light carriers, six heavy cruisers, four light cruisers and nine destroyers. After the battle, Kurita was blamed for his failure to complete the destruction of the American ships in Leyte Gulf, and was banished in December 1944 to the presidency of the Japanese Naval Academy. Ozawa became a hero for successfully completing his part in the battle and in May 1945 relieved Toyoda as commander of the Combined Fleet, although he was not promoted to full admiral.[7]

Chapter 11
Divine Wind

The Kamikaze Corps

While Kurita pounded the escort carriers on the morning of 25 October 1944, Admiral Onishi, commander of land-based naval aviation in the Philippines, realized what was at stake and ordered his kamikazes to make their first organized attack on the American navy. Several escort carriers were attacked that morning. The first bomb-laden Zero hit the *Kitkun Bay,* causing considerable damage. Two others dived on the *Fanshaw Bay,* but were shot down by antiaircraft fire, while others attacked the *White Plains.* One of the kamikazes damaged by antiaircraft fire turned and crashed into the *St. Lo.* In little more than 30 minutes, the *St. Lo* sank, with the loss of about 100 men. It was a taste of the future for the fast carriers.

A few days prior to their debut over Leyte Gulf, Onishi proposed to his First Air Fleet staff that suicide attacks, which had occurred on an individual basis before, be organized as an official operation. Kamikaze means "Divine Wind," a reference to the legendary typhoon that saved Japan from a Mongol invasion in the 13th century. The pilots of the Kamikaze Corps were all volunteers and generally less experienced flyers; the expert aviators served as teachers and escort pilots. Some of the volunteers were motivated by Japanese religious and military traditions of self sacrifice; others were resigned to die in combat anyway and welcomed the opportunity to die magnificently by sinking an enemy warship. Perhaps the simplest explanation came from a young kamikaze pilot who wrote, on the eve of his sacrifice, "I am nothing but a particle of iron attracted by a magnet—the American aircraft carrier."[1] While awaiting their turn to die, kamikaze pilots were treated with great respect and other Japanese often sacrificed their meager food rations to keep them well fed. The kamikazes proved frighteningly effective. In the Philippines 424 kamikazes destroyed 16 ships and damaged 80 others.

Leyte Follow-up Operations

The hectic pace of operations left Task Force 38 at the end of its endurance. By 26 October, the fast carriers were almost out of ammunition and food, which unlike fuel, could not be replenished at sea. Even so, the fast carriers stayed on for a few more days covering Leyte and attacking targets in the Philippines. Pilot fatigue had become chronic. When Halsey rotated McCain's Task Group 38.1 and Sherman's Task Group 38.3 to Ulithi for replacement air groups, two of the returning air groups had only served five of the required six months in a combat zone. ComAirPac ordered emergency replacement air groups to Manus and Guam, but these would not arrive before December. Naturally, the ships crews did not get to rotate and remained aboard for the duration.

Although control of air operations passed to the Army on 27 October, General Kenney could get only one group of P-38 Lightnings in operation from the rain soaked airfields on Leyte. These fighters, used for combat air patrol over Leyte, did not provide close air support for the ground troops. Continuing Japanese air raids caused MacArthur to request that both the fast carriers and the escort carriers stay on for a while longer. Bogan's Task Group 38.2 and Davison's Task Group 38.4 were ordered to strike Visayan and Luzon targets, which were hit 28-30 October. After successfully warding off a Japanese submarine attack, these task groups were hit hard by the kamikazes. *Franklin* and *Belleau Wood* were crashed. The *Intrepid* took a lesser hit when a kamikaze struck one of her portside 20mm gun mounts, killing ten men, but she soon resumed flight operations. The

Franklin had quickly eliminated two of the five planes attacking her, but the remaining three continued to bore in through the thick antiaircraft fire. One plane missed and splashed near the starboard side, another crashed into *Franklin*'s flight deck, setting the deck afire. A fighter nearby fell through the damaged flight deck to the hangar deck below, starting more fires. The third aircraft slipped to within 30 feet of the *Franklin* before splattering into the aft end of the *Belleau Wood*'s flight deck. Aboard *Franklin,* 56 died and 60 were wounded, but all fires were under control within two hours. The *Franklin* returned to Ulithi for temporary repairs before sailing for the West Coast. She would not be back in action until March 1945.[2]

Davison's task group was released to head for Ulithi along with the escort carrier groups on 29-30 October. The Fifth Air Force was scheduled to fly in a group of medium bombers a week later, but rain had delayed airfield construction so much that they were delayed until December. At the end of the month only Bogan's three carriers and a handful of Army P-38s and P-61 night fighters were left to cover Leyte.

Back at Ulithi, a bone-tired Mitscher turned command of Task Force 38 over to Vice Admiral McCain. On 31 October Rear Admiral Montgomery, ComCarDiv 3, took over Task Group 38.1.[3] The slender air defenses over Leyte had invited a Japanese counterattack, which struck 1 November. The attack, combined with decoy reports of the movement of Kurita's and Shima's forces, caused American commanders to send Sherman's Task Group 38.3 back to join Bogan's Task Group 38.2 in protecting shipping off Leyte, with Montgomery's

Task Group 38.1 soon following suit. The three task groups attacked Japanese airfields on Luzon on 5 and 6 November, taking the Japanese by surprise. The Japanese lost over 400 planes, most of them on the ground. Halsey lost 25 carrier aircraft. One of the TBM Avengers from the *Essex* returned from the strikes badly damaged; an antiaircraft shell had exploded in the plane's gun turret, killing the gunner instantly. The *Essex* chaplain administered last rites to the airman, whose body remained aboard. As the torpedo bomber was pushed off the end of the flight deck, the crew stood at attention while the bugler sounded taps.[4] The *Lexington* took a kamikaze hit when a group of kamikazes that had avoided the Combat Air Patrols by hiding in cloud cover dived on the carriers. One splashed 1,000 yards off the *Lex*'s starboard beam, but another, although hit repeatedly, crashed into the signal bridge on the island. Within 20 minutes, all fires were under control and flight operations resumed, but 47 men were killed and 127 wounded.[5] Vice Admiral McCain turned command of Task Force 38 over to Sherman, his senior carrier division commander, and shifted his flag from the *Lexington* to the *Wasp*. McCain returned to Ulithi aboard *Wasp* when she retired to change air groups, with Sherman remaining in command until 13 November. On 11 November, a strike of several hundred carrier planes attacked a convoy carrying 10,000 Japanese troops to Leyte, sinking five transports and four escorting destroyers. Halsey wanted to go after the survivors of the Leyte Gulf battle at Brunei Bay in Borneo or even strike Tokyo, but at a meeting on 10 November between MacArthur, Kenney, and Rear Admiral

Forrest Sherman, Nimitz's Deputy Chief of Staff for Plans, MacArthur decided that the "support of the fast carriers (was) essential" to the Sixth Army, and Task Force 38 stayed on, attacking Luzon airfields and shipping throughout November. On 13 and 14 November, the fast carriers sank a light cruiser and five destroyers plus seven merchant ships, destroying over 75 planes. Five days later they returned to shoot up more aircraft on the ground. Sherman's Task Group 38.3 eventually returned to Ulithi, where it was joined by Davison's Task Group 38.4 which had tried unsuccessfully to use napalm on bypassed Yap on 22 November. A final strike on Luzon by Montgomery's Task Group 38.1 and Bogan's Task Group 38.2 marked the end of fast carrier operations in support of Leyte. The bombing aircraft destroyed several enemy planes and ships, including a heavy cruiser, but the kamikazes struck back, hitting the *Intrepid, Essex,* and *Cabot,* and damaging the *Hancock* with a near-miss.

Two Val dive bombers made suicide runs on the *Hancock* and *Cabot,* but were splashed nearby. The *Essex* received her first major battle damage of the war when a lone kamikaze made it though the antiaircraft fire, skimmed the flight deck, and crashed into the port side. Fifteen men were killed and 44 wounded, but less than 30 minutes later, the fires had been put out and the flight deck was operational. The *Cabot* was also hit by two kamikazes and suffered minor fires and damage.

Intrepid, the "Hardluck I," did not get off as lightly. As a pair of enemy aircraft approached her, the *Intrepid* knocked one of them down only 1,500 yards away, but the other came in low from the stern. One thousand yards from the *Intrepid*, the kamikaze pulled up into a power stall and did a wing-over into the flight deck from 500 feet. Its bomb penetrated the flight deck and exploded in a vacant pilot ready room, killing 32 men in an adjacent compartment. The *Intrepid* maneuvered with starboard turns to spill water and flaming gasoline over the side as fire fighting parties ducked exploding ammunition. The billowing smoke acted as a beacon and, a few minutes later, another enemy aircraft was spotted boring in. At this point the ships frustrated gunnery officer shouted: "For God's sake, are we the only ship on the ocean?" This Zero machine-gunned the deck, released its bomb, and struck the flight deck, sliding toward the bow and starting more fires. The fire fighting parties battled the flames for the next three hours and the aircraft of her air group were forced to land on other carriers or airfields at Leyte. Sixty-five men died in the last attack. The flight deck was ripped apart and the hangar deck was reduced to a twisted mass of hot steel plate. *Intrepid* withdrew to Ulithi the next day. She had earned another ticket to the West Coast—the hard way.[6]

Countering the Kamikaze Threat

The damage done by the kamikazes caused the cancellation of a strike on the Visayas scheduled for 26 November. Task Force 38 returned to Ulithi while the Army air forces assumed responsibility for Leyte's defense.[7] Aboard the *Hornet*, the Plan of the Day reflected just how tired the carrier crews had become of the constant kamikaze threat: "Today will be Field Day. Air Department dust off all overheads, removing any snoopers which

may be adrift and sweep all corners of the Philippines, sending to the incinerator or throwing over the side (first punching holes in the bottom) any Nip cans, APs or AKs still on topside. Gunnery Department will assist as necessary. Engineering, continue to pour on the coal. Medics stand by with heat rash lotion. Damage Control, observe holiday routine."[8] Halsey insisted that the carriers not be exposed in such routine operations as the Philippines support strikes until better defenses could be devised. The immediate need for more fighters aboard the fast carriers led to the Marines being assigned to the fast carriers in early December. The first Marine units to complete the minimum carrier qualification, 12 landings aboard the *Saratoga, Ranger,* or an escort carrier, were Marine Fighting Squadrons 124 and 213 under Lieutenant Colonel William A. Millington. VMF 124 and VMF 213 reported aboard the *Essex* two weeks before the year ended. The Marines brought their own mechanics, who stayed aboard the carriers when the squadrons rotated out, and more air combat intelligence officers were assigned for the new squadrons. As soon as the additional aircraft became available, *Essex* class air groups changed from 54 fighters, 24 bombers and 18 torpedo planes to 73 fighters, 15 bombers and 15 torpedo planes. The faster F4Us eventually supplanted the Hellcats as the primary fighters, which in turn became fighter-bombers, while four radar-equipped Hellcats were retained for night fighters. With 73 planes and 110 pilots, the fighter squadrons became too large to administer as a single unit and so, in January 1945, 18 fighter squadrons were split in two; 36 aircraft in a fighter squadron and 36 in a fighter-bomber squadron, although in practice the two squadrons were interchangeable.[9]

Vice Admiral McCain, with his operations officer Commander John S. "Jimmy" Thach and the rest of the fast carrier staff, developed defensive tactics to best utilize these fighters in countering the kamikaze threat. At the advice of Jocko Clark, who had returned from leave in mid-November, McCain enlarged the task group cruising formations horizontally by stationing radar picket ships, called Tomcats, 60 miles ahead of the carriers. McCain also started several new Combat Air Patrols: JACKCAP, two to four fighters flying at low altitude in each of the four quadrants; DADCAP, patrols at all altitudes launched at dawn and relieved at dusk by the BATCAP of night fighters; RAP-CAP radar picket planes; and SCOCAP scouting line planes stationed over the Tomcat radar picket destroyers. Returning air strikes would circle over the Tomcats to be "deloused" and any aircraft not making the identifying turn would be picked off by the defending fighters. Commander Thach also developed the "Three Strike" system, whereby one fighter patrol would remain over an enemy airfield while a second prepared to take off and a third was either on its way to or from the target or was being readied for another strike. The constant patrol would be continued at night by heckling night fighters flying over enemy airfields to discourage the Japanese from launching any night attacks. These measures were part of what McCain called his "Big Blue Blanket" for protecting the carrier task force.

All these techniques were practiced in simulated "Moosetrap" training strikes during maneuvers off Ulithi in

late November and early December 1944. The first test of the new tactics would be the landings on Mindoro scheduled for 5 December. Task Force 38, reduced to three day carrier task groups because of the damage done in November by the kamikazes, had sortied from Ulithi on 1 December, but was recalled that afternoon when the landings were postponed for ten days. Leyte had been bearing the brunt of Japanese air and kamikaze attacks and the Army air forces had been unable to eliminate Japanese air opposition in the central Philippines, a necessary precondition to successful landings. The Luzon landings also changed from 20 December to 9 January 1945.

At the conclusion of the Leyte operations, more command changes were made. Although Sherman, Davison, and Bogan remained, Montgomery had earned a rest after long duty at sea.[10] His replacement was Rear Admiral Tommy Sprague, still recovering from the ordeal off Samar, where the escort carriers under his command encountered the first kamikazes. Jocko Clark, ComCarDiv 5, and Rear Admiral Arthur W. "Raddy" Radford, ComCarDiv 6, were also available for command at Ulithi. Halsey's three task groups of four day carriers each were supported by a night carrier task group. The *Enterprise,* which spent December converting to a night carrier, later joined the *Independence* under Rear Admiral Matt Gardner as commander of Night Carrier Division 7. Operating the night carriers as a separate task group allowed the crews of the day carriers to get some sleep. All the new carrier division commanders got a chance to practice handling task groups. The two-week respite at Ulithi had given the fast carrier commanders their first real look at McCain as a task force commander and, although he was personably likable, he was resented by the more experienced carrier commanders who felt that he had been forced on them by Admiral King.

Six escort carriers of the newly created Escort Carrier Force Pacific Fleet supported the 15 December Mindoro landings, allowing the fast carriers to strike at strategic targets.[11] Task Force 38 sortied from Ulithi on 10-11 December to strike at targets on Luzon while General Kenney's Army air forces covered all targets south of Manila. To keep the fighters on Luzon grounded, Task Force 38 continuously blanketed Luzon day and night from the 14th through the 16th of December, destroying over 200 enemy aircraft in the process. Only 27 carrier aircraft were lost, and most of the airmen shot down made contact with friendly Filipinos. Task Force 38 then withdrew to refuel before resuming air strikes in support of the Seventh Fleet landings on Mindoro. While searching for a fueling rendezvous in heavy weather on the night of 17-18 December, the task force blundered into what turned out to be a typhoon.

Halsey's Typhoon

As Halsey maneuvered Task Force 38 in the worsening weather, he did not even consider it to be a typhoon until noon on the 18th when he finally cancelled the attempted refueling and strikes planned for Luzon. The task force headed south into a storm blowing east to west. Planes on the light carriers broke their lashings and careened around, starting fires on the *Monterey* and *Cowpens*. Others were lost overboard as the carriers plunged

wildly into the mountainous waves. Being low on fuel and without enough ballast to keep them steady, the destroyers had the worst time of it. Three of them capsized and sank with nearly all hands lost. In a subsequent Court of Inquiry, the "preponderance of responsibility" was placed on Halsey for "errors in judgment under stress of war operations and not as offenses." Poor weather information played its part in the tragedy, but Halsey's sloppy handling of the task force only made the situation worse. Although the damage caused by the storm kept the fast carriers out action for several days, the Army air forces on Leyte were now strong enough to cover Mindoro.

Task Force 38 returned to Ulithi on 24 December and Nimitz arrived to spend Christmas Day with Halsey aboard the battleship *New Jersey*. Rear Admiral Radford relieved Rear Admiral Montgomery as commander of Task Group 38.1 a month early when Montgomery was injured in a boat accident.[12] On 5 January Rear Admiral Gardner arrived with the *Enterprise* to form Night Task Group 38.5 along with the *Independence*.

Fast carrier operations resumed on 30 December to support MacArthur's landings at Lingayen Gulf on Luzon. Starting on 3 January, Task Force 38 spent six days hitting Japanese airfields on Luzon, Formosa, the Pescadores Islands, the Sakishima Gunto, and Okinawa. Heavy weather allowed Japanese aircraft to penetrate the air defenses over the landing area and several ships were damaged or sunk by kamikazes off Lingayen, while an escort carrier was sunk by a kamikaze near Mindoro. Over 150 Japanese aircraft were destroyed and when the landings took place on 9 January. Others were grounded because of strikes on Formosa and the Ryukyus. Losses, however, had been unusually high. Eighty-six carrier aircraft were lost, 40 of them operationally. Many operational accidents involved the inexperienced Marine pilots, who had little carrier landing practice. As Lieutenant Colonel Millington, commander of the Marine squadrons aboard the *Essex,* put it: "We just can't learn navigation and carrier operations in a week as well as the Navy does it in six months."[13]

Halsey still wanted to track down the surviving Japanese surface fleet and Nimitz released Task Force 38 from its support role on the morning of the landings. Naval intelligence had placed the *Ise* and *Hyuga* at Camranh Bay in French Indochina and Halsey hoped to surprise them before they could run south to Singapore. Task Force 38 passed through the Luzon Strait into the South China Sea on the night of 9-10 January and refueled on the 11th. Halsey ignored a reported convoy of over 100 Japanese merchant ships off the Chinese coast and headed for the Formosa Straits in order to surprise the hermaphrodite battleships. When Halsey struck, they had already gone. But targets in Indochina were plentiful. On 12 January alone, Task Force 38 sank 44 enemy ships and destroyed over 100 planes for a loss of 23 carrier planes, with most of the crews being rescued by natives and smuggled into China. Heavy weather made refueling difficult, but Halsey ran north for a series of strikes against Formosa and the nearby China coast on 15 January. Hong Kong, Hainan, Canton, Swatow, and Macao were hit the next day with minimal results. Twenty-two aircraft were lost to Japanese antiaircraft fire.[14] Heavy

monsoon weather forced Task Force 38 south and Halsey wanted to exit the South China Sea through the Surigao Strait. This would take the fast carriers out of the war for a week and expose them to land-based air attack in confined waters. Nimitz rejected the idea and told Halsey to wait until the weather cleared before passing over the top of Luzon. Steaming northward after the weather lifted, the three task groups spent 21 January bombing Formosa, the Pescadores, and the Sakishimas. (Task Group 38.5, Gardner's night task group had been dissolved on 12 January.) The carriers came under fierce kamikaze attack, with two hitting the new *Ticonderoga,* which had joined Task Force 38 at the end of October.

Around noon a single-engine fighter came in out of the sun and hit the "Big T's" flight deck abreast the number two twin 5-inch mount. Over 100 men were killed or wounded when the plane's bomb went off just above the hangar deck, starting many fires. Captain Dixie Kiefer ordered an immediate course change to keep the wind from spreading the fires and to keep smoke out of the ventilation intakes. The *Ticonderoga* was counterflooded to give her a 10-degree portside list, which allowed water and gasoline to drain over the side (gasoline floats on water), and damaged aircraft were pushed overboard. The smoke rising from the carrier made her an easy target; three more kamikazes were shot down before another crashed into the island. Captain Kiefer, severely wounded, remained on the bridge for 12 hours until he was assured that the injured had been cared for. All fires were under control within two hours and the *Ticonderoga* limped back to Ulithi.[15] Another kamikaze hit a radar picket destroyer, while a conventional bomber hit the *Langley.* The same day, an operational accident on the *Hancock* took 52 lives when a stray bomb from a landing Avenger exploded and started a fire. That night seven Avengers sank a tanker off Formosa, and the next day the fast carriers hit the Sakishimas and Ryukyus, photographing the islands, especially Okinawa, in anticipation of later landings. These strikes were the last fast carrier operations in support of the Philippines landings and Task Force 38 headed for Ulithi, arriving on 25 January. Halsey hauled down his flag the next day to begin planning the next series of operations under the Pacific "two platoon" system.

Meanwhile, the Sixth Army had moved inland at Lingayen. General Kenney flew his aircraft into newly seized airfields and relieved the Seventh Fleet from covering the beachhead on the 17th. The Fifth Air Force supported the drive on Manila, picking up close air support tricks from the Marines, who brought seven squadrons of old SBD Dauntless dive bombers from the Solomons at MacArthur's request. The Allies entered Manilla on 3 February and organized resistance on Luzon ended on 14 April 1945. Operations in the southern Philippines continued into the summer. By early February, Army air forces were operating from Luzon and the Navy was using Manila. A major base and anchorage was being built at Leyte-Samar, which would eventually be used by the fast carriers. With the Philippines largely in American hands, the Luzon bottleneck was corked. Japanese ships going from the East Indies to the Japanese home islands had to run a gauntlet of Philippine-based aircraft, submarines, and mine fields laid by B-29 bombers. In losing the Philippines, Japan had not only lost her lifeline to the oil, rubber, and gasoline in Indonesia, but ultimately, the war.[16]

Chapter 12
Okinawa

On 26 January 1945, the Third Fleet again became the Fifth Fleet as Spruance resumed command of the Central Pacific Forces. The Allies, having decided to secure bases from which to launch the final assault on Japan, considered suitable targets within the strategic triangle, with legs 1,500 miles long, formed by Formosa, Saipan, and Tokyo. Back in July 1944, in conferences with Nimitz and King, Spruance had recommended taking Okinawa in the Ryukyus Islands and suggested seizing Iwo Jima in the Bonins for an air base. Spruance added, however, that a method of transferring ammunition at sea would be needed for these assaults because of the distances from friendly bases. Until this time, fuel had been transferred at sea, but ammunition was transferred by lighters in protected anchorages. Although King did not immediately endorse the landings in the Ryukyus and on Iwo Jima, he did adopt resupplying ammunition at sea.[1] Because the Joint Chiefs of Staff eventually rejected Formosa, King's favored target, as being too

costly to take with the forces available, the focus shifted to Okinawa and Iwo Jima. For the Iwo Jima and Okinawa operations, four new *Essex* class carriers would join Task Force 58: *Bennington, Randolph, Shangri-La*, and *Bon Homme Richard*.[2]

By this time in the war, the carrier pilots facing the Japanese were the best. All air group commanders were veterans and all pilots averaged 525 hours of flying time in training before being assigned to combat. By stark contrast, the average Japanese pilot had only 275 hours of training by December 1944 and by July 1945, this number was down to a meager 100 hours. All the fast carrier task group commanders were also veterans: Jocko Clark, ComCarDiv 5, had returned to become Mitscher's right-hand man as commander of Task Group 58.1; Dave Davison, ComCarDiv 2, took command of Task Group 58.2; Ted Sherman, ComCarDiv 1, had his leave postponed to command Task Group 58.3; and Arthur Radford, ComCarDiv 6, continued to command

Task Group 58.4 at sea. Matt Gardner, ComCarDiv 7, led the night carrier group Task Group 58.5. The night carrier task group was changed when it was realized that the *Independence* was too small to operate as a night carrier. The *Independence* returned to Pearl Harbor for conversion back to a day carrier, and plans to convert the light carrier *Bataan* to a night carrier were cancelled. Instead, the old *Enterprise* and *Saratoga* would be the night carriers for Task Force 58.[3] Although carrier doctrine and tactics had not changed from the previous months, Task Force 58 faced two equally demanding roles: softening up the beaches and supporting the troops as well as defending against air attack.

Iwo Jima

The eastern leg of the strategic triangle, Saipan to Tokyo, was the route flown by B-29s on their way to targets in Japan. A halfway point was needed both to recover damaged B-29s unable to make it back to the Marianas and as a base for fighter escorts. Only Iwo Jima met these requirements. The original date for the landings was set at 20 January 1945, but prolonged resistance on Leyte and Luzon pushed the target date back to 19 February.[4] Tragically for the Marines who later assaulted it, this gave the Japanese another month to turn the island into a nearly impregnable fortress.

Fifth Fleet was to conduct carrier strikes in the Tokyo area to reduce the possibility of Japanese interference with the Iwo Jima landings. Task Force 58 sortied from Ulithi on 10 February. After hitting the Bonins on 15 February, the fast carriers launched a series of strikes against airfields and aircraft plants in and around the Tokyo area on 16 and 17 February. This marked the first time aircraft from carriers had attacked the Japanese capital since Mitscher launched the Doolittle raid from the old *Hornet* in April 1942. The first strikes were launched at dawn on the 16th while 60 miles off the coast of Japan and 120 miles from Tokyo. The weather over Honshu was overcast and cold. Although warned not to be drawn off by the Japanese, many inexperienced aviators could not resist breaking formation to dogfight with Japanese fighters. Although the Japanese lost over 300 aircraft to the fighter sweep, Task Force 58 lost 60 carrier aircraft. One of those lost was Phil Torrey, the commander of Air Group 9, who had led the group over Rabaul and Truk. Matt Gardner's night-flying Avengers kept the Japanese night fighters grounded around Tokyo, but they failed to turn up any shipping targets. Foul weather the next day allowed only one strike to be made.

After heading south, Task Force 58 shifted to close support of Iwo Jima. Radford's Task Group 58.4 bombed Chichi Jima 18 February, while two of the battleships and three of the cruisers joined the bombardment forces under Rear Admiral William H.P. "Spike" Blandy. After dawn on 19 February, Marine Corsairs from the *Essex*, along with planes from Task Group 58.2 and the other carriers of Task Group 58.3, swept over the beaches to bomb and strafe just as the Marines landed. The Marines appreciated the support, but neither the carrier strikes, nor the pre-landing bombardment seriously affected the dug-in Japanese defenders; Iwo would be taken yard by yard at terrible cost. Although the distance from other

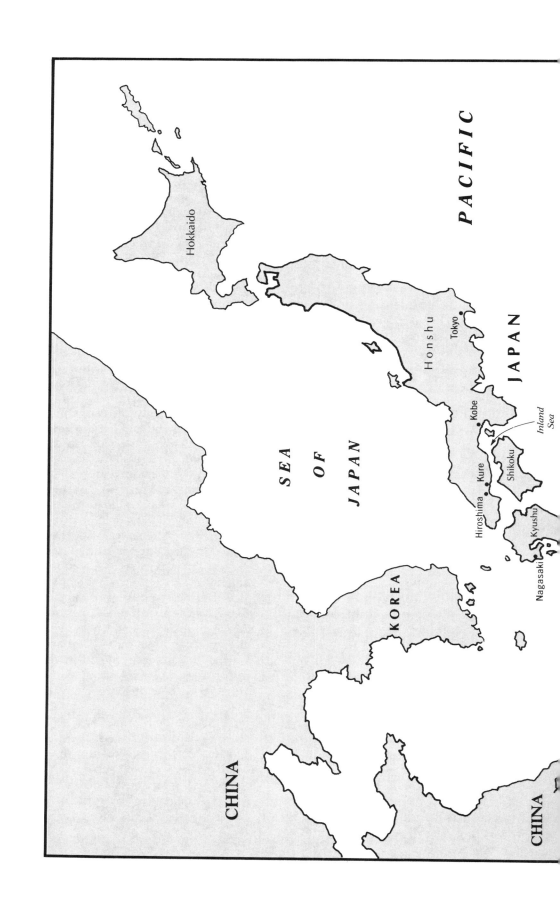

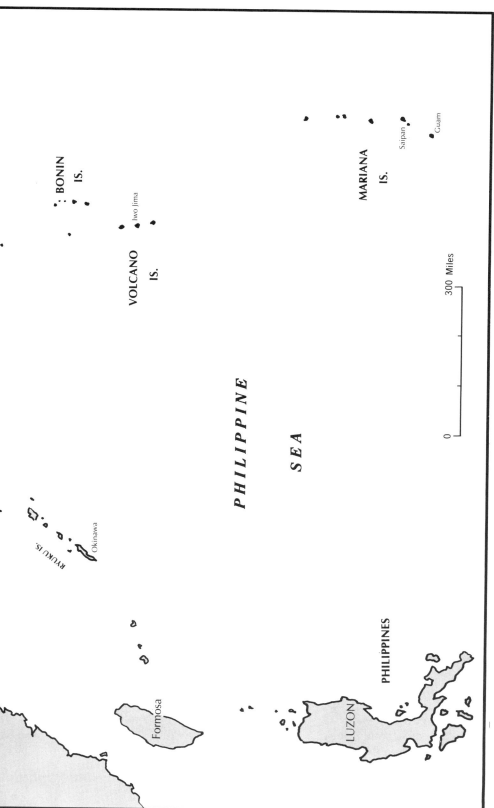

BONIN
IS.

VOLCANO
IS.

Iwo Jima

MARIANA
IS.

Saipan
Guam

RYUKU IS.

Okinawa

PHILIPPINE

SEA

Formosa

PHILIPPINES

LUZON

0   300 Miles

The Western Pacific

Japanese air bases reduced the threat of kamikazes, the old *Saratoga,* detached by Mitscher to provide night cover for the landings and operating with the escort carriers, was hit by three bombs and two kamikazes northwest of Iwo on the afternoon of 21 February. Later that evening, "Sara" took another bomb hit and the escort carrier *Bismark Sea* was lost to a lone kamikaze in the same attack.[5] Task Force 58 continued to support the Iwo landing, sharing close air support duties with the escort carriers until departing late on 22 February. The fast carriers turned to strike Japan again, but bad weather forced the cancellation of strikes against Tokyo, scheduled for the 25th, and Nagoya, scheduled for the next day. Instead, Task Force 58 hit targets on Honshu and the Nansei Shoto, the southwestern islands of Japan which include the Ryukyus and Amami Oshima. Task Force 58 paused to refuel from Servron 6 and Mitscher detached Radford's Task Group 58.4 to Ulithi while the rest of Task Force 58 hit Okinawa again on 1 March. Turning south, the rest of Task Force 58 anchored at Ulithi 4 March.

The escort carriers continued their support until 11 March, when they withdrew to begin preparations for Okinawa. The *Enterprise* stayed behind to provide night cover for the landing force, keeping planes aloft for 174 consecutive hours over Iwo Jima between 23 February and 2 March. By the time the escort carriers departed, Seventh Air Force P-51 Mustangs were providing close support. Even before the island was secured, the first crippled B-29 had landed there. Major resistance ended on 26 March and in April, the Mustangs began flying escort missions to Japan.

Okinawa—Operation Iceberg

The massive preparations for the Okinawa landings called for the neutralization of Japanese land-based air power on Okinawa, Formosa, the China coast, and Japan itself. Extensive minesweeping, underwater demolition, and naval bombardment operations would be carried out under the protection of Task Force 58. The British Pacific Fleet now joined in the Okinawa operation and, although designated Task Force 57, the British carrier force was more comparable to a U.S. task group. The British lacked the at-sea replenishment capabilities of the American navy and could not keep at sea for extended periods. Nevertheless, their contribution to the operation was significant.

While at Ulithi Mitscher reshuffled his task groups in preparation for the Okinawa landings. At a conference with his carrier admirals aboard his flagship, *Bunker Hill,* he admitted that he no idea what the Japanese might do next. For all he knew, he said, they might even use poison gas. The Japanese, it turned out, still had a few tricks to play. The night following Mitscher's conference, 11 March, a long-range twin-engined Frances kamikaze aircraft flew all the way to Ulithi and crashed into the after flight deck of the new *Randolph* as she was lighted while loading ammunition. Like on other carriers anchored at Ulithi, members of the *Randolph*'s crew were enjoying a movie on the hangar deck. The crash killed 25 men and wounded 106 others and the *Randolph* was out of action for nearly three weeks. Because of the ingenuity of a crewmember, however, the she did not have to return to the States. Using undamaged equipment from her arresting gear to replace damaged parts, she was repaired in the forward area and rejoined the fleet off Okinawa on 7 April.[6] The *Lexington* and *Cowpens* went home for overhaul and many air groups rotated out. The overhauled *Franklin, Intrepid,* and *Bataan* rejoined the fleet. Mitscher recalled Gerry Bogan to be a standby carrier division commander and Bogan hoisted his flag aboard the *Franklin* in Task Group 58.2. Tommy Sprague, scheduled to relieve Jocko Clark in the middle of the upcoming operation, was aboard *Wasp.* Matt Gardner, aboard the *Enterprise,* was attached to Radford's Task Group 58.4. The new *Bon Homme Richard,* still in the U.S., would replace the *Saratoga* in the night carrier role, but a two carrier night task group would not be possible until later that year.

Task Force 58 left Ulithi on 14 March, replenishing at sea on the 16th. The next day, Japanese search aircraft located Task Force 58 while it was 160-175 miles from Kyushu. Admiral Ugaki, commander of the Fifth Air Fleet, which controlled most of the aircraft in the Kyushu area, had time to disperse his aircraft to other locations. Task Force 58 struck airfields in the Kyushu area the next day. After bombing hangars and barracks with few Japanese aircraft getting caught on the ground, Mitscher sent his crews farther inland looking for targets. At Kobe and Kure several fleet units were spotted, including the super battleship *Yamato* and the aircraft carrier *Amagi.* That same day, the Japanese counterattacked; 50 Japanese aircraft hit Radford's Task Group 58.4 75 miles south of Shikoku. Early that morning, the *Enterprise* had a lucky escape when a bomb dropped on her failed to explode. The *Intrepid* was damaged by a near miss which spread fires, killing two and wounding 43 of her crew. Three Judy

dive bombers attacked the *Yorktown* around 1300, hitting the signal bridge with a bomb that went through to the next deck before exploding, leaving two gaping holes in her side. Five sailors died and 26 were wounded. The next day Task Force 58 again sent out strikes to the Inland Sea looking for shipping and naval units at Kobe and Kure. Antiaircraft fire was particularly intense around the naval installations and, although 17 ships, including the *Yamato* and *Amagi,* were hit, no serious damage was done. The Japanese counterattacked again in the early morning, hitting Davison's Task Group 58.2 hard. The *Wasp* was hit by an undetected aircraft and suffered heavy casualties since the bomb penetrated down to the mess decks, where breakfast was being served, before exploding. Fires on five decks, ruptured avgas tanks, and broken water mains added to the *Wasp*'s troubles, but excellent fire fighting and damage control allowed her to recover her aircraft within an hour. Casualties on the *Wasp* were high: 101 killed and 269 wounded.

The *Franklin*'s Ordeal

That same morning, the *Franklin,* Davison's flagship, was launching her second strike against Kure while a third was getting ready on the hangar deck below. A few minutes after seven, a lone Japanese aircraft appeared over the bow out of nowhere and dropped two 550-pound bombs on her flight deck. The first went through the flight deck near the forward elevator and exploded on the hangar deck; the second exploded on the flight deck amid aircraft warming up to launch. Both bombs started huge fires fed by the high-octane avgas in the plane's tanks. A series of explosions rocked the ship as bombs burst in their racks. Some of the aircraft in the *Franklin*'s air group carried the large 11.75-inch "Tiny Tim" rockets and, as the flames grew hotter, these began to go off. "Some screamed by to starboard, some to port and some straight up the flight deck," her executive officer later recalled. "The weird aspect of this weapon whooshing by so close is one of the most awful spectacles a human has ever been privileged to see." Hundreds were killed in the first blasts. The entire after end of the "Big Ben" was a mass of flame as explosions tossed aircraft and crewmen into the air. Other men were trapped in spaces below.

The Catholic chaplain, Lieutenant Commander Joseph T. O'Callahan, was eating breakfast in the wardroom when the first explosions shattered the light fixtures, showering the space with bits of broken glass. Making his way to his cabin, he donned his steel helmet with the white cross on it, took out his vial of holy oils for the dying, and "went in search of my proper work." Finding the flight deck littered with the bodies of the dead, dying and injured, Father O'Callahan joined the ship's surgeon, Lieutenant Commander Samuel R. Sherman, to administer spiritual treatment. After their patients had been attended to, they compared notes on their experiences and Sherman patched up a gash on the chaplain's leg caused by a flying hunk of steel. "Amidst the fire and explosion in this moment of respite," Father O'Callahan said later, "the Jewish doctor and the Catholic chaplain said a prayer together." O'Callahan continued to administer last rites to his dying shipmates and helped in whatever ways he could, including carrying hot bombs

and shells to the side of the ship for jettisoning, and leading a damage control party into the main ammunition magazines to wet them down. For his many acts of inspiration and heroism aboard the *Franklin*, he became the first chaplain to be awarded the Congressional Medal of Honor.[7]

Davison ordered a destroyer alongside to take him and his staff off. As he left, he advised Captain Leslie E. Gehres to prepare to abandon the *Franklin*, but Captain Gehres demurred. A few minutes later, he sent a message to Mitscher aboard the *Bunker Hill*: "This is the commanding officer of the *Franklin*. You save us from the Japs and we'll save this ship." As Mitscher watched the clouds of black smoke from the *Franklin* billowing on the horizon, he told his chief of staff, Arleigh Burke, "You tell him we'll save him." Around 0930, the light cruiser *Santa Fe* came along side to pick up survivors and help fight the fires and take off the wounded. Only a skeleton crew remained and the rest went into the water to be picked up. At 1000, the *Franklin* lay dead in the water, listing 13 degrees and still ablaze, but by noon the fires were under control and her list stabilized. The heavy cruiser *Pittsburgh* moved in to take her in tow, eventually working her around to a southerly course as crewmen aboard the *Franklin* worked to free her rudder, which was jammed hard left. The crew managed to free the rudder and relight the boilers. Early the next morning, the *Franklin* had succeeded in regaining power and by 1100, she could make seven knots. At noon, the tow was cast off. Other carriers offered to provide men and provisions, but Captain Gehres replied, "We have plenty of men and food. All we want is to get the hell out of here."

A little later, as *Franklin*'s speed built up, he reported: "Down by the tail but reins up!"

The *Franklin* entered Pearl Harbor on 3 April. After a cleanup to allow her to continue her journey, she departed Pearl on an amazing 1,200 mile voyage to New York Harbor, arriving there under her own power on 28 April. That day, 393 medals, the largest number of decorations ever presented on a single ship, were awarded to the surviving members of her crew. *Franklin* became the most heavily damaged aircraft carrier to survive the war, although at the cost of 724 killed and 260 wounded.[8]

After the 19 March attacks on the *Wasp* and *Franklin*, Task Force 58 slowly retired. Mitscher sent fighter sweeps over the Kyushu airfields to keep Japanese aircraft grounded, but in the afternoon of 20 March, Task Group 58.2, still protecting the crippled *Franklin*, again came under attack. This time flaming debris from a downed Zero kamikaze crashed into the destroyer *Halsey Powell* while she was alongside the *Hancock* refueling. The hit jammed her steering gear and almost caused the destroyer to ram into the *Hancock*. Late that afternoon, 15 to 20 Japanese aircraft closed in on the *Enterprise*. Their bombs missed, but friendly antiaircraft fire caused a flight deck fire, severely hampering her ability to conduct night flying operations. Japanese aircraft continued to shadow the task force throughout the night and around 1400 the following day a large Japanese force was detected to the northwest. About 150 aircraft intercepted a group of 48 enemy aircraft 60 miles from the task force. Eighteen of the Japanese aircraft were Bettys carrying the new Ohka one-man piloted bomb. Capable of speeds up to 600 miles an hour, the Ohka was almost impossible to shoot down once launched. The Ohka bombs were later dubbed "baka" ("fool" in Japanese) by the Americans. The payload made the Bettys difficult to maneuver, however, and easy prey for the defending fighters. No Japanese aircraft got through the fighter screen to the task force.

On 22 March Task Force 58 replenished and was reorganized into three task groups, leaving Davison's Task Group 58.2 as a "cripple" task group to escort the damaged *Franklin*, *Enterprise*, and *Wasp* back to Ulithi. Clark's Task Group 58.1 now included *Hornet*, *Belleau Wood*, *San Jacinto*, and *Bennington*. Sprague had shifted his flag to the *Bennington* after the *Wasp* had been hit. Sherman's Task Group 58.3 now comprised five carriers: *Essex*, *Bunker Hill*, *Hancock*, *Bataan*, and *Cabot* while Radford's Task Group 58.4 had *Yorktown*, *Intrepid*, *Langley*, and the newly arrived *Independence*. Task Force 58 pilots had claimed 528 aircraft destroyed on the ground and in the air.[9] These losses delayed a major Japanese response to the Okinawa landings until 6 April.

The carrier task groups settled in to a routine of fueling and striking in rotation in the week before the 1 April landings, maintaining constant alert to air attack. Visual aircraft detection was necessary as the Japanese had discovered that U.S. radar could detect neither single aircraft coming in low, nor small groups at very high altitude. While the fighters protected the fleet, the bombers worked over Okinawa. During the Okinawa campaign, after the departure of the *Franklin*, the only air group left equipped with the 11.75" Tiny Tim rockets was the *Intrepid*'s. Results with

the large inaccurate rockets were inconclusive and they were withdrawn from
the carriers thereafter. In addition,
Clark's Task Group 58.1 sank a convoy
of eight ships north of Okinawa on 24
March. With the air strikes, Okinawa
got seven days of shelling by the bombardment ships. Beginning 24 March,
and for the next three months, Cal
Durgin's escort carriers also provided
support. With three fast carriers taken
out of the war in one month, *Saratoga,
Franklin*, and *Wasp*, the arrival of four
British carriers on 25 March was most
welcome. Task Force 57 took on the
responsibility of neutralizing the Sakishima Gunto, the islands southwest of
Okinawa used as a staging base for
Japanese aircraft shuttling between
Kyushu and Formosa.[10]

Aircraft from the escort carriers and
the fast carriers also covered the operations in the Kerama Retto. The Kerama
Retto islets, close to the southwestern
tip of Okinawa, were seized before the
main landings to provide a sheltered
anchorage for a fleet base and for flying
boats. Keise Island, between the Kerama
Retto and Okinawa, was also seized to
provide an artillery base to support the
landings on southern Okinawa. About
80 enemy aircraft were destroyed and
many other targets, such as bridges,
small craft and some submarine pens
were attacked. Army Air Force B-29s
struck Kyushu on 27 and 31 March to
further isolate Okinawa from Japanese
aerial attack and in the last seven days
of March, Task Force 58 flew 3,095
sorties. But the Japanese still managed
to launch 50 or so raids against the
American ships off Okinawa during the
period 26-31 March, damaging 10,
including the battleship *Nevada* and the
cruisers *Biloxi* and *Indianapolis*. Eight of

the 10 were hit by kamikazes. The
Japanese, however, lost around 1,100
aircraft.

Vice Admiral Richmond "Kelly"
Turner, commander of the amphibious
phase of the operation, had set up a
series of protective screens around the
vast armada of ships lying off Okinawa.
He placed destroyers around the transport area and antisubmarine and anti-
suicide boat screens and surface forces
positioned to intercept any surface
attacks by Japanese naval units. Beyond
these were the radar picket destroyers.
Task Force 57, the British carrier force,
was positioned to the southwest, between Okinawa and Formosa, while
Task Force 58 was between Okinawa
and Kyushu. The landings on 1 April
went well—too well. The Japanese had
decided not to oppose the landings on
the beaches, choosing instead to pro-
long the struggle and take as many
American lives as possible. The pre-
landing strikes had delayed a major
Japanese counterstroke, although a
limited number of small-scale, but
determined air attacks, including
kamikazes, and suicide boat attacks had
been made against ships off Okinawa.
The breather did not last long. The
Japanese planned to launch the first of
their massed "kikisui" (floating chrysanthemum) kamikaze attacks, which
were intended to destroy the American
fleet.[11] For Task Force 58, tied to Okinawa to protect the invasion, the trial
by kamikaze was only beginning.

At the same time the kikisui attacks
were launched, the Japanese sent the
remains of their once proud surface
fleet on a suicide mission of its own.
The super battleship *Yamato,* the cruiser
Yahagi and seven destroyers were to
proceed at top speed to Okinawa. The

Yamato had only enough fuel for a one-way trip and it was hoped that she could beach herself and sink as many of the American ships with her 18.1-inch guns as possible before being destroyed. The force left Kure on 6 April but was spotted by the submarines *Threadfin* and *Hackleback* around 2000 that evening. Alerted by the submarine contact reports, Mitscher prepared to deal with this new threat.

Meanwhile, the first of the kikisui attacks had been launched during the afternoon of 6 April, with the outer radar picket destroyers being the first to suffer. Before the end of the day, almost 900 planes had attacked the American fleet, and at least 355 of these were kamikazes. Mitscher stowed his bombers below and scrambled all his fighters. By nightfall the Americans had lost three destroyers, two ammunition ships, and one LST and at least eight destroyers, a destroyer escort and a minelayer suffered major damage. Clark's Task Group 58.1 and Sherman's Task Group 58.3 were under constant attack as the many fighters and excellent gunnery took their toll, although *Belleau Wood* suffered a near miss. The *Belleau Wood*'s fighters shot down 47 of the incoming Japanese planes, leading her captain, Red Tomlinson, to signal to his task group commander, Jocko Clark: "Does this exceed the bag limit?" Clark replied: "Negative. There is no limit. This is open season. Well done." Task Force 58 claimed to have downed 249 incoming planes and, of the 182 that had arrived over the fleet, 108 were shot down. Attacks continued the next day, although with reduced intensity. The battleship *Maryland,* the destroyer *Bennett* and the destroyer escort *Wesson* were all rammed by kamikazes. The

Hancock was attacked by a single kamikaze which cartwheeled across her deck and into aircraft spotted on her forward flight deck, the enemy's bomb exploding on the port catapult. She managed to recover her aircraft at 1630, but had lost 72 killed and over 80 injured. The losses were not all one sided, however. That same day, Task Force 58 destroyed the world's largest battleship.

The Death of the *Yamato*

Mitscher had ordered his task groups to take up position northeast of Okinawa, but Davison's Task Group 58.2, returning from Ulithi with the repaired carriers *Randolph* and *Enterprise,* was delayed by refueling and missed the battle. Mitscher launched search-strikes, arming the Helldivers with 1,000- and 250-pound bombs, the fighters with 500-pound bombs, and the Avengers with torpedoes. Task Force 58 search aircraft spotted the *Yamato* force at 0823 on 7 April and Mitscher signalled a warning to the gunfire and bombardment force off Okinawa.[12] Two seaplanes trailed the *Yamato* force for five hours and guided the carrier aircraft in on the Japanese. The first attack started just after noon as Task Group 58.1 and Task Group 58.3 launched 280 planes, including 98 torpedo bombers, at the Japanese ships. Clark's Avengers hit *Yamato* with four torpedoes and she developed a list. More followed from Task Group 58.4 and the Japanese faced air attacks throughout the remaining daylight hours. By 1300, the cruiser *Yahagi* was dead in the water, the destroyer *Hamakaze* sunk, and the *Yamato* had already received two bomb hits and a torpedo hit. Within the next hour, she received another five torpedo hits.

Listing heavily, with her steering impaired and losing speed, the *Yamato* was helpless against the onslaught of carrier aircraft and at 1423 rolled over, exploded, and sank. The *Yahagi* took another 12 bomb hits and nine torpedoes before going down. Of the seven destroyers, only three made it back to port. Task Force 58 lost only 10 planes and 12 men.

Mitscher reshuffled his task groups again. Clark's Task Group 58.1 and Sherman's Task Group 58.3 remained the same, but *Independence* moved from Radford's Task Group 58.4 to Davison's reformed Task Group 58.2, which had returned during the night of 7-8 April. The kamikazes, mostly coming from Kyushu, continued their relentless assault. The *Enterprise* was hit on 11 April and the *Intrepid* on 16 April. The unlucky *Intrepid* received her fourth kamikaze hit, which killed eight crewmen. The kamikaze hit the flight deck in a vertical attitude with such force that the imprint of its wings was smashed into the deck. The plane's bomb exploded on the hangar deck, but the *Intrepid*'s experienced fire fighters soon had the fires out.[13] The radar picket destroyers also continued to suffer. Mitscher reshuffled his task force again on 17 April, dissolving Task Group 58.2 and sending Davison back to Ulithi with the damaged *Hancock* and *Enterprise,* the task force again losing its night carrier. With the detachment of the light carrier *Cabot* for overhaul, there were no reorganizations from 17 to 28 May, although Clark's Task Group 58.1 returned to Ulithi on 28 April for 10 days of rest. Tommy Sprague was to relieve Clark, but Mitscher wanted his right-hand man to stay until the Okinawa operation was over.

While off Okinawa, news arrived that the Commander in Chief, President Roosevelt, died on 12 April 1945. On first hearing of his death, many troops ashore thought it might be a Japanese propaganda trick, but they soon learned it was not. No one had much time to mourn since Japanese attacks continued unabated. By mid-month, everyone aboard the ships off Okinawa was dead tired; the repeated attacks wore down Mitscher's pilots and crews, and sleep was a precious commodity. The general sentiment was expressed in a message sent to "Jocko" Clark by his task group's antiaircraft screen commander: "See Hebrews 13, verse 8." Clark chuckled as the read the passage in the Bible: "Jesus Christ, the same yesterday, and today and forever." Clark circulated the message to his ships, adding "No irreverence intended."[14]

As Army and Marine troops struggled to clear the Japanese from the southern end of Okinawa, the fast carriers provided close air support. Land-based Marine Corsairs occupied two airstrips on Okinawa, but these aircraft were needed to counter increasing kamikaze attacks. One of the airstrips was rained out, then shelled by the Japanese, leaving the Marines only one operational airfield through April. As long as there were not enough Marine aircraft for both roles, the fast carriers had to stay on. On 19 April, a strike of over 650 aircraft, 300 of them from Task Force 58, hit Shuri Castle, the center of Japanese defenses. The strikes could not penetrate the caves sheltering the fanatical Japanese defenders, and Shuri held. The nearby island of Ie Shima was seized for its airfield with Army P-47s arriving in May. Rain halted all airfield construction and repair until June, but by 1 July, when the first Okinawa-based strike on Kyushu was launched, over 750 aircraft were available. In the meantime, the carriers held off kamikaze attacks while striking Japan, Okinawa, and the Sakishima Gunto. Despite heavy commitments, Mitscher rotated his task groups into Ulithi for rest. Task Group 58.4 detached when Task Group 58.1 returned on 12 May, and when Task Group 58.4 returned at the end of May, Task Group 58.3 left for the new base at Leyte.

The *Bunker Hill*

On the morning of 11 May, *Bunker Hill,* Mitscher's flagship, was 76 miles east of Okinawa. Shortly after 1000, 25 of her aircraft were flying strikes against Okinawa, while 30 were ready on her flight deck, and 48 were fueling and arming on her hangar deck. Emerging from low cloud cover on the starboard beam, a Zero headed for the flight deck, dropping a bomb aft of the number three elevator and then crashing into parked aircraft. The bomb penetrated the flight deck, exploding on the gallery deck. About the same time, a second aircraft screamed down in a vertical dive and smashed into the flight deck near the base of the island, spreading fires throughout its passageways. The two kamikaze hits turned the *Bunker Hill* into a blazing inferno. As other ships tried to screen her from further attack, three destroyers and the cruiser *Wilkes-Barre* trained hoses on the fires. The attack killed over 350 men, including 13 of the admiral's staff and most of Fighting 84, asphyxiated in their ready room. Only the *Franklin* had suffered more. *Bunker Hill* limped home and would not return to the war.[15]

After passing command to Ted Sherman, Mitscher shifted his flag from the *Bunker Hill* to the *Enterprise,* which had rejoined the task force on 6 May. Mitscher went north to attack Kyushu. The *Enterprise* got off a successful night heckle mission with 16 night Avengers on the night of 12-13 May, followed by day strikes by the task force. On the 14th, however, a kamikaze found the *Enterprise* and hit her. Good damage control saved her, but she was out of the war for months. Mitscher, who was bald, remarked to Jimmy Flately: "Jimmy, tell my task group commanders that if the Japs keep this up they're going to grow hair on my head yet." The next day, Mitscher shifted his flag to *Randolph,* where Jerry Bogan lent him some of his staff officers. On 18 May Mitscher requested that Task Force 58 be detached from the 60-mile square operating area which was less than 350 miles from Kyushu, where it had been for two months. Spruance, however, had no choice but to keep them on station; they were still needed. The worst was over, however, and no more serious kamikaze attacks threatened the carriers. The British had also suffered from the kamikaze attacks, and although their armored flight decks helped protect them from major structural damage, their aircraft and radars were vulnerable. After replenishing at Leyte in late April, the British carriers rejoined the operation. On 4 May kamikazes hit the *Formidable* and *Indomitable.* On 9 May two more kamikazes hit *Formidable* again and *Victorious.* With the draw down in the intensity of kamikaze attacks later in May, the only other British carrier casualty was the *Indomitable,* which collided with a destroyer in fog and had to return to Sydney on 20 May. Task Force 57 flew its last strikes against the Sakishima air-fields on 25 May and withdrew to Sydney to refit and prepare for the final operations against Japan. Task Force 57's performance had earned it a prominent place in the war in the Pacific. Spruance recommended that the British Pacific Fleet be integrated into the U.S. Fast Carrier Task Force and Nimitz agreed.

Halsey Returns

With the job of taking Okinawa largely done, Nimitz made the last "two-platoon" shift of the war. He had wanted the change to take place on 1 May to allow Spruance to begin planning for the scheduled landings in Japan, but the situation on Okinawa had not permitted that. On 27 May, while at sea, Halsey relieved Spruance, who immediately headed for Nimitz's advance headquarters on Guam. Fifth Fleet once again became Third Fleet and Task Force 58 became Task Force 38. The next day Mitscher turned command of the fast carriers over to Slew McCain, who hoisted his flag in the new *Shangri-La*, which had been in combat for one month. Mitscher, tired and ill, reported back to Washington to become Deputy Chief of Naval Operations (Air).[16] The task group commanders remained the same until the scheduled return to Leyte in June, except for Dave Davison, who was relieved as commander of Task Group 38.2 by Rear Admiral Clifton A.F. "Ziggy" Sprague, ComCarDiv 2.[17] Ziggy Sprague had hoisted his flag aboard the repaired *Ticonderoga* which had rejoined the fast carrier force after a practice strike on the bypassed island of Maloelap on 17 May. Tommy Sprague remained aboard *Bennington* and Gerry Bogan aboard *Randolph*.[18]

Another Typhoon

As Halsey resumed command of the fast carriers, he was not faced with being tied down to defending the beach at Okinawa. He detached Sherman's Task Group 38.3 for a rest period and ran north with the other three task groups to hit Japan. Unfortunately, Halsey's bad luck with weather plagued him again, as Task Force 38 ran into heavy seas. After getting off strikes against airfields on Kyushu on 2-3 June, the task force encountered yet another typhoon. The storm, which was small and tight like the one met the previous December, was discovered on the morning of 3 June. By the early evening of the 4th it was heading north and the task force was heading eastward away from it. Based on the advice of his aerologist, Commander Kosko, who had been involved in the previous fiasco in December, Halsey turned the task force westward to cross in front of and ahead of the storm. Halsey did not consider the effect on Clark's task group, which was refueling from Servron 6.

At 0130 on 5 June, Halsey ordered the task force back into the path of the typhoon. The replenishment force commander, Rear Admiral Donald Beary, realized what was happening and signaled McCain at 0246: "Believe this course is taking us back into the storm." McCain ordered a course change to the north. The turn did not seriously affect Radford's Task Group 38.4, which contained both Halsey's and McCain's flagships, but Clark's task group 16 miles away needed time to get sea room before beginning the maneuver. The typhoon was closing rapidly on Clark, the swells causing ships to roll badly. At 0401 Clark informed McCain that his radars showed the eye of the storm to be 30 miles to the west, but McCain did not reply. At 0420 Clark requested a change of course to the southeast, but McCain replied that his radars showed nothing. When Clark informed him that his radars had for one and a half hours, McCain, after spending nearly 30 minutes debating the matter with his own aerologist, responded: "We (meaning Task Group 38.4) intend holding present course. Use your own judgement." Clark, as Bogan had done in December, decided his superiors must have more complete information and tried in vain to maintain course until 0507, when he began maneuvering to find a better course. His task group was in the midst of the typhoon and at 0535, Clark ordered all ships to maneuver independently. At 0700 Task Group 38.1 reached the eye of the storm and by the afternoon Clark's ships were clear of the storm. No ships were lost, but the bow of the cruiser *Pittsburgh* was broken off and the flight deck overhangs on the *Hornet* and *Bennington* collapsed. Seventy-six aircraft were destroyed and six men were lost overboard. Other ships sustained lesser damage.[19]

Refueling and heading south—the *Hornet* and *Bennington* conducting flight operations by backing down—the task force launched support strikes to Okinawa on 6 June. Also reporting to Task Group 38.1 that day was the *Bon Homme Richard* as the new night carrier. The following day, the task force ran north to bomb the Kanoya airfield on Kyushu on 8 June. Clark detached *Bennington* to return to Leyte for repair, and on 9 June the rest of the carriers dropped napalm on enemy emplacements on Okino Daito Shima. The fast battleships bombarded Minami Daito Shima on 10 June.[20] When Task Force 38 arrived at Leyte on 13 June, they were greeted by the sight of the damaged *Randolph*. Her flight deck was damaged by the crash of stunt-flying Army P-38.[21]

Chapter 13
Closing the Ring

Target Japan

In May 1945, the Joint Chiefs of Staff directed that Operation Olympic, the landings on Kyushu in southern Japan, would be scheduled for 1 November 1945. The follow-on landings on the Honshu coast near Tokyo, Operation Coronet, were tentatively set to follow in March 1946. The Navy leadership opposed the landings in principle, feeling that the growing effectiveness of the air and sea blockade would force Japan to surrender, but continued to make preparations as directed. The first phase of the preparations for the Kyushu landings began when Task Force 38, now organized in three task groups, sortied from Leyte on 1 July. The target would be the Tokyo area. Fueling east of Iwo Jima on 8 July, Halsey launched his strikes on 10 July. Although prepared for counterattack, only two snooper aircraft approached the task force, and these were promptly shot down. Although the antiaircraft fire was stiff, the attacking carrier aircraft met little opposition over Tokyo as the Japanese had dispersed their aircraft to revetments away from the airfields. The Japanese had apparently given up on trying to destroy the American fleet and were conserving their strength for the final battle for the home islands. Despite this the fighter-bomber sweeps destroyed over 100 enemy aircraft on the ground. Moving north, Task Force 38 was to hit targets in northern Honshu and Hokkaido, but Halsey, who seemed to attract typhoons like a magnet, had to delay the strikes until 15 July. Again, the Japanese did not respond and the dispersed aircraft were difficult to find, although the carrier aircraft did sink over 50,000 tons of coastal shipping and light naval craft. A battleship-cruiser force also bombarded the Kamaishi and Muroran iron factories.

As the Third Fleet refueled on 16 July, the British carrier force, which had departed Sydney on 28 June, joined the American fleet as Task Force 37, marking the first time British carriers became part of an American tactical carrier formation. Refueling from Servron 6 oilers, the British could maintain the same operational tempo as the Americans, but were frustrated by the maneuvering of the night carrier *Bon Homme Richard*, as they were "constantly altering course to keep clear of the erratic and unpredictable movements of the *Bon Homme Richard*." After inconclusive air strikes and shelling in the Tokyo area 17-18 July, refueling, and intermittent heavy weather, the fast carriers launched the last strikes of the war against the immobile Mobile Fleet on 24 and 25 July. Strikes by Army B-24s and the carrier aircraft severely damaged several warships at Kure naval base, some of which sank, settling on the shallow bottom. The ships included the elusive hermaphrodite battleships *Ise* and *Hyuga,* and the battleship *Haruna.* The carriers *Amagi* and *Katsuragi* and the light carrier *Ryuho* were also severely damaged. The incomplete carriers *Kasagi, Aso* and *Ibuki* were also hit. Night attacks kept up the pressure. Task Force 38 paid a high price, however— 133 aircraft and 102 airmen. The British were diverted to other targets, as Halsey wanted the U.S. Navy alone to have the satisfaction of destroying the Japanese surface fleet.

The month ended with heavy weather. Honshu was shelled on 29 July and air strikes hit Kobe and Nagoya the next day. Typhoons in the area delayed refueling and, at the order of Nimitz, Task Force 38 withdrew from southern Japan. Unknown to most of the commanders in the Pacific, the atomic bomb was going to be dropped on Hiroshima on 6 August. Nimitz wanted the fleet to be far away from the then unknown effects of the revolutionary new weapon. The second atomic bomb was dropped on Nagasaki on 9 August. Meanwhile, MacArthur had requested

carrier strikes on Misawa air base in northern Honshu, where intelligence had reported a large air fleet and airborne troop unit being assembled for what was thought to be a large-scale suicide landing on Okinawa.[1] After his battleships shelled the Kamaishi factory on 8 August, Task Force 38 aircraft hit Misawa the next day, destroying over 200 aircraft in revetments and breaking up the attack. More strikes were flown over Honshu on 10 August and the battleships continued shelling targets. On 9 August the Soviet Union declared war on Japan and its armies swept into Manchuria. Halsey reasoned that the raids on northern Japan would help the Russian effort by preventing long-range Japanese strikes against the Russians. For the first time since June, the Japanese counterattacked, sending about 20 aircraft at the fleet. Although most were shot down, one crashed a radar picket destroyer, causing heavy casualties. Until 10 August, all operations were according to the plan for Olympic, but now, with signs that surrender was near, Task Force 38 stayed on, refueling on 11 August. Task Force 38 had planned to refuel and retire to Eniwetok, while the British were to retire to Manus. Because of a lack of tankers, the British commander, Rawlings, conferred with Halsey to leave *Indefatigable* and several escorts as a token force to represent the British should word of the surrender come through. Task Force 37 departed for Manus the next day.

On 12 August a typhoon caused Halsey to stand clear of his proposed operating area off Tokyo. On the 13th and again on the 15th, with a refueling in between, the last air operations of the Fast Carrier Task Force against Japan took place. On 13 August, full deckload strikes claimed over 250 aircraft destroyed on the ground, while the Combat Air Patrol shot down 18 more. A smaller strike of 103 planes hit Tokyo after dawn on 15 August, shooting down 30 to 40 enemy aircraft. Another small strike of 73 carrier aircraft was on its way when Halsey received word from Nimitz to suspend all further air attack operations. As Japanese pilots, either uninformed of the surrender or unwilling to accept defeat, continued to attack the fleet, Halsey ordered them to be shot down "in a friendly fashion." Although four *Yorktown* Hellcats were lost over the coast, no Japanese aircraft got through.[2]

Although the war was now over, the Third Fleet continued to maintain constant vigilance as preparations for the actual surrender were worked out. Halsey ordered Task Force 38 to an area 100 to 200 miles southwest of Tokyo known as "Area McCain." The three task groups maintained their normal wartime patrols through 23 August. On the 16th and 17th, the task force steamed in unusually tight formations while commemorative aerial photographs were taken. On the 22nd and 23rd, the aircraft took their turn, massing overhead for photographs.

There were also some command changes as the war closed. As part of the final preparations for the invasion of Japan, the Third Fleet and the Fifth Fleet would, for the first time, operate as separate fleets. Spruance remained in command of the Fifth Fleet and Ted Sherman, long in line to command the fast carriers, became Commander, First Fast Carrier Force and commander of Task Force 58. Sherman received his third star in July while in Washington. On 18 August Vice Admiral Sherman

hoisted his flag in *Lexington,* shifting to the *Wasp* two days later. In July, it was decided that Vice Admiral Jack Towers, a long-time advocate of the fast carriers who had risen to become Nimitz's deputy, would replace McCain as Commander, Second Fast Carrier Force and commander of Task Force 38.[3] On 22 August, Vice Admiral Jack Towers raised his flag in *Shangri-La,* formally relieving McCain as commander of Task Force 38 on 1 September. McCain was bitter over his relief and wanted to leave, but Halsey convinced him to stay on for the formal surrender ceremony.

Late on 23 August, Halsey assigned the carriers new operating areas. While some carrier aircraft flew surveillance over Japanese airfields, others dropped food and supplies to prisoners of war. Halsey had planned to take many of his surface ships into Tokyo's outer bay, Sagami Wan, on 26 August, but two typhoons appeared on the day before. Unfortunately, one of these storms made an unexpected turn and hit Bogan's Task Group 38.3 off Shikoku. *Randolph* lost steering control for four minutes and the forward flight deck overhang on the *Wasp* buckled, causing her to be detached and sent home for repairs on 31 August. Bogan was exonerated in his handling of the task group during the storm because of its unpredictable nature. Ted Sherman, who had been riding on *Wasp,* had to shift his flag back to the *Lexington.* The day after the typhoon, 27 August, Towers had boarded *Randolph* and stood by to relieve Bogan as scheduled. That same day, ships of the Third Fleet entered Sagami Wan, with only the light carrier *Cowpens* representing the fast carriers. Sherman protested that the carriers had earned the right to be in on the surrender ceremony, but Halsey, who feared the Japanese might commit some act of treachery, wanted his carriers where they would have the sea room to act if needed and sent Sherman a sharp rebuke to mind his own business.

Not to be outdone by MacArthur's forces, a fighter pilot from VF-88 landed at Atsugi airfield on 27 August and ordered the Japanese to put up a banner for the Army paratroopers arriving the next day. It read: "Welcome to the U.S. Army from the Third Fleet." On 28 August two of Tower's staff officers landed at Atsugi in a VT-85 Avenger to begin preparatory talks with the Japanese for the ceremony arrangements. VF(N)-91 from the *Bon Homme Richard* flew the last night Combat Air Patrol on the night of 27-28 August and the next night, the entire fleet lighted ship. On 30 August, the ships in Sagami Wan entered Tokyo Bay and Halsey shifted his flag ashore from the *Missouri* to the Yokosuka naval base. The surrender ceremony took place on the deck of the *Missouri* on 2 September. MacArthur signed on behalf of the Allies and Nimitz on behalf of the United States. Just as the ceremony ended, 450 carrier planes roared overhead in massed formation at low altitude. Above the carrier planes droned formations of B-29s. The war had ended. A few days after the second atomic bomb had been dropped on Nagasaki, Mitscher, back in Washington, D.C., issued a press release in his new capacity as the head of naval aviation. While careful to acknowledge the indispensable contributions made by the rest of the Navy, Army troops, Marines, and land-based air forces, he left no doubt that the starring role had been played by the aircraft carriers. "Japan is beaten," he asserted, "and carrier supremacy defeated her."[4]

Chapter 14
The "Peaceful" Years

With the victory won, America immediately began dismantling its military and naval forces and demobilizing personnel. Of the three million men and women in naval service at war's end, only a half-million remained a year later. Construction halted on 9,800 ships and craft, another 2,000 were decommissioned and "mothballed," and even more declared surplus. While some forces remained on occupation duty, the only thing that mattered to most Americans overseas after the war was "getting home." As the postwar era unfolded, the Navy struggled to adapt to the growing demands of the Cold War while justifying its continued existence in an age dominated by atomic weapons and jet-propelled aircraft. The competition for resources and the debate over roles among the services continued into the Korean War.

Even as the Navy stressed the need for balanced forces and the importance of sea power in the postwar world, it developed its own nuclear capability. To learn how survivable naval ships would

be in nuclear combat, the Navy conducted underwater atomic tests, appropriately named Operation Crossroads, at Bikini Atoll in July 1946. The lessons learned had profound impact on the Navy's future. The first members of the Navy's family of guided missiles were also developed at this time. For the carrier force, the first shock of the new era was contending with jet aircraft; the second was the development of heavy carrier attack aircraft capable of delivering nuclear weapons.

"Magic Carpet"

Between October 1945 and May 1946 over a million men were transported home in what the Navy called Operation Magic Carpet.[1] A few of the *Essex* class carriers involved in the final operations against Japan—the *Essex, Intrepid,* and *Lexington*—stayed in the Far East on occupation duties after the surrender. They were joined by the *Boxer* and *Antietam*; both carriers arrived too late to serve in combat, but stayed in the Far

East until August 1946, the *Boxer* operating out of Guam as the flagship of Task Force 77, and the *Antietam* supporting the occupation of China and Korea. The rest of the *Essex* class carriers were pressed into service transporting troops home as quickly as possible. Crew complements were reduced and extra galley facilities and three to five tiers of bunks were installed on the hangar decks to accommodate the returning troops. The *Yorktown, Hornet, Ticonderoga, Bunker Hill, Hancock, Bennington, Bon Homme Richard,* and *Shangri-La* transported troops from the Pacific area, while the *Randolph, Wasp* and *Lake Champlain* transported troops from the European theater across the Atlantic.[2] The newly commissioned *Lake Champlain* set an Atlantic speed record, crossing from Cape Spartel in Africa to Norfolk, Virginia, in 4 days, 8 hours and 51 minutes.[3]

Operation High Jump

After completing her shakedown cruise in late 1946, the *Philippine Sea* returned to the Boston Navy Yard for alterations in preparation for the Navy's first Antarctic Expedition, "Operation High Jump." Rear Admiral Richard E. Byrd and his staff embarked on 2 January 1947 as the *Philippine Sea* sailed for Little America, where Byrd and his party were launched from the ship on 29 January in six twin-engine R4D transport planes (the Navy designation for the C-47) to begin their exploration. The *Philippine Sea* returned to Quonset Point and resumed normal peacetime operations.

As Operation Magic Carpet wound down, the wartime *Essex* class carriers were laid up in reserve, most of them in

1947. Their replacements were *Essex* class carriers commissioned postwar: the *Leyte, Kearsarge, Tarawa, Valley Forge,* and *Philippine Sea.* Those kept active received only minor refits, mostly radar and communications equipment. On the *Boxer, Leyte, Antietam, Princeton, Valley Forge, Philippine Sea,* and *Kearsarge* the SK or SK-2 radars were replaced with the SX radar, which combined long-range air search and height-finding capability. This also allowed the removal of the SM and SP radars. The three starboard outboard quad 40mm mounts by the island were also removed from earlier ships not immediately placed in reserve. When war in Korea broke out in June 1950, only four *Essex* class carriers were on active duty: *Valley Forge, Philippine Sea, Boxer,* and *Leyte.*

Down to the Sea in Jets

The first Navy jet, the McDonnell FD-1 Phantom, a twin jet, straight-wing design, made a series of takeoffs and landings from the deck of the large carrier *Midway* in July 1946. The Navy ordered a small number, primarily for use as jet familiarization aircraft, and began three major jet fighter projects: a more powerful derivative of the Phantom, the F2D Banshee (later redesignated F2H), the Grumman F9F Panther, and the Douglas F3D Skynight. The Skynight, the Navy's first jet night fighter, was a twin-jet aircraft with side-by-side seating for the pilot and radar operator. Operating from land bases, it saw extensive service with the Marines during the Korean War. Several other projects were dropped after limited production runs or abandoned completely: the Ryan FR-1 Fireball and its successor the XF2R-1

Dark Shark were both hybrid jet-propeller designs, the Vought XF6U-1 Pirate was an aircraft only noteworthy for its experimental afterburner, and the North American FJ-1 Fury was the straight-winged progenitor of the famous F-86 Sabre.

The McDonnell F2H Banshee, originally planned as a day fighter, featured the same layout as the Phantom, with twin Westinghouse J34 engines buried in the wing roots. The first production models were ordered in 1947 and the F2H-1 Banshee entered squadron service in 1949. The F2H-2 model, with improved 3,200-pound thrust J34 engines, was used in combat over Korea. Known affectionately as the "Banjo," the F2H became the Navy's primary jet fighter-bomber and was adapted to a variety of roles, including photo reconnaissance.

The Grumman F9F Panther was conceived in 1946 as the XF9F-1 night fighter with four jet engines. But the design was too complex and Grumman developed the XF9F-2, a completely different aircraft using a single British Rolls-Royce Nene engine, instead.[4] The powerful Nene engine, built under license by Pratt & Whitney as the J42, produced 5,000 pounds of thrust.[5] Short and stubby, the Panther was a typical "Grumman Iron Works" design, but thanks to its leading edge wing slats, it landed at speeds of only 85-90 knots and could take off in less than 800 feet at a time when Air Force jet fighters, such as the Lockheed P-80, needed 4,000 feet of runway. Another prototype was flown with the Allison J33, an engine with characteristics similar to the Nene, and production models alternated between versions of the J33 and J42. The F9F-2 also entered squadron service in

1949. Both the Banshee and the Panther had four 20mm cannon in the nose, an improvement over Air Force fighter designs of that era, which were still armed with .50 caliber machine guns.

Despite the new jet programs, many piston-engined aircraft remained in the inventory. Most Navy fighter squadrons were equipped with the F4U Corsair and Reserve units still flew the F6F Hellcat, TBM Avenger, and SB2C Helldiver. The twin-engine F7F Tigercat and F8F Bearcat, produced in limited numbers, entered service too late to participate in the war against Japan. The single-engine Grumman AF Guardian, originally developed as a replacement for the TBF Avenger, became an antisubmarine aircraft operating in hunter-killer pairs from the smaller aircraft carriers incapable of handling jets.

The separate dive bomber and torpedo aircraft of World War II were replaced by a single attack aircraft, the Douglas AD Skyraider. The Skyraider was a single-engine, single-seat piston aircraft that had the performance of a World War II fighter and the ability to carry an amazing amount of ordnance.[6] The "Able Dog" was powered by a 2,700 horsepower eighteen-cylinder Wright R-3350 radial engine and armed with four 20mm cannon in the wings. The Skyraider, described as a "dump truck with wings," performed a variety of roles. These special mission aircraft were identified by a suffix to the basic designation: N for all-weather, W for radar surveillance, or Q for electronic countermeasures. The AD-4 model was used in Korea.

Operating jets from aircraft carriers posed many problems. Jet engines provided speed and high altitude capability, but they burned fuel voraciously.

The early engines were heavy and produced too little thrust per pound of engine to serve as load carriers, so the first Navy jet carrier aircraft were all fighters. With their higher gross weights and approach speeds, jets were more difficult to bring aboard a carrier and since jet engines took time to "spool up" when power was applied, they could not accelerate as quickly as a piston-engine aircraft during a wave off. Jets also had too little low-speed lift for rolling takeoffs and launching the heavier jets by catapult strained the capability of the existing H-4 catapults.

Strategic Bombing and the Atomic Bomb

The Navy had plans for the construction of a new super carrier, the *United States*, which would be capable of operating jet aircraft large enough to carry the early atomic bombs, which were nearly as massive as the original weapons used against Japan. The existing *Essex* and *Midway* class carriers were too small for jets capable of carrying atomic weapons, so the Navy developed the North American AJ-1 Savage, a large carrier-based attack bomber with two piston engines and a jet engine in the tail.[7] The contract for developing the Savage was awarded in 1946, but the first aircraft did not deploy in the Mediterranean, operating from the large *Midway* class carriers, until 1951. Modernization of both the *Essex* and *Midway* class carriers was necessary to allow them to operate in the jet and atomic ages. The AJ-1 Savage first operated aboard the new *Oriskany* in May 1951, which marked the beginning of a nuclear attack capability for Pacific Fleet attack carriers.

Unification

There had long been talk of unifying the armed services under a single Department of Defense, and even before the war had ended the Army Air Forces saw unification as their best chance of becoming a separate service, co-equal with the Army and Navy. The Army felt that a unified command would be best and American public opinion supported unification in the belief that it would lead to economies in procurement and increased coordination between the services. The Navy held back, fearing that the Army and Air Force did not understand sea power and would team up to outvote it when it came to dividing up the dwindling defense appropriations. The Navy also feared that the Marines would be absorbed by the Army and that both Navy and Marine air would be absorbed by the Air Force. The Royal Naval Air Service had been absorbed by the Royal Air Force in 1918, and the results for British naval aviation had been disastrous. Many "strategic air power" advocates felt that with the atomic bomb and long range bombers, all other forms of warfare were obsolete. After much wrangling and maneuvering, the National Security Act was finally approved by Congress and signed into law by President Truman in July 1947. The Air Force achieved its goal of becoming an independent service and the individual service secretaries were now subordinates under the Secretary of Defense. But the Navy won some important concessions. The law ensured that land-based naval antisubmarine aircraft would not be absorbed by the Air Force, and protected the Marines from any takeover by the Army. The first Secretary of Defense was James V. Forrestal, a Wall Street financier who came to Washington to serve as the first Undersecretary of the Navy and later as Secretary of the Navy, following the death of Frank Knox in 1944. The new Department of Defense, under Forrestal's strong leadership, kept inter-service squabbling to a minimum and things remained on a somewhat even keel—for the time being.

SCB-27A

As early as February 1945, BuAer was proposing jet modifications to the *Essex* class. Meanwhile, plans were made to incorporate missiles into ship design. The new *Midway* class carriers were too valuable to take out of service for experimental work, so in August 1946 construction on the *Oriskany* was suspended to await completion to a new design under the FY 48 program. The Ship Characteristics Board drew up two different schemes, called SCB 27A and SCB 27B, incorporating various new features. But fiscal reality set in and it was realized that money would not be available to convert a valuable ship solely for experimental purposes.

In January 1947, the Vice Chief of Naval Operations, Vice Admiral DeWitt C. Ramsey, made changes to the SCB 27A design that were "the minimum alterations necessary to permit *Essex* class carriers to operate present or prospective fighter type aircraft and the largest and heaviest attack type aircraft now considered feasible without requiring major structural changes. . . ."[8] The revised conversion cleared the flight deck by removing the deck gun mounts and reduced the size of the island by removing the antiaircraft mounts, rebuilding the uptakes and angling them aft. The redesigned island allowed a

massive pole mast to be built to support antennas without the interference problems of the wartime arrangements. The flight deck was strengthened to take 52,000-pound airplanes; the centerline elevators were strengthened to 40,000-pound capacity and enlarged to 58 feet by 44 feet. The deck edge elevator was strengthened to 30,000-pound capacity. Heavy aircraft could be armed and fueled on the hangar, raised to the flight deck on the centerline elevators and struck below on landing by the deck edge unit. New H-8 catapults replaced both H-4Bs, and the newer Mark 5 arresting gear replaced the Mark 4 gear. The forward bomb elevator was enlarged to handle "a package 15 feet long weighing 16,000 lbs." i.e., a nuclear weapon. Internal avgas capacity increased almost 50 percent to 300,000 gallons. Three ready rooms were relocated from the gallery deck to protection below the hangar deck. Since pilots had a considerable climb to the flight deck, a prominent escalator was installed outside of the island structure on the starboard side. These alterations called for more electrical power and the original 250 kW emergency diesel generators were replaced by 850 kW units. New sponsons for four open single 5"/38 guns on the starboard side were built. The 5-inch guns were supplemented by 14 twin 3"/50 mounts: two each at the bow and stern, three outboard of the island structure, one aft of the island at the hangar deck level, one each beside the port forward and port and starboard aft 5-inch sponsons, and three at sponson level along the port side of the flight deck. The twin 3"/50 was originally developed in 1945 as a replacement for the quad 40mm Bofors as a defense against kamikaze attack. Underwater protection was revised according to the ideas prevailing in 1945. These features and other top weight would have to be compensated for by hull blisters, which were designed to be flush with the ship's sides, extending all the way up to the hangar deck. The side armor was removed entirely and 1.5-inch thick Special Treatment Steel was used for the blister plating. Wartime experience had taught the Navy the danger of hangar deck fires. As BuShips argued: "hangar damage resulting from fires has far exceeded the hangar damage resulting from the initial bomb or suicide plane crash. . . hangar deck fires primarily result from the presence of gasoline in planes in that space. . . these fires readily detonate, by roasting, major ordinance material with ensuing great extension of damage. STS hangar bulkheads. . . would be provided for the main purpose of preventing and limiting the damage resulting from gasoline fires on the hangar deck. . . ." To improve fire fighting capability the hangar deck was subdivided by two fire and splinter bulkheads, and a new fog/foam fire-fighting system, improved water curtains, and a new cupronickel fire main were installed.[9]

The *Oriskany*

The *Oriskany* was built to the revised SCB 27A design under the FY 48 program, her conversion approved by the Chief of Naval Operations in June 1947. Launched in October 1945, she was decommissioned shortly afterward while plans for her were being recast. She was 85 percent complete when construction was suspended and had to be torn back to 60 percent before recon-

struction could begin. The *Oriskany* was commissioned in September 1950, the last of the *Essex* class carriers to reach active status. The *Oriskany* also had 16 twin 20mm weapons, justified at the 1950 General Board hearings as useful for morale.

The next two ships chosen for SCB-27A conversions for the FY 49 program, the *Essex* and *Wasp,* were drawn from the reserve fleet. The two selected for the FY 50 program were made to come from the active fleet, which would save money, particularly since the active fleet was to draw down in FY 51 anyway. The *Kearsarge* was decommissioned for reconstruction, but the *Leyte,* scheduled to be modernized after the completion of the *Oriskany,* remained on active service when the war broke out in Korea. Her place was taken by the *Lake Champlain.* In the end, the *Kearsarge* was the only carrier active in 1949 that got an SCB-27A conversion. Korea caused a rethinking of the drawdown in carrier strength and four conversions were ordered for FY 51 and four more in FY 52 for a total of 13 of the original 24 *Essex* class carriers. By the time the tentative FY 53 program showed four more conversions, the SCB-27C conversions were approved and only nine ships were finished to SCB-27A standards: the *Essex, Yorktown, Hornet, Randolph, Wasp, Bennington, Kearsarge, Oriskany,* and *Lake Champlain.*

The Revolt of the Admirals

In March 1949 a nervous breakdown, resulting from overwork, forced Secretary Forrestal to resign. His replacement was Louis A. Johnson, a lawyer-politician active in veteran's affairs who was given the post as a reward by President Truman for his fund-raising efforts during the 1948 presidential elections. He was tactless and overbearing and did not understand the Navy's role in national defense. It was not long before the wrangling over missions and roles among the services became a crisis.

Throughout the unification struggle, planning for the proposed 60,000-ton super carrier *United States* had continued. With the approval of Congress and the White House, funds had been appropriated and the keel of the carrier laid at Newport News, Virginia, on 18 April 1949. Five days later, while Secretary of the Navy John L. Sullivan was out of town, Johnson ordered all work on the carrier halted, ostensibly for budgetary reasons. The Chief of Naval Operations, Admiral Louis E. Denfield, learned of the action from a press release and Secretary Sullivan resigned in protest. Sullivan was replaced as Secretary of the Navy by Francis P. Matthews, who had no experience or appreciation of the Navy, let alone naval aviation. Naval leadership was in a state of shock, and regarded Johnson's actions as part of an Air Force campaign to retain its monopoly on atomic warfare. These views seemed credible when funds allegedly saved by cancelling the *United States* were earmarked to pay for more B-36 bombers. The Navy was repeatedly outvoted in meetings of the Joint Chiefs of Staff and feared that its appropriations would be continually cut. When Captain John G. Crommelin, a distinguished naval pilot,

supplied documents to the press showing that key naval officers, including Admiral Denfield, considered Johnson's policies dangerous to national security, the resulting uproar led to a Congressional investigation.

In what became known as "The Revolt of the Admirals," naval officers, led by Admiral Arthur W. Radford, attacked Johnson's policies and the Air Force claims for strategic bombing. The Navy especially criticized the B-36 as "a billion dollar blunder." With a range of 5,000 miles, the B-36 was designed to carry an atomic bomb from American bases to any point on the globe without refueling. The B-36 was a piston-engine design that had originated in 1940. Capable of a top speed of only 375 miles an hour and with a service ceiling of 40,000 feet, the B-36 was vulnerable to the new Russian MiG-15 jet fighters. In October 1949, as the Congressional hearings got under way, the Russians exploded an atomic bomb, ending the American nuclear weapon monopoly. In the end, the budget cuts remained, although the B-36 program was trimmed. Admiral Denfield was relieved as Chief of Naval Operations and replaced by Admiral Forrest P. Sherman. Sherman set about tempering many of the hotheads within the Navy and worked to strengthen the Navy's support in Congress and restore funding for Naval Aviation. Though hard work and perseverance salvaged much of the Navy, Johnson's cuts had left conventional forces, Army, Navy, and tactical air, ill prepared to fight the "limited" war in Korea.[10]

As part of Operation Magic Carpet, carriers are lined up at the docks at NAS Alameda, November 1945. The ships are (from the front): Saratoga CV-3, Enterprise CV-6, Hornet, *and* San Jacinto CVL-30.

A gun crew loads shells into a twin 3"/50 mount during gunnery drills aboard the Hornet, *September 1954. Rushed into development in 1945 as a replacement for the 40mm Bofors, it became the Navy's standard antiaircraft weapon in the postwar era.*

The Leyte, *seen here in March 1952, was typical of the* Essex *class carriers completed after the war. They were completed without the additional armament fitted to so many of the wartime carriers and were not significantly modernized during their service careers.*

Two F9F Panthers passing up the starboard side of the Princeton *in Korean waters, May 1951. (Although completed without outboard sponsons for 40mm mounts, two were added to the* Princeton *during the Korean War to provide additional antiaircraft protection.)*

An F2H2 Banshee lands aboard the **Essex** *after its initial combat mission over Korea, 23 August 1951.*

Weather conditions in Korea were often miserable. Crewmen of the Valley Forge *sweep snow from the flight deck during her second deployment to Korean waters during the winter of 1950-51.*

An F9F about to catapult off the Boxer *on a bombing mission over North Korea, July 1952.*

AD Skyraiders from the Bon Homme Richard *going into divebombing runs against a supply center near Tanchon in North Korea, November 1952.*

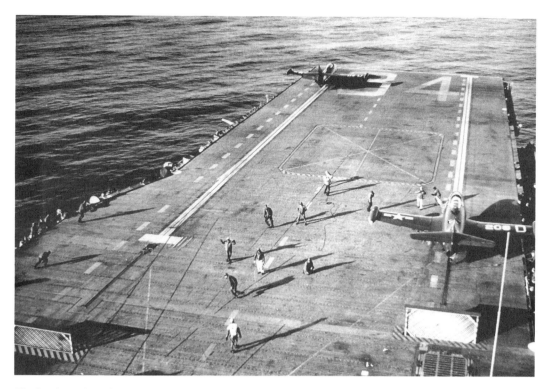

The Oriskany *launches F9Fs for a strike on Korean targets, November 1952. Improved catapults and other features, such as the jet blast deflectors seen in this photograph, enabled the modernized SCB-27 ships to handle jets much more efficiently than the older members of the class.*

The modernized Essex, *underway in the South China Sea, August 1956.*

The Antietam *underway in the Virginia Capes during flight operations to evaluate the new "canted" flight deck, January 1953. The angled deck, along with the steam catapult and the mirror landing system allowed the aircraft carrier to truly enter the jet age.*

The Bennington *receiving her angled deck and enclosed "hurricane" bow during modernization at the New York Navy Yard, September 1954.*

A view looking forward from the port side of the 18-foot barricade installed on the modernized Intrepid. *The new emergency barricade was designed to stop the larger and faster jets then coming into service.*

In 1962, the Lexington *became the Navy's training carrier and served in that role for nearly thirty years. Here a student Naval Aviator in his T2A Buckeye is about to catapult off the Lady Lex as she steams in the Gulf of Mexico.*

Older Essex *class carriers were often adapted to other roles. In response to a Marine Corps requirement, the* Boxer, Princeton *and* Valley Forge *were converted to helicopter carriers. HUS helos are seen here aboard the* Princeton *LPH-5 during an amphibious assault exercise.*

Essex *class carriers often served as recovery ships for space shots. The* Hornet *served as recovery ship for Apollo 11, the first manned landing on the moon. Here, the Apollo 11 command module is lowered onto a dolly before being moved to the hangar bay.*

RADM Donald C. Davis, commander of the Hawaiian Sea Frontier, welcomes Apollo 11 astronauts Neil Armstrong, Edwin "Buzz" Aldrin, and Michael Collins aboard the Hornet. *(The Mobile Quarantine Facility the astronauts are in was a converted Airstream trailer.)*

Chapter 15

Korea

By June 1950, the Navy was poorly prepared to fight a limited conventional war, especially in Asia. Secretary of Defense Louis Johnson's efforts to "trim the fat" had reduced the active Navy forces to 15 carriers of all sizes, most of which were in the Atlantic.[1] Of the two major sea commands in the Western Pacific, the Seventh Fleet and Naval Forces Japan, only the Seventh Fleet had a carrier assigned, the *Valley Forge*. She had arrived in the Western Pacific in May and was just north of Hong Kong when the North Koreans invaded South Korea on 25 June. She immediately headed for the Philippines to replenish and stand ready. Her air group was typical of the period: two fighter squadrons with 30 F9F-2B Panther jet fighters, two squadrons with 28 F4U-4B Corsairs, an attack squadron with 14 AD-4 Skyraiders, and 14 special mission Corsairs and Skyraiders for photo reconnaissance, early warning, and radar countermeasures[2]. President Truman ordered naval and air support of South Korea's efforts to resist the invasion on 27 June, and

the *Valley Forge* departed Subic Bay in the Philippines that same day. While standing by for possible action in Korea, the *Valley Forge* flew her Corsairs and Skyraiders over the Formosa Strait as a show of force to the Chinese Communists. The Communists had taken over mainland China from Chiang Kai-shek's Nationalists only the year before. Since that time, a Communist invasion of Formosa (as Taiwan was still called then) was considered a strong possibility, hence the need for an aerial demonstration of American support for the Nationalist Chinese on Formosa.[3]

Task Force 77, with the *Valley Forge* and the British light carrier *Triumph,* steamed for the Yellow Sea. Before dawn, both carriers launched their strikes; the *Valley Forge* hit the area around Pyongyang, the North Korean capital, while the *Triumph* hit Haeju, on North Korea's west coast. The propeller driven aircraft were launched first, but the faster jets got to the target area ahead of them to attack North Korean aircraft on the ground before the strike

Line of
Allied Advance,
November 1950

Armistice Line,
July 1953

40°

Sea of Japan

MANCHURIA

Miles
0   75

Antung

Yalu River

Suiho

Sinuiju

Ch'osan

Kanggye

Hyesanjin

Kapsan

Ch'ongjin

Fusen
Reservoir

Chosin
Reservoir

Hagaru

Sonch'on

Ch'ongch'on River

River

Taedong River

Sunch'on

Hamhung

Yongp'o

Hungnam

Wonsan

Huwach'on
Reservoir

River

P'yonggang

Yangdok

Nan River

PYONGYANG

Chinnamp'o

Cho'do

Korea
Bay

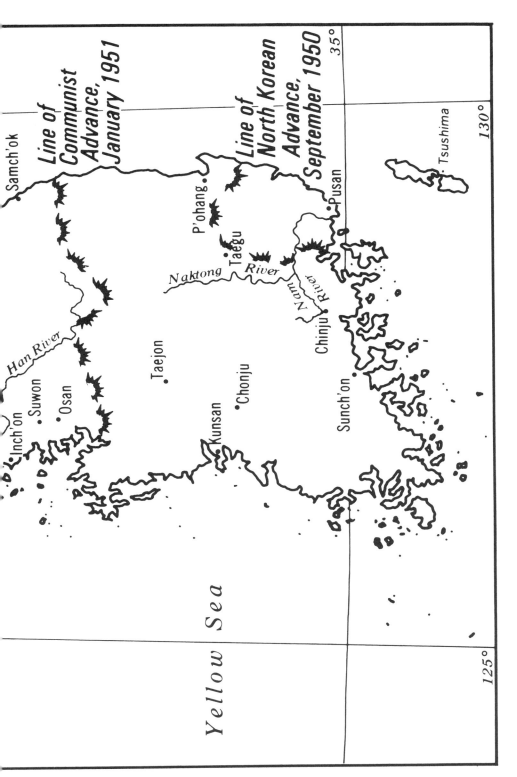

Line of
Communist
Advance,
January 1951

Line of
North Korean
Advance,
September 1950

Samch'ok

P'ohang

Taegu

Naktong River

Pusan

Nam

Chinju River

Tsushima

Taejon

Chonju

Chinju

Sunch'on

Kunsan

Han River

Inch'on

Suwon

Osan

Yellow Sea

35°

130°

125°

Korea

aircraft arrived. The North Koreans were taken by surprise—Pyongyang was 400 miles from the nearest U.S. airfields—and two Yak fighters were shot down and nine other aircraft destroyed on the ground. The Panthers then worked over the ground installations moments before the Corsairs and Skyraiders arrived. That afternoon the two carriers went back to hit rail facilities in their respective target areas. No carrier planes were lost during these strikes. On 4 July, the *Valley Forge* hit the Pyongyang area again, attacking railroads and dropping a span of a vital railroad bridge. This time four Skyraiders were hit by antiaircraft fire, but all made it back to the carrier. One of the damaged Skyraiders was unable to reduce speed, approached too fast and too high, and bounced over the barrier into the aircraft parked forward, destroying two Corsairs and damaging six other aircraft. Because of the Communist threat in the Formosa Straits, the carriers withdrew toward Okinawa after their strikes.

After ten days, Task Force 77 again sailed for Korean waters to cover the unopposed landing of U.S. troops at Pohang, 65 miles north of Pusan. From the Korea Strait between Korea and Japan, the two carriers steamed 50 miles off the east coast of South Korea and sent off strikes against highways, railroads, airfields and industrial plants in the north while conducting antisubmarine and Combat Air Patrols. The strikes destroyed key facilities at a petroleum plant in the North Korean port of Wonsan, which earlier attacks by Air Force B-29s had failed to destroy, and about two dozen aircraft were destroyed on the ground. Two carrier planes were lost, but their pilots were recovered.

While the *Triumph* departed for maintenance in Japan, the *Valley Forge* steamed around the "bottom" of Korea, fueled at sea, and launched strikes from the Yellow Sea into North Korea on 22 July. After a brief call at Sasebo, Japan, to rearm, the "Happy Valley" hurriedly returned to action as the situation in Korea deteriorated. The *Valley Forge* flew direct support and interdiction missions throughout the day on 25 July and was joined by the *Triumph.* The effectiveness of the support strikes was hampered by poor coordination with the ground troops and lack of up to date intelligence information, problems which continued throughout much of the war. Different concepts of "Close Air Support" between the Navy and Marines, who often bombed and strafed within 50 feet of friendly troops, and the Air Force, which operated further behind the front lines, also created problems.

The two carriers steamed through the night to launch support strikes on 26 July from the Sea of Japan. Withdrawing to refuel, they raced around the southern coast into the Yellow Sea to launch strikes against the western coast on 28 and 29 July. Again withdrawing to Okinawa to replace lost aircraft and stand by to respond to any crisis in the Formosa Strait, the *Valley Forge* anchored in Buckner Bay on 31 July. The next day she was joined by the *Philippine Sea,* which had transferred from the Atlantic just before hostilities began. The *Triumph* returned to Japan and later engaged in blockade operations.

The *Philippine Sea*'s air group was similar to that of the *Valley Forge,* but it had just received its Panthers and was not ready for combat. The carrier had ten days of training off Hawaii en route to the Western Pacific and, upon reaching Okinawa, went to sea with the *Valley Forge* for two days of joint operations. While the fast carriers worked up off Okinawa, the escort carriers *Sicily* and *Badoeng Strait,* known to her crew as "Bingding," went into action. The escort carriers, operating Marine aircraft, provided close air support throughout the Korean War.

The *Boxer* had just completed a six month deployment in the Western Pacific before the war broke out and needed overhaul, but was instead hastily made ready for sea. Loaded with Air Force F-51 Mustangs and other equipment urgently needed in Korea, the *Boxer* departed San Francisco on 1 July. She crossed the Pacific in a record-breaking eight and one-half days and, after unloading in Japan between 22 and 27 July, she broke her own record returning to San Diego in seven days, ten and one-half hours.

Returning to Korean waters, the fast carriers flew off strikes against targets in southwest Korea on the morning of 5 August. The *Philippine Sea* concentrated on rail and highway bridges, while the *Valley Forge* provided close air support to the ground forces, again hampered by poor air-ground coordination. The rest of the month was spent in close support and interdiction missions, with the fast carriers ranging up and down the eastern and western coasts. Most strikes were flown over the south, but some went as far north as Chongjin on the east coast, only 50 miles from Soviet Siberia, and Sinuiju on the west coast, some 75 miles from the Yalu River and Communist China. During a lull in fighting in late August, the *Valley Forge* and *Philippine Sea* put into Sasebo to replenish. The carriers resumed strikes on 26 August with rocket and strafing

close air support attacks. By the next day, the carriers were north of the 38th parallel and launched strikes against the North Korean east coast ports of Wonsan, Songjin, and Chongjin. Steaming around Korea, the carriers refueled at sea and took aboard replacement aircraft before entering the Yellow Sea to launch strikes against the west coast between 29 August and 4 September. On 4 September, as the carriers operated astride the 38th parallel between China's Shantung peninsula and the Korean coast, a destroyer reported an unidentified radar contact out of Port Arthur heading toward the task force. A four plane division of Corsairs was ordered to intercept the contact. The contact split in two; one aircraft turning north, the other continued to close on the task force. When the Corsairs intercepted the twin-engine bomber, it nosed down and began taking evasive action and headed east toward Korea. As the fighters closed, the bomber opened fire on them. Upon reporting this, the Corsairs were authorized to return the fire. The first Corsair missed on its firing run, but the second caught the bomber, sending it spinning down in flames. A destroyer spotted the crash and recovered the body of a Russian flier. Meanwhile, the carriers had launched more fighters and prepared to defend the task force against further attack. When the weather over North Korea turned bad the next day, the carriers turned south.

Inchon

By September 1950, the Pusan perimeter had been reinforced and MacArthur, the commander of all United Nations forces in Korea, planned to outflank the North Koreans with an amphibious landing at Inchon, on the west coast near Seoul. Because of the difficult tidal conditions at Inchon, the landings were set for 15 September, the earliest date possible. The 230 ships assembled for the landings were supported by the three fast carriers of Task Force 77. The veteran *Valley Forge* and *Philippine Sea* were joined by the *Boxer,* which had just returned after her record breaking crossings to deliver aircraft to Japan at the start of the war. She had been quickly repaired on the West Coast and sailed for Korea with a hastily formed air group made up of four fighter squadrons of Corsairs, one squadron of Skyraiders, and the usual special mission aircraft. She arrived off Inchon on the day of the assault. The escort carriers *Sicily* and *Badoeng Strait* operated with the invasion forces, while the *Triumph* operated off the east coast as part of a diversionary operation and then raced around Korea to join in supporting the landings. (The *Triumph* was relieved by the *Theseus* later in September.)

For two days before the landings, the carriers pounded the area around Inchon and Seoul. The landings were brilliantly successful and the North Koreans, caught in a giant pincer movement by the landings at Inchon and an offensive from the Pusan perimeter, began to fall back. Seoul fell on 27 September after bitter fighting. With the North Koreans in full retreat, MacArthur planned another amphibious landing, this time at the North Korean port of Wonsan on the east coast. Task Force 77 steamed around Korea to begin the intensive pre-landing bombardment, this time joined by the *Leyte,* which had been transferred from the Mediterranean. The *Leyte* air group had only one

squadron of Panthers, two squadrons of Corsairs, one squadron of Skyraiders, and the usual special mission aircraft. Ten days before the scheduled landings, minesweepers arrived off Wonsan to clear channels for the invasion forces. The mines proved to be the greatest menace to naval operations. By the time the Marines landed on 25 October, Wonsan had already been occupied by the South Koreans for two weeks. U.S. troops took Pyongyang on 19 October, but mines and difficult geography delayed the opening of the capital's port of Chinampo to deep draft ships.

Except for difficulties with mines, the war was going well and Allied commanders expected all organized enemy resistance to end before Thanksgiving. The Allied forces had complete control of the ground and air, but South Korean and U.S. troops were overextended and beginning to suffer shortages of food and supplies. With the pace of carrier operations easing, the *Boxer* and *Philippine Sea* departed for Japan on 22 October. The *Boxer* was to continue on to the West Coast for her long delayed overhaul; the *Valley Forge* was to follow soon after. A week after the *Boxer* and *Philippine Sea* departed, the *Leyte* and *Valley Forge* headed for Japan. The British carrier *Theseus* had sailed for Japan and then on to Hong Kong, leaving the *Sicily* and *Badoeng Strait* the only carriers in Korean waters. Plans were made for the two escort carriers to send their Corsairs ashore and have the *Sicily* return to Guam to embark her antisubmarine squadron.

The Chinese Intervene
During October, as Allied aircraft clashed with Communist aircraft along

the Yalu, there were indications that the Chinese might enter the war. Between 24 and 28 October, South Korean troops were attacked by forces positively identified as Chinese. On 1 November a flight of six swept-wing fighters streaked across the Yalu from Manchuria and fired upon a light observation plane and a flight of Mustangs. The U.S. planes escaped with the news that the Soviet MiG-15 had entered the war. The MiG-15 was the world's most advanced fighter at the time and could fly faster and higher than the Navy Panther or the Air Force F-80 Shooting Star. Air superiority over Korea would now be challenged. On the ground, the attacks by the Chinese on South Korean forces were soon followed by attacks on U.S. troops, and on 3 November, an American division was forced to retreat some 50 miles to protect its overextended supply lines.

On the morning of 5 November, Task Force 77 sortied from Japanese ports with the *Leyte* and *Valley Forge*; the *Philippine Sea* joined the task force shortly after. The *Boxer* was already en route across the Pacific, but the escort carriers *Sicily* and *Badoeng Strait* were recalled to Korean waters. Task Force 77 was to provide close support of ground units and interdict enemy communications, assembly areas, and troop columns. Washington countermanded General MacArthur's order to bomb the Yalu River bridges and imposed a bombing suspension of all targets within five miles of the Yalu. When the general protested, he was given permission to attack the Korean side of the spans as long as U.S aircraft did not fly over Manchuria. There were six major and 11 lesser bridges across the Yalu, which forms nearly all of the North Korean border with Manchuria. Most of

the bridges were constructed by the Japanese before World War II and were solidly built. They were defended by heavy antiaircraft batteries and jet fighters and the restrictions on violating Manchurian air space meant that in many places along the twisting Yalu, level bombers could not do the job. On 9 November Task Force 77 began "bridge busting" with three days of attacks against the top priority rail and highway bridges at Sinuiju, near the mouth of the Yalu, that had survived attacks by Air Force B-29s. The highway bridge was "dropped," but the railway bridge resisted destruction.

Between 9 and 21 November the carriers flew nearly 600 sorties against the Yalu bridges. The strikes usually consisted of Skyraiders carrying 1,000-pound bombs to drop the spans (in one case 2,000-pounders were used), Corsairs with bombs and rockets to hit gun positions along the southern bank of the river, and Panthers to provide cover against MiGs. At the time, the carriers were operating from the Sea of Japan, forcing aircraft to make overland flights of up to 225 miles to reach their targets. Even as the bridges were being attacked the Chinese were erecting pontoon bridges across the river and when the water froze, men and supplies moved directly across the river on ice.

On the first day of the bridge strikes, a Panther from the *Philippine Sea* shot down the first MiG to fall to a naval fighter after a chase that went from 4,000 feet up to 15,000 feet and down again.[4] On 18 November Panthers from the *Leyte* and *Valley Forge* shot down two more MiGs. These kills were remarkable considering the MiG's superior performance and the restrictions on "hot pursuit" over the Yalu.

General MacArthur repeatedly sought permission to attack the concentrations of men and equipment on the northern side of the Yalu as well as key communication and industrial centers in Manchuria, but was turned down by Washington as the U.S. attempted to keep the war within the limitations imposed by the Allied members of the United Nations. Although bombing of Manchuria would have slowed the Chinese advance, the forces available were simply not enough to take on the Chinese and Russians. All of Korea and much of Japan was within range of Communist air bases in China, Manchuria, and Siberia, and Soviet-designed Russian and Chinese aircraft outnumbered the available Allied aircraft, both in total number and in the number of modern jets.

Although the North Korean army had been virtually destroyed, by late November there were more than 250,000 Chinese troops in North Korea. Of the 267,000 Allied troops facing them, nearly half were South Koreans, another 10,000 were from various members of the United Nations, and the rest were U.S. soldiers and Marines. On 26 November, in the midst of an Allied offensive, the Chinese launched an all out ground attack, catching the Allied forces off guard. The Allied military command had underestimated the numbers of Chinese troops and thought the bridge strikes had cut them off from their supplies and support. The escort carriers had been withdrawn and the *Valley Forge* departed on 19 November for overhaul on the West Coast, leaving the *Leyte* and *Philippine Sea* in Task Force 77. As the Chinese offensive threw the Allied ground forces into a desperate holding action and then into retreat,

Task Force 77 began flying maximum support for the Allied forces. The *Sicily* and *Badoeng Strait,* along with the British carrier *Theseus,* hurriedly returned to Korea. The light carrier *Bataan* had just arrived with a deckload of North American F-86 Sabre fighters. The swept-wing Sabre was the first Allied fighter considered to be the equal of the MiG-15, although it did have range and firepower limitations. After unloading the Air Force fighters, the *Bataan* took aboard a squadron of Marine Corsairs and reached Korea in December. The *Valley Forge,* halfway across the Pacific, was ordered to continue on to the West Coast, exchange her air group for the *Boxer*'s, and return to Korea. The *Princeton,* which had been recommissioned a few months earlier, arrived in Korea on 5 December.[5]

While help was on the way, the *Leyte* and *Philippine Sea* supported the withdrawing Allied ground forces in North Korea. Fighters and bombers strafed and bombed within 50 yards of Allied positions; napalm could be used close in, in part because the 25-degree-below-zero temperatures reduced the danger zone around friendly troops. Two carrier aircraft from the *Leyte* were lost during this period. One was a Skyraider which crashed after being hit by ground fire; its pilot was captured before a rescue helicopter could pick him up. The other was a Corsair piloted by Ensign Jesse L. Brown, the U.S. Navy's first black pilot. His Corsair made a forced landing near the Chosin Reservoir, five miles behind enemy lines. Brown was alive, but unable to free himself from the burning wreckage. One of his squadron mates, Lieutenant (j.g) Thomas Hudner, deliberately crash landed his aircraft nearby and attempted to free Brown, packing snow around him with his bare hands to keep the flames away before returning to his own aircraft to radio for a rescue helicopter with cutting tools. The helicopter arrived, but Ensign Brown died before he could be freed. For his valiant efforts Lieutenant Hudner became the first Navy man to receive the Medal of Honor in the Korean War.[6]

As the Chinese pushed the Allied forces south, plans were made to evacuate troops through the ports of Hungnam, Chinampo, and Inchon and redeploy them further south. Early in the new year the Chinese advance had lost momentum. The drive had been costly due to the fierce fighting retreat of the Allied ground forces and the constant pounding by Allied aircraft. By late January 1951, the Allies began to advance again and the Chinese decided to withdraw to defensive positions just above the 38th parallel. As the front lines stabilized, the carrier forces that had been hastily thrown together to deal with the crisis were sorted out. The *Leyte* was returned to the Atlantic and departed for the East Coast late in January. Task Force 77 was left with the *Philippine Sea, Princeton,* and *Valley Forge* and a rotation schedule was drawn up where two carriers would remain on station while the third was in Japan for a ten-day rest and replenishment period. The light carrier *Bataan* rotated blockade duty off Korea's west coast with the British carrier *Theseus,* while the escort carrier *Bairoko* took aboard an antisubmarine squadron and operated out of Japan. The hardworking *Sicily* and *Badoeng Strait* departed for the West Coast and a well-deserved rest. In March 1951, the *Boxer* returned after her long-delayed overhaul and relieved the

Valley Forge. The *Boxer*'s new air group was composed entirely of reserve squadrons recalled to active duty. In April Task Force 77, along with the *Boxer* and *Philippine Sea,* left Korean waters to operate off the China coast. Intelligence reports indicated that the Communist Chinese were about to launch an amphibious landing on the Nationalist island stronghold of Formosa and so, from 11 to 14 April, the carriers flew aerial parades off the Chinese mainland as a show of force. The carriers had returned to conduct interdiction operations when the Communists launched a major spring offensive late in April. All three carriers were kept on the line by daily underway replenishments, taking on fuel and ammunition from late afternoon until midnight. (The term "underway replenishment," or "unrep," refers to refueling and resupply at sea.) The light carriers also stayed at sea; the *Theseus* was relieved by the *Glory* late in April.

On 1 May, Skyraiders from the *Princeton* made the only aerial torpedo attack of the Korean War—against a dam. The Hwachon reservoir and dam controlled the water level on several rivers in Korea. By closing the sluice gates the Communists could facilitate their own crossing of these rivers and by opening them impede Allied movements. Army Rangers had failed to capture the dam and B-29s using six-ton guided bombs had failed to destroy it. On 30 April, the Army asked Task Force 77 to have a try and a flight of six Skyraiders, escorted by five Corsairs, launched from the *Princeton.* Each of the Skyraiders carried two 2,000-pound bombs and made a dive bombing attack on the dam, succeeding in holing one of the sluice gates. The Army asked the

Navy to try again and the next morning 12 Corsairs and 8 Skyraiders, each armed with a torpedo set for surface run, attacked the dam. The approach was difficult because of the hills surrounding the reservoir. One torpedo was a dud and one ran erratic, but the other six hit and blasted the dam open, destroying Communist control of the reservoir.

Even before the Communist drive ended in mid-May, the Allied forces, supported by land and carrier-based aircraft, went on the offensive. The recommissioned *Bon Homme Richard* replaced the *Philippine Sea* in Task Force 77 and the "Bonnie Dick" launched her first air strikes over Korea on the last day of May.[7] The Allied drive continued until June 1951, when the Soviets showed some interest in negotiating an armistice. The talks began in Korea in early July. While the Allied and Communist delegations talked, fighting on the ground continued along a relatively fixed front. The air war, however, continued over much of the Korean peninsula.

Operation Strangle

Late in May, the U.S. command in Korea had proposed severing the battlefield from all Communist supplies and reinforcements. Highways, which carried most of the materiel to the front, would be cut in a one-degree "belt" across Korea.[8] Within this belt, Air Force aircraft would cut roads, drop bridges, and block tunnels on the three westernmost highways, while Task Force 77 took the two central routes and land-based Marine aircraft took the three easternmost routes. The interdiction effort, which began on 5 June, was to be

an around-the-clock effort, with roads and other bottlenecks hit with regular bombs, delayed action bombs, napalm, rockets and gunfire. But although hundreds of trucks were destroyed and roads and bridges holed and cut, reconnaissance still showed supplies getting through. Dirt roads and slave labor made highway repair simple and the delayed action bombs were ignored; the number of trucks moving supplies over the highways at night remained unchanged.

In late August 1951, the arrival of the *Essex* to replace the *Princeton* marked the first deployment of a modernized *Essex* class carrier. Besides being better suited to operate jet aircraft, the *Essex* air group included a squadron equipped with an aircraft new to Korea, the McDonnell F2H Banshee. She arrived off Korea in the middle of Operation Strangle, but was soon called upon to provide escort for B-29s bombing the key port city of Rashin, only 17 miles from the Soviet frontier.[9] Rashin was linked to Vladivostok by rail, road, and sea, and was where supplies from the Soviet Union were loaded onto trucks bound for the front lines. Rashin had been hit by B-29s twice before, but was placed off limits because of the risk of wandering into Soviet air space. It was the only North Korean city that had not been pounded by Allied aircraft.

After the U.S. Joint Chiefs of Staff had obtained permission from President Truman, 35 B-29s took off on 25 August to hit the Rashin railroad yards. Since the B-29s could not overfly Soviet territory, they had to fly over North Korea en route to the target and, because no Allied fighters flying from bases in South Korea could escort the bombers so far north, the B-29s were met on the way by 12 Banshees and 11 Panthers from the *Essex*. The 29 B-29s that reached the target smashed the marshalling yards and no MiGs challenged the mission.

Operation Strangle continued with unsatisfactory results through 20 September. Flight operations aboard the *Essex* were interrupted late on 16 September when one of her Banshees, returning with battle damage, missed the arresting wires, floated over the barrier, and crashed into aircraft parked forward. Before the fires were extinguished, four planes were destroyed, eight men killed, and 27 injured. The *Essex* had to retire to Japan for repair until 3 October. In October the interdiction effort shifted to railroad tracks and bridges in North Korea as there were indications that the Communists were relying more heavily on railways. Task Force 77 now included the *Essex*, the *Bon Homme Richard*, and the *Antietam*, which had relieved the *Boxer*. The *Valley Forge* soon returned to relieve the *Bon Homme Richard*. The rail attacks were another multi-service, around-the-clock effort. In contrast to the night operations of World War II carriers, the night attacks by Task Force 77 were an important factor in the interdiction campaign. Using radar and light from searchlights and flares to hit trains and trucks that hid during the day and moved only at night, F4U-5N night Corsairs and AD-4N night Skyraiders added significantly to the destruction of enemy equipment and installations.

During the rail effort, the *Essex* was given another unusual mission when Allied guerrillas reported that an important meeting of Chinese and Korean Communist party leaders was to take place at Kapsan, 60 miles inland in a mountainous area of North Korea. On the morning of 30 October, the *Essex* launched eight Skyraiders from a hundred miles off shore. The Skyraiders, each armed with two 2,000-pound bombs, a napalm bomb, eight 250-pound bombs, and a full load of 20mm ammunition, flew low over the water and through valleys overland to avoid detection. Almost 15 minutes after the meeting was to have started, the Skyraiders rolled in on their target, bombing and strafing until the meeting compound was destroyed. Over 500 attendees were killed and all of the party records in North Korea destroyed. The pilots who returned to the *Essex* were labled the "Butchers of Kapsan" by Communist radio and a price put on their heads.

The train-busting efforts continued as Air Force, Navy, and Marine aircraft cut railways, destroyed marshalling yards, dropped bridges, plugged tunnels, and destroyed rolling stock. Interdiction efforts against these targets continued throughout the war, but late in June 1952, the emphasis shifted to transportation centers, manufacturing areas, and supply depots in order to force Communist concessions at the truce talks. On 23 June, the *Boxer, Philippine Sea,* and *Princeton* flew off a major strike against the Suiho dam, whose hydroelectric plant was the fourth largest in the world. The Suiho dam had been off limits to Allied bombers because its location on the Yalu made it difficult to attack without violating Manchurian air space; the B-29s could not hit it because their level runs would take them across the river. Thirty-five Skyraiders armed with 2,000- and 1,000-pound bombs launched first; once on their way, 35 Panthers followed, 24 armed with

250-pound bombs, the others with extra fuel tanks. The bomb-carrying Panthers streaked in to suppress antiaircraft fire while the others remained high to watch for MiGs as the Skyraiders rolled in on the dam. All the bombs struck the target, smashing the power plant and all but two aircraft made it back to the carriers. A badly damaged Skyraider and its wingman diverted to Seoul, where the pilot made a wheels-up landing. Air Force F-84s and F-80s arrived to begin follow-up strikes as the carrier aircraft pulled off the target. As Suiho was being attacked, 12 other power plants were being hit in North Korea as the *Bon Homme Richard, Boxer, Philippine Sea,* and *Princeton* combined their strikes with the Air Force and Marines in an intensive two-day effort. Eleven of the power plants were knocked out and all others at least sustained damage. Two navy aircraft were lost, but their pilots were rescued.

Early on 6 August 1952, a fire broke out on the *Boxer*'s hangar deck, igniting gasoline, bombs, ammunition, and planes being readied for the next day's strikes. Seven men were killed in the fire and explosions and 12 aircraft were destroyed. Flames forced 63 men over the side, where they were picked up by destroyers and helicopters. After being quickly repaired in Japan, the *Boxer* returned to Korea to launch the first guided missile attacks of the Korean War. F6F Hellcats were fitted as remotely controlled drones and loaded with high explosives. With their engines running, they were catapulted into the air and guided by drone control aircraft to hard-to-hit bridges where they were crashed into the structure. Between 28 August and 2 September, six of these guided missile strikes were flown; most

hit their targets and only one failed because of faulty control.

On 1 September 1952, the *Boxer, Essex,* and *Princeton* sent a major strike into a target too difficult for the B-29s when they struck the oil refinery at Aoji, only four miles from Manchuria and eight miles from Siberia. On 8 October there was another joint Navy-Air Force strike, this time against a railroad junction at Kowan in eastern Korea. Ten B-29s, escorted by 12 Banshees, carpeted the area with 500-pound bombs to suppress antiaircraft fire before the Navy strike arrived to bomb and rocket the rail yards and supply depots. The air pressure strategy of joint Air Force and Navy strikes against selected North Korean targets, well established by the fall of 1952, continued to the end of the war, though the number of suitable industrial targets quickly dwindled.

The Cherokee Strikes

Throughout the Korean War, command of Task Force 77 had rotated on a short-term basis among several admirals. "Jocko" Clark had been among them and, following his promotion to Vice Admiral, he returned to Korea in May 1952 to command the Seventh Fleet. An inspection trip of the forward areas convinced him that the Communists had to maintain their supplies close to the front in order to survive the Allied air interdiction effort. He reasoned that a large number of worthwhile targets must be just beyond the maximum range of Allied artillery. In contrast to the Air Force concept of spontaneous Close Air Support by on-call aircraft under the control of a Tactical Air Control Party (TACP) or T-6 "Mosquito" forward air controller, the

"Cherokee" strikes, named in honor of Clark's Indian heritage, involved up to 50 aircraft in carefully preplanned strikes against specific targets. Flak suppression escort was also provided and targets were inside or outside the bomb line (the area beyond the front line where tactical aircraft could not bomb for fear of hitting friendly troops) as necessary. The first of the Cherokee strikes were launched on 9 October 1952 and by the end of the month, the Navy had set a new wartime record, 13,000 flights, for Korean air operations.

Following a November conference with the Eighth Army and Fifth Air Force, the Navy agreed to operate above the bomb line only, coordinate with the Eighth Army and Fifth Air Force, and use the T-6 Mosquitos to mark their targets. Complementing the Cherokee strikes were the "Call-Shot" strikes which supported ground troops confronted by mass human wave assaults by Chinese and North Korean troops as the war degenerated into a brutal contest for small gains along a static front. The area behind the bomb line to a depth of about 20 miles became known to pilots as the "Cherokee strip." Flak was intense, but losses were encouragingly low. The Cherokee strikes continued for the rest of the war and, despite a few incidents of bombing friendly troops, they were important in preventing the Communists from building up enough men and materiel to mount a major offensive for the rest of the war.[10]

In late October 1952 the *Oriskany* arrived off Korea with two fighter squadrons equipped with a newer version of the Panther, the F9F-5. The first aerial combat for the new fighters came on 18 November when four Panthers were on patrol over Task Force 77 as it supported a surface bombardment of the extreme northeast Korean coast, about a hundred miles south of the Soviet base at Vladivostok. One of the Panthers had fuel pump difficulties and its wingman stayed with it while the other two Panthers climbed to investigate seven aircraft detected by the Task Force 77 radar. The bogies had broken off from a larger group that was operating north of the task force. The bogies were identified as MiGs and the Panthers were ordered to close on them. Two, and then three, of the Panthers fought a brief but fierce battle with the MiGs. Two MiGs were shot down and another was believed damaged; all of the Panthers made it back to the *Oriskany.* The task force continued to monitor the aircraft to the north, some approached within 40 miles, and twice vectored carrier fighters out to intercept approaching aircraft. There was one sighting, but the MiGs turned away.

When the *Boxer* returned to Korea in May 1953, she had three squadrons of F9F-5 Panthers and one of Skyraiders, but she could not operate three jet squadrons effectively and traded one to the *Lake Champlain* for a squadron of Corsairs. The *Lake Cham*plain was a modernized *Essex* class and could operate the three squadrons, two with the Banshee and the Panther squadron from the *Boxer,* as well as her Skyraider squadron and special mission aircraft.

The use of night aircraft in Korea was highly successful, but mixing day carrier operations with night operations was always taxing and difficult. The *Princeton* was selected for Operation No Doze and night detachments from the other carriers shifted to her. However, when she joined Task Force 77 in March 1953, she was needed for other operations. She then needed repairs in Japan and did not see action as a night carrier. Night attacks continued to be successful, however, and before dawn on 3 May 1953, three AD-4N Skyraiders from the *Valley Forge* struck a power plant at the Chosin reservoir, a difficult target because of heavy antiaircaft fire and interference by MiGs. During the last few months of the war, the Communists flew night heckling missions over Allied lines using slow propeller-driven aircraft, including biplanes. These "Bedcheck Charlies" would drop small bombs and generally make nuisance attacks designed to keep Allied troops awake. Since they were too slow to be intercepted by jet night fighters, Task Force 77 sent several F4U-4N night Corsairs ashore to operate from an airfield 35 miles south of Seoul. On the night of 29 June, Lieutenant Guy P. Bordelon from the *Princeton* shot down two Communist planes; the next night he shot down two

more and on the night of 17 July he shot down a fifth aircraft, becoming the Navy's only ace of the Korean War.

During the summer of 1953, both sides attempted to gain advances that would give them a better bargaining position in the peace talks. In June and July, as the fighting on the ground reached a crescendo, the pace of air operations also intensified as Task Force 77 provided close support to Allied ground forces, despite difficult weather. Unable to prevail over the Allies, the Communists agreed to a cease fire and, at 1000 on 27 July 1953, the armistice was signed. During the 12 hours before the cease fire took effect, Navy aircraft continued to strike, hitting transportation networks and airfields to knock them out by the time of the truce. Shortly after the last aircraft had pulled out of their divebombing runs, the war was over. An uneasy peace had returned to the Korean peninsula.[11]

Chapter 16
The Golden Age

For the Navy, the Korean War had positive results. Experience in Korea had irrefutably silenced critics who had felt that navies were obsolete. Aircraft carriers in particular had proven their usefulness and, starting with FY 52, Congress appropriated funding for six of the new 60,000-ton *Forrestal* class carriers. By the mid-1950s, the steam catapult, angled flight deck, and mirror landing system all combined to make the aircraft carrier truly jet-capable. The Navy, recognizing the primary role played by the aircraft carrier in offensive operations, changed the designation of aircraft carriers from CV to CVA for "attack aircraft carrier" in October 1952. Other carriers, older *Essex* class carriers no longer capable of handling the latest jets and those operating with antisubmarine air groups aboard, assumed the specialized role of antisubmarine warfare (ASW). In July 1953, these ships were redesignated CVS, for "antisubmarine warfare support carrier." (The mothballed *Bunker Hill* and *Franklin* were also included under this

category.) As new carriers entered service, more *Essex* class carriers converted to antisubmarine duties. The helicopter had also proven itself in the Korean War and as newer and more capable helicopters were developed, they were used in both antisubmarine and amphibious warfare roles. Later, as the Marines developed their doctrine of amphibious assault using helicopters, other *Essex* class carriers were adapted for use as helicopter carriers under the designation LPH.

New aircraft also entered the inventory as the swept-wing fighters of the second generation replaced the first generation straight-wing jet fighters. Swept wings allowed jets to deal with the Mach effects of supersonic flight and the performance of carrier based aircraft again compared favorably with their land-based counterparts. The first new fighters were derivatives of older straight-wing designs: the F9F-6 Cougar, based on the F9F Panther, and the FJ-2 and FJ-3 Fury, based on the FJ-1. Both entered service too late for combat over Korea. There was also a new anti-submarine aircraft to replace the single-engine Grumman AF Guardians and AD Skyraiders used earlier. These single-engine aircraft had to be operated in hunter-killer pairs, limiting their usefulness. They were replaced by the twin-engine Grumman S2F Tracker, which was large enough to accommodate both search equipment, such as radar and MAD (Magnetic Anomaly Detection) gear, and attack weapons, such as depth charges and homing torpedoes. When they first deployed with squadrons in early 1954, the Trackers were larger than any other carrier aircraft except the AJ-1 Savage. Other variants of the S2F were later developed for airborne early warning as the WF-2 Tracer, more commonly called "Willy Fudd" and the TF-1 *Trader* carrier on-board delivery (COD) transport. Helicopters were also developed as antisubmarine aircraft and, combined with the fixed-wing Trackers, gave the fleet an impressive antisubmarine capability.

Three or four years behind the second generation jet fighters came several new truly supersonic designs in the "golden years" of the mid-1950s and early 1960s. These included the McDonnell F3H-1 Demon, the Douglas F4D Skyray, the Grumman F11F-1 Tiger, and the Vought F7U Cutlass. A trailing member of this generation of fighters was the Vought F8U Crusader. The Crusader later became known as the "MiG master" in Vietnam, and was the last of a long line of fighters to fly from the *Essex* class carriers. New jet attack aircraft were also introduced. In a reversal of the trend toward larger and heavier aircraft, Douglas designed the outstanding A4D Skyhawk. At the other end of the scale was the Douglas A3D Skywarrior, a

large twin-jet attack bomber which began as a nuclear heavy attack aircraft and wound up in roles such as photo reconnaissance, aerial refueling, and electronic warfare.[1]

As these new aircraft appeared, the new super carriers of the *Forrestal* class began entering service. Along with them, the *Essex* class carriers were modernized to prepare them to operate in the new age of jet carrier operations.

SCB-27C

Studies for more improvements to the SCB-27A design began in 1951. These included a more powerful slotted tube catapult using a powder charge, new Mark 7 arresting gear, and a new starboard deck-edge elevator to replace the after centerline elevator, which interfered with traffic flow along the deck. Since stability had become critical in the *Essex* class, new five-foot wide blisters were designed to improve stability over that of the SCB-27A design. The SCB-27C was to be applied to the *Hancock* and later conversions. Although not all SCB-27A conversions had been fitted with the "improvement program," i.e., capacity for handling nuclear weapons, all SCB-27C conversions would be so fitted. One of the two H-8 catapults would be replaced with a C-10 powder charge catapult with its breech in the extreme bow. All SCB-27Cs would have a new fuel blending system that allowed tanks used for the ship's bunker oil to be used for JP-5 jet fuel storage, although this reduced the steaming radius.[2] The starboard after pair of 5"/38s were moved further aft to a position across from the port guns and all 14 twin 3"/50s were retained. Other features included: catapult blast deflectors, deck cooling, mechanical positioning of aircraft at the catapults, and a new nylon barricade. Delays in the C-10 catapult program caused the Navy to consider delaying the conversion of the first three ships, the *Hancock, Intrepid,* and *Ticonderoga,* or installing the H-8-1 catapult, a lengthened version of the H-8. The steam catapult came to the rescue and the three ships were finished to the original SCB-27C design. The final three ships, the *Lexington, Bon Homme Richard,* and *Shangri-La,* all had the later angled decks and enclosed "hurricane" bows included with their SCB-27C modernizations; they also had their forward centerline elevators enlarged at the same time. All the SCB-27C ships had the new C-11 steam catapult. To compensate for weight, the gun battery was reduced to eight 5"/38s and five twin 3"/50 mounts.

As the SCB-27A conversions displaced unconverted *Essex* class carriers in the attack carrier force, the unmodernized ships were assigned to antisubmarine warfare missions. After the Korean War, as the *Forrestal* class carriers were commissioned, they and the SCB-27C conversions displaced the SCB-27A ships into the ASW role. All the *Essex* conversions were marginal in their stability by this time and the only means of compensating was to reduce the gun battery. By 1960 few of these ships retained any 3"/50s, after which 5"/38s were removed as well. At the end of her career, the *Oriskany* had only two 5"/38s; other surviving *Essex* class ships had four.

The Steam Catapult

The H-8 had taken hydraulic catapult technology about as far as it could

go. For the most efficient catapult stroke, nearly constant acceleration is desired and, given that the ultimate limit of a catapult is its overall length, the shorter the braking cycle is, the longer the power stroke can be. With its hydraulic-pneumatic brake, the H-8 catapult needed 50 feet to decelerate. While Americans worked on powder charge designs, the British worked on steam catapults. A young Scottish engineer, Colin Mitchell, had begun design and development work on the first steam catapult in 1948. A remarkable feature of Mitchell's design was a water brake, which could bring a 5,000-pound shuttle to a halt within a distance of only five feet. When his design work was complete and the concept demonstrated, the first full scale steam catapult was installed on the *H.M.S. Perseus.*

The first U.S. steam catapult, the C-11, while based on the British BXS-1, used higher pressure steam. The BXS-1 was 203 feet long and used a pair of 18-inch diameter power cylinders. Test shots aboard the *Perseus* began at the Philadelphia Navy Yard on 9 December 1953 with the destroyer *Greene* supplying the high pressure steam.[3] The C-11 launched a 23,670-pound deadweight at 138 knots and 55,300 pounds at 109.5 knots, all well beyond U.S. requirements. The first C-11 was installed in the *Hancock* in May 1954.[4] The H-8 generated more than 9,000,000 pounds of energy over a 190-foot deck run, but the C-11-1, the follow-on version of the original C-11 with higher steam pressure and a longer deck run of 215 feet, generated over 36,000,000 pounds of energy. In practical terms this meant that the H-8 could accelerate a 25,000-pound aircraft to an end speed of about 95 knots. If the takeoff speed of the aircraft were 135 knots, 40 knots of wind over the deck would be needed. Since the *Essex* class carriers, in their modernized form, could only make slightly over 30 knots, there would have to be 10 knots of natural wind available. The C-11-1, however, could launch the same aircraft with an end speed of 132 knots, greatly improving operational flexibility and safety.[5]

The Angled Deck

The idea of angling the landing area of a carrier flight deck was a simple, but revolutionary concept that originated with the British. By landing at an angle, aircraft "go arounds" were possible without hitting the barricade. At first, the British thought that a 4-degree angle would be the technological limit, but this meant sacrificing too much area on the forward flight deck and did not fit in with the American ideas of high tempo air operations. When an 8-degree angle was tried, the U.S. became interested because much less deck space forward would have to be given up. The Navy began to give the angled deck concept serious consideration in 1951 and in the spring of 1952, two carriers, the large carrier *Midway* and the *Wasp,* were given superficial modifications to test the 8-degree angle deck.[6] While the carriers were made over, 16 carrier suitability pilots practiced landings on a simulated carrier deck painted on one of Naval Air Station Patuxent River's runways using a power on approach instead of the traditional level approach with power cut to land. The power on approach allowed the pilots to touch down in the arresting gear area and immediately apply full power to lift off and go around again. More than 300

landings in March and May convinced the Navy of the value of the new technique and the *Antietam* was chosen to become the Navy's first angled deck carrier.[7]

The *Antietam*

At first the *Antietam* was fitted with an 8-degree angled deck and later a 10.5-degree deck. On 12 January 1953 an SNJ trainer made the Navy's first true angled deck landing on the *Antietam.* Shortly afterward, carrier suitability pilots from the Naval Air Test Center brought down a variety of current aircraft for carrier landing tests. In August 1953, the *Antietam* was reclassified as a CVS and served in the Atlantic until April 1957, when she reported to Pensacola, Florida, for duty as a training carrier. *Antietam* was not included in later modification programs; her angled deck installation was considered an experimental modification and, except for her angled deck and some minor alterations, she was otherwise much the same as she was at the end of World War II.

The Mirror Landing System

To take advantage of the capabilities offered by the angled deck and the steam catapult, a new method of controlling aircraft as they came aboard had to be devised, since an LSO could only control one aircraft at a time and the limitations of the human eye made control using paddles limited to no more than one-half mile. Fortunately, the British again came up with a simple and elegant solution. The system used a large mirror, concave around its horizontal axis, placed alongside the landing area at the edge of the angled deck. The mirror pointed astern at the angle of the glide path and was mounted on gimbals connected to the ship's fire control system, which was gyro stabilized. This allowed the mirror to compensate for any movement of the ship. Aft of the mirror, a powerful light source was aimed at the mirror so that a cone of light was reflected back along the glide slope. The pilot would see a spot of light, the "ball," when he flew in the middle of the beam. To position his aircraft more precisely, a horizontal row of green datum lights was mounted on either side of the mirror. If the pilot was a little high on the glide path, the ball appeared to be slightly above the reference lights, if too low, the ball was below the reference lights. Later, the mirror was replaced by a Fresnel lens and colors added to the ball, but the principle was the same. The three elements together: angled deck, steam catapult, and mirror landing system, allowed the aircraft carrier to truly enter the jet age.[8]

SCB-125

SCB-125, which was intended to apply the angled deck to the *Essex* class carriers, also included the fitting of an enclosed "hurricane" bow. Three groups of ships were affected by the SCB-125 program. The first group included the *Lexington, Bon Homme Richard,* and *Shangri-La,* which were modernized to both SCB-27C and SCB-125 standards during a single dockyard period. The second group included the *Intrepid, Ticonderoga* and *Hancock,* which were SCB-27C ships modernized again by SCB-125 between 1954 and 1957. In the third group were ships originally mod-

ernized under SCB-27A. Because the C-11 steam catapult differed enough from the earlier hydraulic catapults to prevent easy conversion of the SCB-27A ships to steam catapults, the SCB-27A ships were given the angled flight deck, enclosed bow, and the after starboard deck-edge elevator, but not other features of the SCB-27C. The *Lake Champlain* was the only SCB-27A which did not get an angled deck. The *Oriskany,* originally finished to SCB-27A standards, received a one-of-a-kind SCB-125A conversion which brought her up to full SCB-27C standard with Mark 7 arresting gear, C-11-1 steam catapults, and enlarged elevators of increased capacity. Thus, by 1959, *Oriskany* was the last ship to be brought up to the latest standards.

Helicopter Carriers

By the late 1950s some of the older unmodernized *Essex* carriers were marked for decommisioning, but the Marine Corps, in need of amphibious assault ships, requested that some of them be converted into helicopter carriers. The *Boxer,* which had already been redesignated as a CVS in 1955, was equipped as an amphibious assault carrier and flagship in October 1958. In January 1959 she was reclassified as an amphibious assault helicopter carrier, given a new hull number, LPH-4, and assigned to the Atlantic Fleet. The *Princeton,* as LPH-5, followed her in March and was assigned to the Pacific Fleet. The *Valley Forge,* LPH-8, followed the first two conversions in July 1961 and was assigned to the Pacific. These ships had never received any of the SCB modernizations and looked much as they had at the end of World War II.

Most of the changes involved internal rearrangements to accommodate a Marine Battalion Landing Team. Other changes were aimed at reducing maintenance and operating costs: four of the eight boilers were taken out of service, dropping the speed to 25 knots; the radar suite was greatly reduced; and armament was reduced. (The *Boxer* retained all eight 5-inch guns on the flight deck and all sponson guns were removed. The *Princeton* and *Valley Forge* had four flight deck guns and two guns in the sponsons.) Using helicopters in place of fixed-wing aircraft, the LPHs practiced "vertical envelopment." The evolving concept called for landing Marines behind "enemy" beach fortifications, providing logistic and medical support as they attacked from the rear to seize key points, cut supply and communications lines, and linked up with Marine assault forces landing on the beaches. Many of the tactics and concepts developed would later be used in support of contingency operations around the world and in combat in the Dominican Republic and Vietnam.

When tension over missiles in Cuba mounted in October 1962, the *Boxer* joined two other LPHs, *Thetis Bay* and *Okinawa*, in the blockade imposed by President Kennedy. The *Boxer* was also on hand during the Dominican Republic crisis in April 1965. After standing off Santo Domingo for two days, Marines from the *Boxer* landed in Santo Domingo to protect American lives. During the week that followed, over 1,000 American women and children were evacuated from danger areas. After 47 days of continuous operations, the *Boxer* returned to Norfolk, her home port, late in June. In August of that year, the *Boxer* transported helicopters of the Army's

First Cavalry Division (Air Mobile) to Vietnam, arriving in Cam Ranh Bay, South Vietnam in September. The *Boxer* made another deployment to Vietnam the following year. Arriving in May, she delivered units of the First Marine Aircraft Wing to Danang and units of the 3rd Force Reconnaissance Company to Okinawa before returning to the Atlantic.

The involvement of the Pacific Fleet helicopter carriers in Vietnam began when the *Princeton* delivered Marine advisors and helicopters to Soc Trang in the Mekong Delta area in April 1962. As American combat forces began building up in 1964 and 1965, the *Princeton* and *Valley Forge* rotated support for the Amphibious Ready Groups off the coast of South Vietnam, supporting ground operations, transporting helicopter units and, on occasion, providing flood relief assistance to the Vietnamese. In all, the *Princeton* and *Valley Forge* each completed four deployments to Vietnam between 1964 and 1969. As newer ships designed and built from the keel up as helicopter carriers were commissioned, the *Essex* conversions were withdrawn from service and eventually scrapped. The *Boxer* was stricken from the Navy List in December 1969, followed by the *Princeton* and *Valley Forge* in January 1971.

The Antisubmarine Carriers

As the carrier force entered the 1960s, air groups changed to reflect new missions and capabilities. Antisubmarine Carrier Air Groups, CVSG, were established in 1960-61 and given numbers between 50 and 60. These antisubmarine air groups continued to be called air groups even after the attack carrier air groups were retitled as wings, CVW, in 1963. An antisubmarine air group included two VS fixed-wing antisubmarine squadrons flying the S-2 Tracker, an HS helicopter antisubmarine squadron equipped with SH-3 Sea King helicopters, and a VAW airborne early warning squadron with E-1 Tracers. Operating in the Pacific and Atlantic, the antisubmarine carriers monitored the growing Soviet submarine force, and, as ASW gained in importance, the ships themselves were again modernized under an overall Navy effort known as the Fleet Rehabilitation and Modernization II program. SCB-144 was the FRAM II modernization aimed at improving the ASW capabilities of the SCB-27A CVS carriers. The principal modifications included the installation of a bow-mounted sonar dome for the SQS-23 sonar, a stem hausepipe and bow anchor (to clear the sonar dome), and modifications to the Combat Information Center. By 1965 all the FRAM II conversions were back in service.

As American involvement in Vietnam grew, the antisubmarine carriers of the Pacific Fleet performed the vital, if less conspicuous, role of providing ASW protection for the naval forces in the South China Sea. In addition to antisubmarine screening, they performed surface surveillance and combat search and rescue missions. Occasionally, their detachments of A-4 Skyhawk "fighters" were used to launch strikes at ground targets. During the peak years from 1964 through 1969 the *Yorktown,* *Hornet, Bennington* and *Kearsarge* all rotated through deployments to Vietnam. One Atlantic Fleet antisubmarine carrier, the *Intrepid,* was lent to the war effort as a "special attack carrier" and completed three combat deployments,

though she retained her CVS designation. The ASW carriers responded to other hot spots in the Pacific as well. The *Yorktown,* on her way to South Vietnam, was diverted to the Sea of Japan following the seizure of the spy ship *Pueblo* off Wonsan, North Korea, on 28 January 1968. She maintained a readiness patrol for 48 days before being released to continue her deployment. Trouble with the North Koreans flared again the next year. In April, the *Hornet,* nearing the end of her deployment to the Western Pacific, was diverted to the Sea of Japan when a Navy reconnaissance aircraft was shot down. She remained in the area for two weeks before continuing on her way to Long Beach.

Space Support Operations

When Commander Alan B. Shepard, Jr., splashed down in the Atlantic on 1 May 1961 after completing a 115-mile suborbital flight in the Freedom 7 capsule, the *Lake Champlain* was standing by. Within minutes America's first astronaut was aboard a recovery helicopter headed for the carrier.[9] It was the first of many such recoveries as America began its drive to put men on the moon before the decade was over. Beginning with the Project Mercury launches in the early 1960s, *Essex* class CVS carriers were often used as the primary recovery ships supporting America's space program as it evolved through Project Gemini and Project Apollo. These space support missions were interspersed with routine ASW operations and continued into the late 1960s even as America's involvement in Vietnam grew. The Apollo 11 mission in July 1969 represented the high point of

America's massive effort to land men on the moon and the role played by the *Hornet* is typical of these space support operations. The Apollo 11, with Lieutenant Colonel Michael Collins, Neil Armstrong, and Colonel Edwin E. "Buzz" Aldrin aboard, was boosted into space on 16 July 1969 by a powerful Saturn 5 rocket to begin their historic journey to the moon. On 20 July 1969, as Collins remained in the Command Module orbiting the moon, Armstrong and Aldrin landed the Lunar Module on the moon's surface. Later that evening the world watched by live television as Neil Armstrong became the first man to set foot on the moon, uttering the now famous words, "That's one small step for a man, one giant leap for mankind." The two blasted off from the moon the next day to rendezvous with the orbiting Command Module before returning to earth. On 24 July, the Columbia space capsule splashed down in the Pacific, only 12 miles from the *Hornet* and within 1.75 miles from the aiming point 950 miles southeast of Hawaii. Two of *Hornet's* helicopters took off and headed for the capsule, as it wallowed in the ocean. The first diver from the recovery crew attached a sea anchor to the capsule as others attached a floatation collar. Wearing special garments to protect against possible contamination from space, the divers sprayed down the spacecraft and the astronauts, who were then hauled aboard a helicopter for the trip to the *Hornet*. Armstrong was the first to board, followed by Collins and Aldrin. The ships band struck up "Columbia, Gem of the Ocean" as the astronauts stepped onto the *Hornet's* flight deck. The astronauts quickly stepped into a special trailer, again to prevent possible contamina-tion, and the *Hornet* headed for Pearl Harbor, where the trailer was flown to Ellington Air Force Base aboard an Air Force C-141 transport.[10]

The Cold War

In the late 1950s and early 1960s, carrier forces were often called upon to support America's policy of "containment" of Communist aggression, becoming effective instruments of American foreign policy during the "Cold War." Aircraft carriers could quickly provide an American presence in "hot spots" around the globe. Merely moving a carrier task force into an area demonstrated American capability and resolve, yet at the same time did not interfere with any nation's sovereignty or commit American forces to any particular course of action. One of the earliest of several Cold War "incidents" occurred in June 1954. While searching for a downed British airliner in the South China Sea, planes from the *Hornet* were attacked by two Chinese communist fighters, both of which were promptly shot down.

Lebanon

American sea power was frequently used as a stabilizing influence in the volatile Middle East, where America's efforts to balance its support of Israel against relations with other Middle Eastern states were in conflict with Soviet efforts to dominate the region through Arab client states and deny Western access to Arab oil. When the pro-Western government of Iraq was overthrown by a coup in July 1958, President Camille Chamoun of neighboring Lebanon asked for American assistance in preventing a similar occurrence in his country. Within hours naval forces of the Sixth Fleet, including the carriers *Saratoga, Wasp,* and *Essex,* went into action. Marines quickly moved ashore and secured Beirut. With the situation stabilized, the Marines were promptly withdrawn. Although the landings met no opposition, the American capability to rapidly intervene did not go unnoticed by either the Soviet Union or the more radical Arab states in the region, such as Nasser's Egypt.

Quemoy and Matsu

While the Sixth Fleet supported American policy in the Middle East, the Communist Chinese began a build-up of forces opposite the Nationalist-held islands of Quemoy and Matsu, only four miles from the mainland. The Nationalists intended them as stepping stones for their eventual return to the mainland and garrisoned them with 100,000 men; the Communists regarded them as key to their conquest of the Nationalist stronghold on Taiwan. In August the Communists began intensive shelling of Quemoy, and as the shelling continued, the Seventh Fleet moved into position to intervene if needed. The Eisenhower administration had formally agreed to defend Taiwan itself, but it was unclear whether this would include the offshore islands and the actions taken by the Seventh Fleet were meant to keep the Communists guessing about what the American response to an invasion would be. The major problem facing the defenders was resupply. By providing amphibious tractors and escorting them to within three miles of Quemoy, the Nationalists

were able to land supplies. The air groups from five carriers provided air cover over Taiwan itself, allowing the Nationalist air force to take on the Communists over the islands.[11] One of the five carriers, the *Essex,* had just provided six weeks of air cover over Lebanon and then transited the Suez Canal to join the Seventh Fleet units supporting the Nationalists. The combination of American presence and support thwarted any Communist plan for taking over the islands.

The Bay of Pigs

When President John F. Kennedy took office in 1961, he inherited a plan from the Eisenhower administration for the invasion of Communist Cuba, taken over by Fidel Castro in 1959. The plan called for Cuban exiles, transported and supplied by the American government, to liberate Cuba. Although the administration planned and supported the operation, great pains were taken to conceal official involvement. But the rules of engagement prevented any interference by American naval forces unless actually fired upon, and at a critical point in the invasion when U.S. air support was vital to the survival of the invaders, the *Constellation* and *Essex* could only stand by helplessly as the Cuban exiles were defeated, rounded up, and either killed or captured. For the Bay of Pigs operation the *Essex,* which had been converted to a CVS only the year before, reverted to a limited attack role with A-4 Skyhawks embarked.

The Cuban Missile Crisis

Throughout the summer of 1962 there were indications of unusual activity in Cuba. In October, high altitude reconnaissance flights by a U-2 spy plane showed that the Soviets were constructing missile bases in Cuba. Along with the Il-28 twin-engine jet bombers arriving in Cuba, these missiles could reach U.S. targets within minutes. Faced with a choice of ignoring the threat or perhaps starting a war between the two superpowers, President Kennedy opted for a naval blockade, euphemistically called a "quarantine." Kennedy announced the quarantine on national television on 21 October. To give the Russians time to think things over, the blockade did not actually go into effect until the morning of 24 October. Task Force 136, with some 483 ships deployed in an arc about 500 miles to the northeast of Cuba, stood ready. The Soviet premier, Nikita Khrushchev, called the American allegations of missile bases in Cuba lies and threatened that if the American navy carried out any act of "piracy" the Soviet Union would react accordingly. Tension mounted as the Russian cargo ships en route to Cuba approached the American naval forces. Fortunately, Khrushchev backed down and the crisis abated. The Russians dismantled their missile bases and removed them from Cuba.

Four *Essex* antisubmarine carriers participated in the naval blockade. The *Essex* had been at sea off Guantanamo Bay when President Kennedy announced the quarantine. For the next 26 days, she conducted 624 consecutive hours of flight operations, returning to Quonset Point only after the crisis passed. The *Lexington* had been slated to replace the *Antietam* as the Navy's training carrier in the Gulf of Mexico in January and had been redesignated as a CVS on 1 October, but during the Cuban Missile Crisis, she operated as an attack carrier. It was not until the end of December that she relieved the *Antietam* as a training carrier. In the summer of 1962 the *Randolph* was deployed to the Mediterranean, but returned to the Atlantic when the crisis broke, operating in the Caribbean from October through November. The *Wasp*, which had been operating off the East Coast, participated in the quarantine through most of November, returning to Boston on 22 November.

President Kennedy, encouraged by his success in the Cuban missile crisis, was determined to blunt other Communist moves around the world. Special emphasis was placed on Indochina, where bloody wars of "national liberation" had been going on since the end of World War II, first against the French colonial authorities and then between the Communist North Vietnam and the anti-Communist South Vietnam. When Kennedy was inaugurated in 1961 there were only 800 Americans in South Vietnam; at the time of his assassination in November 1963, the number had grown to 23,000, two-thirds of them military advisors. The guerrilla campaign had not been stopped, and the American commitment grew. President Lyndon B. Johnson continued that commitment and the Navy's carrier forces again became involved in a war in Asia.

The Intrepid *in the South China Sea, September 1966.*

An F-8 Crusader recovers aboard the Hancock, *December 1970.*

The Hancock *operating in the Gulf of Tonkin, March 1971.*

A catapult crewman prepares to hook up the "bridle" to an F-8 aboard the Oriskany *as she prepares to launch a strike against North Vietnam.*

As the Hancock *steams in the South China Sea, an A-4F Skyhawk is ready for launch, May 1972.*

The Intrepid *during underway replenishment with the Camden AOE-2. CH-46D Seaknight helicopters are being used for "vertrep" (vertical replenishment).*

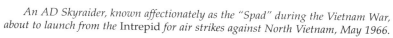

An AD Skyraider, known affectionately as the "Spad" during the Vietnam War, about to launch from the Intrepid *for air strikes against North Vietnam, May 1966.*

Decks awash in heavy seas, the Ashtabula *AO-51 refuels the* Ticonderoga *off the coast of Vietnam.*

Pilots aboard the Oriskany *man their planes as crewmen wrap up last minute details.*

A-4 Skyhawks landing on the Intrepid, *May 1966.*

F-3H Demons, A-4 Skyhawks and AD Skyraiders aboard the Ticonderoga.

An F-8 Crusader takes off to strike targets in Vietnam while the Ticonderoga *loads more bombs and ammunition from the Wrangel AE-12.*

A-4 Skyhawks landing on the Intrepid, *May 1966.*

An A-4 Skyhawk is ready to launch from the Intrepid, *May 1966.*

The Oriskany *is decommissioned at*
NAS Alameda, 30 September 1976.

CAPT William "Bill" Kennedy, last
commanding officer of the Lexington,
was the last to leave the ship during
decommissioning ceremonies at
NAS Pensacola, 8 November 1991.
(CDR S. Silverio courtesy
Naval Aviation News).

The Oriskany *was the last of the* Essex
class still operating with the fleet as an
attack carrier to be decommissioned.
Here, the tug Winnemucca *tows the*
"O-boat" from NAS Alameda to the
inactive ships facility in Bremerton.

The Lexington *is now a museum ship in Corpus Christi, Texas. She was the last* Essex *class carrier to be decommissioned and will probably be the last to be preserved as a museum ship. (Courtesy U.S.S. Lexington* Museum on the Bay*)*

The Intrepid *has become the centerpiece of the* Intrepid *Sea-Air-Space Museum in New York Harbor. Besides the submarine* Growler *SSG-577 and the destroyer* Edson *DD-946, numerous aircraft (including an SR-71 Blackbird) and spacecraft are on display. (Courtesy* Intrepid *Sea-Air-Space Museum)*

Chapter 17

Vietnam

Throughout the late 1950s and early 1960s, U.S. carriers maintained a presence in the South China Sea as the turbulence in Vietnam grew following the French withdrawal from Indochina in 1954. The whole of Southeast Asia seemed on the verge of a Communist takeover as guerrilla warfare continued in what had become South Vietnam and as the conflict spread into neighboring Cambodia and Laos.[1] American involvement began with supplying equipment and advisors, and, after Lyndon B. Johnson assumed the presidency, contingency planning began for possible attacks against North Vietnam.[2]

The Gulf of Tonkin

By 1964 the ships of the U.S. Seventh Fleet were operating off the Indochina coast on a routine basis, gathering intelligence, supporting anti-Communist activities and launching carrier-based reconnaissance flights. On the afternoon of 2 August 1964, as she operated off the coast of North Vietnam, the destroyer *Maddox*'s radar detected three unidentified high speed craft.[3] The North Vietnamese torpedo boats ignored a warning shot from the *Maddox* and two of them fired torpedoes. The *Maddox* evaded the torpedoes and returned the fire, possibly hitting the third North Vietnamese boat. Meanwhile, a training flight of four F-8 Crusaders from the *Ticonderoga* was vectored to the area. After contacting the *Maddox* the Crusaders were ordered to attack the torpedo boats as they headed north. Armed with 20mm cannon and unguided Zuni rockets, they made several strafing runs over the craft, sinking the third torpedo boat. The whole affair lasted about three and one-half hours. President Johnson ordered the destroyer *Turner Joy* to join the *Maddox* and the carrier *Constellation* (CVA-64) was routed from Hong Kong to the Gulf of Tonkin. Meanwhile, the *Ticonderoga* maintained daylight patrols and the destroyers retired to about a hundred miles offshore during the night to reduce the danger of torpedo boat attack.

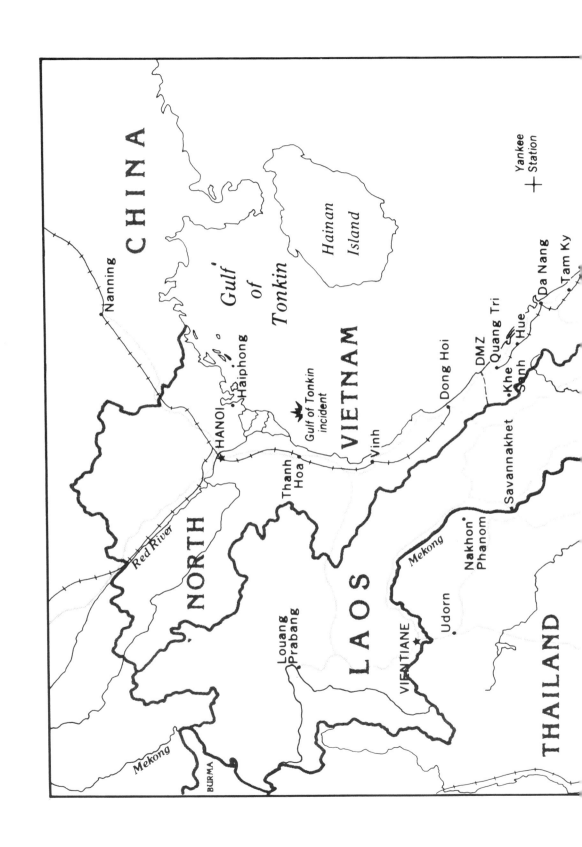

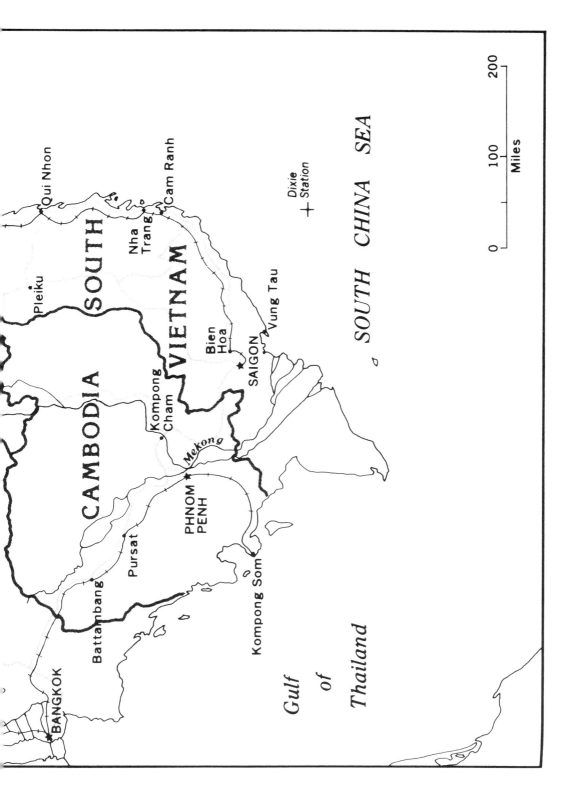

Vietnam

On the night of 4 August, the *Maddox* picked up five high-speed radar contacts, identified as North Vietnamese torpedo boats about to make nighttime runs. In bad weather, the two forces exchanged gunfire and torpedoes from the boats narrowly missed the destroyers. *Ticonderoga* launched two A-1 Skyraiders to provide air cover, but by then the destroyers had lost radar contact.

Retaliation was not long in coming. Even as President Johnson went on national television to speak about the two unprovoked attacks on American warships in international waters and to announce the actions he would take, aircraft from the *Ticonderoga* and *Constellation* were heading for four major North Vietnamese torpedo boat bases.[4] Crusaders, Skyhawks, and Skyraiders bombed and rocketed the four bases, damaging all the facilities and destroying or damaging an estimated 25 torpedo boats and more than half of the North Vietnamese air force.[5] With the passage of the Gulf of Tonkin Resolution by Congress a few days later, Task Force 77 stood ready to launch further retaliatory attacks against the north. The *Ranger* (CVA-61) and the *Kearsarge* (CVS-33) joined Task Force 77 in the Gulf of Tonkin, giving the task force three attack carriers and one anti-submarine carrier.[6] The Communists shifted a few fighter units from China into North Vietnam and the Americans brought Air Force units into South Vietnam, along with support personnel and equipment. The buildup had begun. For the next six months, American carriers continued to patrol off Vietnam.

Although there were occasional reports of Communist terrorist activities in Saigon and in the countryside, things remained quiet until February 1965. Dissatisfaction with General Khanh's government had led to street demonstrations and Viet Cong attacks, and a U.S. advisory team, led by national security advisor McGeorge Bundy, was sent to observe the South Vietnam situation and make recommendations. On 7 February, shortly before the team was to leave, the Viet Cong attacked the American compound in Pleiku in the Central Highlands, killing nine Americans and wounding a hundred. To the American officials in South Vietnam, there seemed little choice but to retaliate and President Johnson authorized a Navy strike, coordinated with South Vietnamese aircraft, against the military barracks and staging area at Dong Hoi, north of the demilitarized zone (DMZ) along the 17th parallel. The strike, named Flaming Dart I, involved the *Coral Sea* (CVA-43), the *Ranger* (CVA-61), and the *Hancock,* but weather in the South China Sea caused a delay.[7] By noon, however, the carriers were ordered to launch their aircraft. *Coral Sea* and *Hancock* were to hit the barracks at Dong Hoi while the *Ranger* would hit barracks 15 miles inland at Vit Thu Lu. The *Ranger*'s aircraft could not hit their target because of the weather, but the strikes against Dong Hoi destroyed much of the facility. The Communists responded with an attack on a hotel in Qui Nhon used as American enlisted quarters. Twenty-three American soldiers were killed and many wounded. Flaming Dart II began the next day, 11 February, with strikes against the Chanh Hoa barracks 35 miles north of the DMZ. Flying in the northeast monsoon, this strike faced the same rain and fog that had hampered the 7 February strike. The Chanh Hoa strike had limited success and the attacking aircraft faced heavy antiaircraft fire. Three aircraft were shot down and others damaged. These strikes were the first of the so-called Alpha Strikes, which involved using all available aircraft from a carrier's air wing, from fighters to tankers. The Communists, unimpressed by the American carrier strikes, continued their periodic attacks against American installations in South Vietnam. The monsoon weather continued to plague carrier operations for the rest of the war.[8]

Rolling Thunder

Because merely responding to Communist attacks did not prove effective, President Johnson gradually allowed a program of interdictive air strikes. The Air Force and Navy were tasked to bomb targets successively farther north of the DMZ. As the bomb line of these "Rolling Thunder" operations approached their capital of Hanoi, the North Vietnamese were expected to sue for peace. Severe restrictions imposed on the operational commanders hamstrung the operation from the start: no pre-strike photography was permitted, reconnaissance aircraft had to accompany the strike or fly in immediately afterward, no follow-up strikes were authorized, unexpended ordnance could not be dropped on targets of opportunity, and enemy aircraft had to be positively identified before engaging in air-to-air combat.[9] Specific targets were assigned to the Navy and Air Force, and later these were organized into "route packages" to relieve some of the confusion in planning missions. Two geographic stations were picked in the Gulf of Tonkin—Yankee Station in the north

and Dixie Station in the south.[10] Yankee Station served as the center of carrier operations against North Vietnam, while Dixie Station became a "warm up" area where newly arrived carrier air wings could gain experience while supporting ground operations in South Vietnam before rotating to the "big league" up north. The first Navy Rolling Thunder strikes were launched from the *Coral Sea* (CVA-43) and the *Hancock* against supply buildings at Phu Van and Vinh Son on 18 March 1965. All the aircraft returned with light damage, but successive Rolling Thunder strikes brought increased losses as the attacks moved north to within 70 miles of Hanoi. Although Rolling Thunder was somewhat effective, the Communists continued the war by moving and resupplying their units at night. What eventually became known as the Ho Chi Minh Trail was set up from North Vietnam into Laos.[11]

As the tempo of strikes increased, the North Vietnamese responded with stronger air defense measures and in April, the first surface-to-air missile (SAM) site was photographed 15 miles southeast of Hanoi. By July several SAM sites were detected, but it was not until August, after several aircraft were lost, that permission was given to attack the SAM sites. These missions became known as Iron Hand in the Navy and Wild Weasel in the Air Force, with the first actual strike against a SAM site taking place on 17 October 1965.[12] SAMs were not the only problem; the North Vietnamese set up early warning radar sites as fast as possible and introduced growing numbers of MiG-17 jet fighters. The MiG-17 was the follow-on improvement of the famous MiG-15 from the Korean War. Although slower than the American fighters, the MiG-17 was very maneuverable and its cannon armament could be deadly.[13] Later, the more advanced delta-winged MiG-21 appeared over North Vietnam, posing an even greater threat. Also, as attacking aircraft were forced down to lower altitudes to get out of the performance envelope of the Soviet-designed SA-2 Guideline missiles, they faced radar-controlled antiaircraft guns. The flak, according to some veterans, was as intense as any they experienced in World War II. The three carriers on station at the end of 1965, the *Enterprise* (CVAN-65), *Kitty Hawk* (CVA-63) and *Ticonderoga,* wound up the year with one of the biggest strikes flown up to that time. One hundred aircraft hit the thermal power plant at Uong Bi on 22 December 1965, marking the first time an industrial target, as opposed to bases and support installations, had been hit.

By the time the Christmas truce began on 24 December 1965, ten carriers had seen combat since August 1964 and many of them now rotated home—first the *Coral Sea,* then *Midway, Independence, Bon Homme Richard,* and *Oriskany.* The *Enterprise* and *Kitty Hawk* were left to carry on. The bombing halt lasted for 37 days and while the Americans waited for peace talks to begin, the North Vietnamese rebuilt their damaged bridges and facilities and added to their air defenses. Rolling Thunder had failed. Nearly 57,000 combat sorties had been flown, with over a hundred aircraft lost, and 82 men killed, captured or missing. Forty-six were rescued. Ironically, the carriers had shown their worth by carrying the war to North Vietnam and in supporting operations in the south.

Under pressure from senior military commanders, the administration gave approval for a resumption of the bombing campaign, although many restrictions, such as avoiding foreign shipping, MiG airfields, and large industrial targets north of Hanoi, remained. Gradually, the strikes were directed more at interdicting the flow of men and supplies into the south than "punishing" the North Vietnamese. The northeast monsoon, which runs from November through April, was at its height in the South China Sea when the bombing resumed in January 1966. Although SAMs were a threat, most of the losses were due to heavy flak. Pilots had learned that the SA-2 Guideline missile could be beaten with the right tactics. When a pilot sighted a missile, which was described as looking like a flying telephone pole, coming at him, he would wait until the proper moment and then execute a hard turn across the missile's flight path. With luck, the missile seeker would break lock and eventually explode without effect. Only the pilot being shot at could decide when to pull the stick and waiting for the right moment took courage, skill, and stamina.

During the early months of 1966, shortages of both pilots and aircraft began to effect operations. Aircraft production was not keeping pace with attrition and the pilot shortage was aggravated by a combination of combat losses and pilots leaving the service either out of frustration over the restrictions imposed or the lure of lucrative airline jobs. Pilots flew an average of between 16 and 22 combat missions a month over the North with some going as high as 28 a month. The Defense Department eventually decided that a pilot could not fly more than two complete deployments within a 14-month period, but even with these restrictions there were individuals who completed over 500 missions. More pilots were training, but it was 18 months, the normal training cycle for a pilot to earn his wings, before any improvement would be felt. In March, the monsoon abated slightly and the air crews welcomed the clearer weather, but better weather meant increased operations in March and April. Loss rates climbed as strikes against the industrialized areas of the North increased. During April North Vietnam was divided into target areas with the Navy assuming responsibility for the coastal areas, especially Haiphong. Crews could get to know the defenses of their areas and plan to avoid them as much as possible.

Responding to General Westmoreland's request for more carrier air support for American ground forces in the South, the ASW carrier *Intrepid* was designated a "limited attack carrier" and began operating on Dixie Station in May 1966 after having traded her S-2 Trackers, SH-3 helicopters, and E-1 Tracers for 28 A-4 Skyhawks and 24 A-1 Skyraiders. She began her first strikes against the Viet Cong on 15 May and, over the next two months, flew over 5,000 sorties, earning the personal praise of General Westmoreland.

In March, the first MiG-21s had been sighted and more MiG-17s were appearing, but it was not until 12 June that the first MiG kill was scored by an F-8, when a pilot from the *Hancock* scored one kill and one probable kill out of four MiG-17s encountered while escorting A-4s. Another *Hancock* pilot scored again nine days later, after a prolonged chase.

At the end of June Secretary of Defense Robert S. McNamara

announced the beginning of a campaign directed against the North's petroleum facilities. The POL (for Petroleum, Oil, and Lubricants) campaign, known as Rolling Thunder 50, marked a new and more dangerous phase of the air war as the oil and industrial areas in the northeast were attacked. The POL campaign continued throughout 1966 and into 1967. Large strikes in July and August took out major parts of the Communist facilities, including transportation equipment, such as trucks, rolling stock, and barges. Strikes from the *Franklin D. Roosevelt* (CVA-42), *Constellation* (CVA-64), *Ranger* (CVA-61), and *Hancock* ranged from the DMZ to Haiphong. During September and October, the *Intrepid* joined the carriers from Yankee Station to hit Ninh Binh, Than Hoa, and Phy Ly. On 9 October 1966, an F-8 from the *Intrepid* scored the Navy's first victory over a MiG-21. Although the crews were elated that they could finally hit the right targets, their efforts were a year too late. The North Vietnamese had used the time to cache much of their oil supply in underground bunkers and tanks. The free zone around Hanoi, in which no bombs could be dropped for fear of hitting population centers, and the restrictions on striking ports such as Haiphong for fear of hitting foreign ships, remained. Despite American efforts, the North was determined to carry on the war.

On 26 October 1966, the *Oriskany* fell victim to the threat that all carriers face—fire. As two sailors returned some unused flares after a strike, one of the flares ignited. Panicking, one of the sailors threw the flare into a locker. The resulting fire spread to the nearby hangar bay, setting off other ordnance. Flame and smoke spread through four levels, reaching officer staterooms and trapping pilots just returned from the mission. Forty-four men died, including the air wing commander. Two helicopters were destroyed and four A-4s damaged. The *Oriskany* made her way to the Philippines for repairs and then on to the San Francisco Naval Shipyard for major work.[14]

At the beginning of 1967, air-to-air combat picked up, with the Air Force tangling with MiGs over North Vietnam. The MiG activity died down, but resumed in March. Airfields could no longer be kept off limits and on 24 April, the airfield at Kep, 37 miles northeast of Hanoi, was struck by the *Kitty Hawk* and *Bon Homme Richard.* The runway was damaged along with several MiGs on the ground. F-4s from the *Kitty Hawk* downed two MiG-17s as they took off to intercept; two more MiGs fell to the F-8s from the *Bon Homme Richard.* As the Air Force struck air bases in the North, April and May became periods of intense air-to-air combat as MiGs rose to challenge the strike groups. Except for the two MiGs scored by the *Kitty Hawk* on 24 April, all of the kills scored by the Navy during this period were by aircraft from the *Bon Homme Richard.* One of the two MiG-17s scored on 1 May was brought down with Zuni rockets by an A-4 pilot who had joined the landing pattern above a Communist airfield. The other MiG kill, and the other four scored in May, were by F-8s.[15] After several losses, the North Vietnamese again laid low until resupplied by the Soviets and the Chinese. The MiGs reappeared in August.

Early in 1967, the decision was made to begin mining selected rivers as the mounting air attacks on road and rail traffic forced the Communists to shift more to the rivers leading into the South.[16] In March, the new Walleye television-guided air-to-surface glide bomb made its combat debut when A-4s from the *Bon Homme Richard* attacked the military barracks at Sam Son on 11 March. *Ticonderoga* was also active throughout this period, hitting industrial facilities such as POL depots and power plants. Bridges became a favorite target. But although they formed a major part of the Vietnamese road system, they proved to be extraordinarily difficult targets. They were not only difficult to hit and destroy, but were also heavily defended and therefore costly targets. The resourcefulness shown by the North Vietnamese in repairing damaged bridges or bypassing them added to the frustration. The emphasis on bridges was due in part to the prohibition on attacking Hanoi and Haiphong. If Haiphong, a center of supply operations, could not be hit, then it could at least be isolated by destroying approaches outside the main area. As the months wore on, attacks on bridges, roads, and canals, were met with intense flak. At one point, Haiphong apparently ran out of ammunition as striking aircraft met no SAMs and only light flak. The respite lasted for two days before weather precluded strikes for the next three. When the rain cleared and operations resumed, so did the flak and missiles. Haiphong had been resupplied.

At the height of this effort, the *Oriskany* stood by to help another victim of fire. On the morning of 29 July, the *Forrestal* (CVA-59), an East Coast carrier on her first deployment to Vietnam, was preparing to launch her second strike of the day when a Zuni rocket from an F-4 on the aft end of the flight deck accidentally fired into the fuel tank of an A-4. In the resulting fire and explosions, 134 men had lost their lives, 21 aircraft were destroyed, and 43 others damaged.

With the *Forrestal* heavily damaged and out of action, the *Constellation* (CVA-64), *Oriskany,* and *Intrepid* continued to hit bridges, depots, SAM sites, and airfields before the monsoon set in. On 21 August, some 80 SAMs were fired in response to major strikes from the *Constellation, Intrepid,* and *Oriskany* which hit supply depots, rail yards, and airfields. *Oriskany* also hit torpedo boat bases near Haiphong in August, sinking three vessels. The *Constellation, Oriskany,* and *Intrepid* were joined by the *Coral Sea* in September. By November the rains and fog had returned and only the A-6 Intruders flew regularly. Intensive mining efforts were made to deter supply traffic as much as possible before the upcoming Christmas bombing halt. Although MiG activity remained constant, only three MiGs fell to Navy fighters in the last three months of 1967. In December the *Ranger* arrived on Yankee Station with a new aircraft, the Vought A-7 Corsair II. The A-7 bore a superficial resemblance to the F-8, but was an entirely new design. It was shorter (the engine did not have an afterburner) and its wing did not have the variable incidence feature of the Crusader. With six underwing pylons, two "cheek" attachment points on the fuselage for Sidewinders, and 20mm cannon in the nose, the Corsair was heavily armed. It was intended to replace the A-4 Skyhawk, but the two aircraft continued to operate side by side during the war.

Over the Christmas stand down, reconnaissance flights confirmed that a massive supply effort into the South was under way and that something big was being planned. When the New Year's truce period ended, strikes were launched to staunch the flow of men and supplies. F-8s from the *Oriskany* even used heat-seeking Sidewinder air-to-air missiles to attack rail traffic; the Sidewinder proved to be very effective against locomotives. From 2-11 January, aircraft from *Oriskany, Ranger,* and *Coral Sea* struck bridges around Hanoi and Haiphong, SAM sites, and storage depots. During that same month an incident occurred that momentarily diverted American attention from the war in Vietnam.

The Pueblo Incident

On 22 January 1968, the intelligence gathering ship *Pueblo* was seized by the North Koreans in the Sea of Japan and her crew imprisoned. In response, the *Enterprise,* en route to Vietnam, was diverted to act as the flagship of Task Force 71. Task Force 71 remained in the Sea of Japan as a contingency force. By the time the *Enterprise,* relieved by the *Kitty Hawk* on 6 February, arrived off Vietnam, the North's invasion of the South had begun.

Tet and Khe Sanh

On 30 January 1968, the day before the Vietnamese holiday of Tet, the Viet Cong struck at several points in South Vietnam—Nha Trang, Pleiku, Da Nang, and Qui Nhon—and even penetrated the American embassy in Saigon the next day, only to be repulsed. The Tet offensive was primarily a land campaign with little air or naval involvement. Within two weeks the Communists lost thousands of men and had failed to rally the South Vietnamese people to their cause. In the northwest, however, the camp at Khe Sanh was fighting for its life. American forces had occupied Khe Sanh, only six miles from the Laotian border, since 1962. An important block to Communist supplies coming south from Laos, it was reinforced by Marines in January 1967. The Communists began their attacks on 21 January 1968 and for the next 71 days, in a siege reminiscent of Dienbienphu, the Marines held on. Overwhelming American air superiority, including B-52s used in a tactical role, eventually prevailed. When the siege of Khe Sanh was lifted in April, President Johnson imposed a partial bombing halt that prohibited attacks north of the 20th parallel in order to motivate the Communists for projected peace talks. (Only the southernmost part of North Vietnam was below the 20th parallel.)

The Tet offensive, while a military failure, was a political victory, and served to divide American opinion on the conduct of the war. Some wanted to reinforce our troops in Vietnam, others wanted the United States to disengage. President Johnson decided that reinforcement was not the answer and felt a dialogue between the Communists, the South Vietnamese, and the Americans was the only way to resolve the conflict. He announced that he would not seek reelection in 1968 and, in a misguided gesture of good faith, imposed the partial bombing halt on 31 March. With the restrictions imposed on attacking the North, tangles with MiGs were rare. The first Navy victory did not come until 26 June, when a *Bon Homme Richard* F-8 returning from an escort mission shot down a MiG-21. On 19

September, an F-8 from the *Intrepid* scored the last confirmed Crusader kill of the war.[17] The year 1968 also marked the end of the venerable A-1 Skyraider's career. Known affectionately as the "Spad," the propeller-driven workhorse could no longer survive in the dangerous skies over Vietnam and was supplanted by the A-7.[18]

The Communists used the partial bombing halt to their advantage and continued to press their attacks in the South. President Johnson, in response to mounting criticism of the war at home, imposed a complete bombing halt on North Vietnam on 1 November. When Richard M. Nixon was inaugurated as president in January 1969, he was left with few options in light of the stalemate in Vietnam and the antiwar sentiment at home. During the first half of 1969, operations concentrated on South Vietnam as the bombing halt imposed the year before was observed. By February four carriers were on station: *Hancock, Kitty Hawk, Ranger,* and *Coral Sea,* but the *Hancock* left mid-month. The *Ticonderoga,* coming back on station, brought two new A-7 squadrons to Vietnam, the first equipped with the A-7B version.

The beginning of 1969 saw another major carrier flight deck fire. On 14 January, the nuclear-powered *Enterprise* was conducting exercises off Hawaii when a Zuni on an F-4 ignited during startup procedures. Within minutes, the fire reached major proportions, but was brought under control within three hours. Twenty-eight men died and 15 aircraft were destroyed.[19]

Withdrawal

The bombing halt continued, but on 5 June, strikes into North Vietnam were launched in retaliation for the downing of an RF-8 reconnaissance Crusader. Three days later, President Nixon, during a meeting with South Vietnamese President Thieu, announced that a phased withdrawal of American troops would begin. Twenty-five thousand men were withdrawn from South Vietnam by the end of August and, over the next year, over 100,000 troops were pulled out. The carriers, however, remained on station, hitting targets in the northernmost region of South Vietnam, the I Corps area. In August, the North Vietnamese unexpectedly released three prisoners of war and the brutal treatment suffered by the POWs was confirmed. Although air operations continued, encounters with MiGs were infrequent. The next Navy MiG kill was not until 28 March 1970, when an F-4 from the *Constellation* brought down a MiG-21. This happened just three days after the *Hancock* with her F-8 Crusaders had left the line. The F-8 pilots, always in a friendly rivalry with the F-4 crews of the big deck carriers, were convinced that the Communists were more afraid of the F-8.

In the new year of 1970, the war went on much as before as the withdrawal of ground forces continued. The *Bon Homme Richard,* after completing her sixth combat deployment in November, was scheduled for decommissioning by mid-1971, leaving the *Hancock* and *Oriskany* as the only "Twenty-Seven Charlie" (SCB-27C) *Essex* class carriers still in combat. The *Oriskany* made her fifth combat cruise with two A-7 squadrons replacing her three squadrons of A-4s.

Cambodia and Laos

In March 1970, a military coup in Cambodia deposed Prince Norodom Sihanouk while he was in Moscow seeking to reduce Communist activity in his country. General Lon Nol took over the government and requested American help in dealing with Viet Cong infiltration and camps in Cambodia. By the end of April a full-scale invasion, spearheaded by South Vietnamese troops, was under way. The campaign did not stop the Communists from using Cambodia and only served to intensify antiwar protests within the United States.

Although the bombing halt of November 1968 ended attacks over North Vietnam, operations neither stopped nor diminished, they merely shifted to the infiltration routes through Laos. The routes making up the Ho Chi Minh Trail were subjected to day and night surveillance using an ever increasing number of remote acoustic and seismic sensors. A-4s operating from the *Hancock* were active over Laos in anti-truck attacks and to support Marine ground operations in South Vietnam. Occasionally, retaliatory raids were made into southern North Vietnam. By early 1971, a buildup of North Vietnamese forces in the panhandle region of Vietnam seemed to indicate that an invasion of Cambodia or Laos and South Vietnam was imminent and American help in countering this threat was needed. In February, Operation Lam Son 719, a name that commemorated a Vietnamese victory over the Chinese in the 15th century, was launched as South Vietnamese troops jumped off from Quang Tri province in Southern Vietnam. Under American air cover, South Vietnamese units crossed into Laos. The North Vietnamese put up heavy resistance and in several areas South Vietnamese troops had to be picked up by helicopter under enemy fire. Before March ended, the last South Vietnamese troops had left Laos. Both Hanoi and Saigon claimed victory, but within weeks, the supply routes that had supposedly been disrupted were again carrying traffic south.

The anti-truck campaign in Laos ground on through 1971 as frustrated pilots from the attack squadrons faced daily risks in a futile effort to slow down the flow of supplies to the south. The fighters flew escort for photo missions and stood ready for a MiG threat that never materialized.[20] The stage was set for major North Vietnamese efforts, and, as the new year approached, American air activity was stepped up as protective-reaction raids below the 20th parallel increased. The North Vietnamese brought mobile SAMs into sites near the DMZ and during the last three weeks of 1971, ten American aircraft were lost over Laos and North Vietnam from a variety of combat measures. In February 1972, the *Hancock* joined the *Coral Sea* and *Constellation* off Vietnam; her A-4 squadrons flew missions day and night as part of the anti-truck campaign.

The Easter Invasion

On 30 March 1972, the Thursday before Good Friday, three North Vietnamese divisions pushed through the DMZ to kick off the long awaited invasion of South Vietnam. Twelve of the North's 13 regular divisions, with over 120,000 troops, were eventually sent into South Vietnam and, as the South's troops fell back under heavy pressure, the North used tanks in significant numbers for the first time in the war. In response, B-52 Arc Light operations

expanded almost immediately and Marine air squadrons that had left South Vietnam were returned. Only the *Coral Sea* and *Hancock* were on station in the Gulf of Tonkin; the *Constellation* was on her way to Hong Kong, but was recalled. The *Kitty Hawk* soon joined, while the *Enterprise* was on duty in the Indian Ocean. The *Saratoga,* the first carrier to be redesignated under the "CV concept" was recalled from the Atlantic fleet in April and others were transiting the Pacific.[21] By July, six carriers were off Vietnam: *America, Hancock, Kitty Hawk, Midway, Oriskany,* and *Saratoga.* This was the greatest number of carriers on station during the war. The carriers hit targets in the North and South; the *Hancock,* still flying A-4s, concentrated on truck and troop positions in the South, leaving the AAA sites, bunkers, and supply depots to the more sophisticated A-7s and A-6s from the big deck carriers. The *Oriskany* did not have an easy time during her last combat cruise. A faulty screw swung her into the ammunition ship *Nitro* during a night replenishment, damaging her starboard aircraft elevator. She continued operations, but had to put into Yokosuka, Japan for major repairs when she lost a screw during the same line period.

Linebacker

For two years, in public and secret meetings with the North Vietnamese, Dr. Henry Kissinger, President Nixon's National Security Advisor, had tried to get the North to agree to a ceasefire. Le Doc Tho, the North's representative, played for time, alternately agreeing, then disagreeing with American negotiators. In May, after the North had unleashed a major attack, Dr. Kissinger, after a frustrating session with Le Doc Tho, reported to the president that the Communists were intransigent. Faced with an upcoming summit meeting with Soviet leader Leonid Brezhnev, presidential elections, and the strong possibility of public outrage at home, President Nixon decided to take the gamble and ordered the mining of North Vietnamese ports to cut off the supply of materiel into the South. On 8 May A-6s from three carriers mined the waters of Haiphong, Hon Gai, and Cam Pha to the north and Thanh Hoa, Vinh Quang Khe, and Dong Hoi in the southern part of North Vietnam. The strikes against the North had been given the name Freedom Train, but now, with the mining operations, the air offensive was given the code name of Linebacker. The effort was more intense than the previous Rolling Thunder operations and the Communists were pushed back by the South Vietnamese backed by American air power. The North began to show signs of willingness to negotiate.

The October 1972 Paris peace talks produced little; the North Vietnamese were again unwilling to agree to a ceasefire once President Nixon had halted bombing north of the 20th parallel. Instead, they used the respite to resupply and rebuild their defenses. In December, their delegation walked out of the negotiations. With few choices left, President Nixon ordered a maximum bombing effort directed at the Hanoi-Haiphong area. Linebacker II began on 18 December with waves of Air Force B-52s and F-111s. Before the B-52s struck, the Navy sent in airfield suppression strikes, particularly at Kep, the main MiG base in the Hanoi area. By the end of December, the North

Vietnamese showed a willingness to negotiate in earnest and returned to the peace talks. On 23 January 1973, a ceasefire was announced. America would have "peace with honor"—for the time being.

Eagle Pull and Frequent Wind

The ceasefire did not end the war itself. North Vietnam and the United States had agreed on ending the fighting, returning prisoners of war, and clearing the mines from North Vietnamese harbors, but Cambodia and Laos continued fighting against Communist insurgents. While Americans continued withdrawal from Vietnam and the POWs returned home, strikes were flown into Laos. The capital of Cambodia, Phnom Penh, was under siege; its only access routes to the outside were through convoys of ships along the Mekong River. The Communists protested American strikes supporting the convoys as violations of the Paris peace accords; the American response was to halt mineclearing operations. By June all sides agreed to better enforcement of the ceasefire and by August American strikes had stopped. Laos accepted a coalition government and Cambodia was left to fend for itself. The Communists had only to wait until American support was too little to make any difference. The end came in 1975. Cambodia fell first, as the Khmer Rouge, along with thousands of North Vietnamese and Viet Cong troops, put the final strangle hold around Phnom Penh. On 12 April Marine helicopters operating off the *Hancock* evacuated the American embassy in Operation Eagle Pull. The Communists swept up city after city in

South Vietnam and by the end of the month were at the outskirts of Saigon. During Operation Frequent Wind, thousands of Americans and their South Vietnamese allies were evacuated during the "night of the helicopters," 29-30 April. North Vietnamese tanks rolled through the gates of the Presidential Palace in Saigon the next morning.

The Mayaguez Incident

After the fall of South Vietnam, there was one final act in America's involvement in Southeast Asia. The American merchant, *S.S. Mayaguez,* was steaming in international waters en route to Thailand when she was boarded on 12 May 1975 and her crew seized by the new Communist government of Cambodia. Following so closely on the heels of the humiliation of the fall of Saigon, President Gerald Ford, who had taken over from President Nixon less than a year before, felt he had to move quickly. On 15 May, a force of Marines was landed by helicopter on Koh Tang, a small island off the Cambodian coast where the crew was believed to be held. Carrier aircraft strikes were sent in to support the Marines. Two of the helicopters had been shot down by the Cambodians before it was learned that the crew had been released. Fifteen men were killed, three missing and 50 wounded. It was a bitter footnote to a long and costly war.[22]

Chapter 18

The End of the Line

Even before the Vietnam War ended, there was less need for large numbers of aircraft carriers and many *Essex* class carriers were either put into mothballs or broken up for scrap. The *Franklin* and *Bunker Hill* never returned to active service after World War II and were reclassified as "auxiliary aircraft transports," AVT, in 1959, along with the *Leyte* and *Philippine Sea*, which were inactivated that year. They were joined by the *Tarawa* two years later. Beginning in the mid-1960s, these carriers were the first to be broken up and, as they were scrapped, their places in the reserve fleet were taken by more modern ships recently withdrawn from active service. The *Essex* class attack carriers dwindled, but a few were kept on until the end of the Vietnam War. The CVS carriers had also operated off Vietnam during the war, operating alongside the attack carriers and supporting the Seventh Fleet by monitoring Soviet and Chinese submarine activity in the area. A-4 Skyhawks often operated as "fighters" on these carriers to give them a limited

strike and self defense capability if needed. Through the late 1960s and early 1970s, the antisubmarine carriers continued to soldier on, even as more of them were decommissioned. Although they did not receive the attention that the attack carriers did, they performed a vital function until supplanted by newer carriers.

1972 was the "Year of the Carrier" and marked the 50th anniversary of the commissioning of the *Langley*. It also marked the introduction of the "CV concept" where the large deck carriers would embark a new jet antisubmarine aircraft, the S-3 Viking, and more capable antisubmarine versions of the SH-3 Sea King helicopter. This was a return to the "general purpose" carrier and, as the big deck carriers were modernized, the specialized antisubmarine carriers were decommissioned. The *Essex* class attack carriers could not operate the F-4 Phantom, A-6 Intruder, and E-2 Hawkeye, which had become the main aircraft in the air wings on the larger and newer carriers. With the end of the

Vietnam War, those *Essex* class carriers that had been extended beyond their expected service lives were now deactivated. By 1976 all had been withdrawn from active service except the *Lexington,* which had replaced the *Antietam* as a training carrier in 1962.[1]

Museum Ships

With so many decommissioned aircraft carriers now available, there were several efforts to save individual ships as memorials or museums. For a variety of reasons, it is no simple matter for the Navy to turn a warship over to an organization. The vessel in question must meet certain criteria, such as availability, historic significance, and restorability, and a suitable site must be found and approved. Organizations must demonstrate that they can meet the financial requirements and that all environmental concerns have been addressed.[2] Efforts to resolve these difficulties often take years and are not always successful in the end.

The first of the *Essex* class carriers to successfully become a museum ship was the *Yorktown.* The *Yorktown,* known as "The Fighting Lady," was redesignated CVS-10 in 1957 and decommissioned in 1970. She was struck from the Navy list in 1973 and towed from New Jersey to Charleston in 1975. She is now the centerpiece of the Patriots Point Naval and Maritime Museum in South Carolina. Several vintage aircraft are on display on her flight and hangar decks and other spaces have been converted to house displays and exhibits. The Patriots Point complex also includes the nuclear-powered ship *Savannah,* the *Sumner* class destroyer *Laffey,* the submarine *Clamagore,* and the Coast Guard cutter *Ingham.*

In August 1982, after a five-year campaign, the *Intrepid* was opened as a museum in New York City. Since then the submarine *Growler* and the destroyer *Edson* have been added. The *Intrepid* Sea Air Space Museum is located on Manhattan's Westside at 46th Street and the Hudson River. "The Fighting I" has a large collection of aircraft from various periods, most notably an SR-71 Blackbird reconnaissance aircraft.

Other than the *Lexington* and the museum ships, the only other *Essex* class carriers left as the 1980s closed were those still awaiting final disposition at the Puget Sound Naval Shipyard in Bremerton, Washington: the *Bennington, Oriskany,* and *Hornet.* The *Oriskany,* decommissioned in 1976, was the object of an offer in 1991 from a group of Japanese investors to purchase the ship for about $2 million, its scrap-metal value, in order to make it the center of a $150 million cultural center in Yokohama Harbor. The project drew criticism from various veterans groups and did not get far, although talks continued into 1993. The *Hornet* was considered for a museum ship to be located in Tacoma, Washington, but this proposal also fell through. The *Bennington* was offered for sale as scrap, but due to the high cost of environmental cleanup, the bids were not satisfactory. She has since been offered up for scrap again.[3]

The "Lady Lex"

The last *Essex* class carrier in service, the *Lexington,* was decommissioned in 1991, having served as the Navy's training carrier for 27 years. On 8 November, a cold and windy overcast day, 13 former commanding officers of the *Lexington* watched as her commissioning pennant was struck. Captain William "Bill" Kennedy, her last skipper, presided over the ceremonies. The Chief of Naval Operations, Admiral Frank B. Kelso II, was the principal speaker and Vice Admiral Dick Dunleavy, the Assistant Chief of Naval Operations (Air Warfare), read the decommissioning directive. Other dignitaries on the platform made brief remarks.[4] When the orders to "march off the crew, haul down division colors, secure the watch" were given, *Lexington*'s officers, chief petty officers and sailors began marching down the gangway. A T-2 Buckeye training jet in the orange and white colors of the Naval Air Training Command flew by. Taps played as the commissioning pennant was lowered, to be presented to the Commanding Officer by the Command Master Chief. The ship's log and spyglass were also presented to the C.O. In tribute to those who served aboard the Lexington over her 48-year career, came fly-bys of an F4F-3 Wildcat, a group of SNJ Texan trainers, and the Blue Angels. For virtually every Naval Aviator now on active duty, as for countless others before them, the *Lexington* was the first carrier they had ever flown from. The last *Essex* class carrier on active service is now the latest, and last, to be saved for history. Although her home port was Pensacola, Florida, the *Lexington* often operated out of Corpus Christi, Texas, which is where she was opened to the public as a museum ship in October 1992.

It is ironic, that so few *Essex* class carriers have been saved for posterity out of the 24 that were built. Their careers have spanned three wars and they have gone from propeller-driven aircraft into the jet age and the space age. Their very success was the reason for building the newer carriers that followed, carriers which eventually replaced them when they simply became too small, too cramped, and too old to operate the latest generation of carrier aircraft. The *Essex* class design began at a time when the aircraft carrier had not proven itself as the new capital ship of the world's navies and they embodied several design compromises— they were not the best ships that could have been built, but they were the right ships, at the right time, and in large enough numbers to overwhelm their opponents in the largest naval battles in history. None of them were lost in combat, although many were grievously damaged, and they are all the more remarkable for their later adaptability to new requirements and new roles. For many, the words "aircraft carrier" will always conjure up an image of an *Essex* class carrier, steaming into the wind to launch her aircraft.

Technical Data

***Essex* (CV-9) Characteristics—December 1942**

Length (overall):	872'0" (888'0" in "long hull" ships)
Length (waterline):	820'0"
Beam (extreme):	147'6"
Beam (waterline):	93'0"
Flight Deck:	862' x 108'
Hangar Deck:	654' x 70'
Elevators:	2 48'3" x 44'3" (capacity 28,000 lbs.)
	1 60'0" x 34'0" (capacity 18,000 lbs.)
Catapults:	1 H 4A, 1 H 4B (2 H 4B in later ships*)
Arresting Gear:	Mk 4
Design Standard Displacement:	27,500 tons
Design Displacement:	33,400 tons
Design Full Load:	36,380 tons
Draft:	26' (optimum battle); 27'6" (full load)
Machinery:	8 Babcock & Wilcox boilers (565 psi, 850 F.)
	4 1,250 kW ships service turbine generators
	2 250 kW diesel generators
Shaft Horsepower:	150,000 (design); 154,054 (trial)
Fuel Capacity:	6,330 tons (design)
Speed:	33 knots (design); 32.93 knots (trial)
Endurance:	20,000 nautical miles at 15 knots (design)
	15,440 nautical miles at 15 knots (service)
Tactical Diameter:	765 yards at 30 knots

Armament:	12 5"/38 (4 x 2, 4 x 1)
	32 40mm (8 x 4)
	(up to 72 40mm [18 x 4] in later ships)
	46 20mm (up to 60 20mm in later ships)
Fire Control System:	2 Mk 37; 8 Mk 51 **
Protection:	Flight deck, gallery deck - none
	Hangar deck - 2.5" STS
	Protective deck(s) - 1.5" STS
	Armor belt - 4" tapered to 2.5" (508' x 10')
	Bulkheads - 4"
	Conning tower - 1.5" STS top
	- 1" STS side of pilot house
	Steering gear - 2.5" deck
Aircraft:	36 F6F fighters
	37 SB2C bombers
	18 TBF torpedo bombers
Aviation Ordnance:	625.5 tons
Aviation Gasoline:	231,650 gals.
Complement (ship & air group):	268 officer; 2,363 enlisted

Notes

* *Essex* completed without catapults; only *Yorktown, Intrepid, Hornet, Bunker Hill,* and *Wasp* were
    completed with H 4A hangar deck catapult.

** Mk 51 directors added as 40mm mounts increased; some Mark 51 directors were replaced by Mk
    57 or Mk 63 directors.

SCB-27A

This was the first *Essex* class modernization program and was carried out on CV-9, CV-10, CV-12, CV-15, CV-18, CV-20, CV-33, and CV-39 between 1948 and 1953. (CV-34 was completed to SCB-27A standard in 1950.) The principal features of SCB-27A included: removal of the side belt armor and replacing it with a hull blister which increased the beam at the waterline to 101 feet; removal of the island twin 5-inch turrets and relocation of the new open 5-inch mounts to the starboard side along the edge of the flight deck; modifications to the island which replaced the tripod mast with a single pole mast and redesigned the smokestack; strengthening the flight deck in the landing area; installation of larger and more powerful elevators; replacement of the H-4-1 hydraulic catapults with H-8 hydraulic catapults capable of launching aircraft up to 40,000 pounds gross weight; more powerful bomb and ammunition elevators; equipment for the handling of jet aircraft, including jet blast deflectors behind the catapults; increased aviation fuel capacity; installation of higher capacity aircraft cranes; three ready rooms relocated below the hangar deck; installation of an escalator along the starboard side of the island for aircrew to reach the flight deck; and division of the hangar deck space by two fireproof steel doors.

SCB-27C

The SCB-27C program was a further refinement of the SCB-27A program. The SCB-27C ships fall into two groups: the first group (CV-11, CV-14, and CV-19) received the basic SCB-27C modifications between 1951 and 1954; the second (CV-16, CV-31, and CV-38) received an advanced SCB-27C that included most of the features of the later SCB-125 program. The principal features of the basic SCB-27C that differed from SCB-27A included: a revised hull blister which increased the waterline beam to 103 feet; installation of two C-11 steam catapults; strengthening the flight deck; replacement of the number three elevator with a starboard side deck edge unit (this required moving the starboard side open 5-inch guns further aft to a position opposite the port side guns); and installation of a stronger arresting gear system.

SCB-125

SCB-125 introduced the angled deck and enclosed "hurricane" bow to the *Essex* class. Three groups were covered by SCB-125. The first (CV-16, CV-31, and CV-38 as mentioned above) received both their SCB-27C and SCB-125 modifications in one dockyard period between 1951 and 1955. The second group (CV-11, CV-14, and CV-19) included those SCB-27C ships brought up to SCB-125 standards during a later dockyard period between 1955 and 1957. These ships were also given longer (70-feet 3-inches) forward centerline elevators. The third group (CV-9, CV-10, CV-12, CV-15, CV-18, CV-20, CV-33) included SCB-27A ships which did not get all the features that the SCB-27C ships did. (CV-39 was the only SCB-27A ship that did not get the SCB-125 modernization. CV-34 is covered under SCB-125/A below.) Apart from the hurricane bow and angled deck, the principal features of the SCB-125 included: installation of the improved Mark 7 dual arrestor wire system with half the cross-deck pendants of the previous systems; introduction of air conditioning in some spaces; strengthening of the crash barriers; primary flight control (prifly) was moved to the aft edge of the island, two decks high; better soundproofing of the island; and improved deck lighting. (*Antietam*'s angled deck installation was not considered part of the SCB-125 modernization program.)

SCB-125A

This modernization program was a one-of-a-kind effort that brought the *Oriskany* (CV-34) up to full SCB-27C and SCB-125 standard. CV-34 was the last ship to receive the SCB-27C modernization (1959) and many features were improved over the older SCB-27C ships. Besides the angled deck, hurricane bow, C-11 steam catapults, and lengthened centerline elevator, CV-34 had a light metal cladding for the flight deck and an arresting gear system that was stronger than on the older SCB-27C ships.

SCB-144

SCB-144 was part of the Navy Fleet Rehabilitation and Modernization (FRAM) II program intended to improve the ASW capability of the SCB-27A CVS carriers. All the SCB-144 FRAM II modernizations were completed by 1965. The principal modifications included: installation of the SQS-23 bow-mounted sonar dome; installation of a stem hawsepipe and bow anchor; and modifications to the Combat Information Center.

Characteristics of World War II *Essex* Carriers
(listed in order of commissioning)

Name / Builder / Commissioned	Hull Type	Bridge Type		Catapults Flight Deck			SK Radar			SK-2
		Early	Late	Hangar	Stbd	Port	Mast Top	Stbd Stack	Plat Aft	
CV-9 *Essex* Newport News 31 Dec 42	Short	12/42	4/44	–	4/44	4/44	12/42	4/44	–	3/45
CV-16 *Lexington* Bethlehem, Quincy 17 Feb 43	Short	2/43	5/45	–	3/43	12/43	–	2/43	–	5/45
CV-10 *Yorktown* Newport News 15 Apr 43	Short	4/43	9/44	4/43	4/43	9/44	–	4/43*	–	–
CV-17 *Bunker Hill* Bethlehem, Quincy 24 May 43	Short	5/43	1/45	5/43	5/43	1/45	–	5/43	–	–
CV-11 *Intrepid* Newport News 16 Aug 43	Short	8/43	6/44	8/43	8/43	6/44	8/43	11/43	6/44	–
CV-18 *Wasp* Bethlehem, Quincy 24 Nov 43	Short	11/43	6/45	11/43	11/43	6/45	–	11/43	–	4*
CV-12 *Hornet* Newport News 29 Nov 43	Short	11/43	9/45	11/43	11/43	9/45	–	–	11/43	9/45
CV-13 *Franklin* Newport News 31 Jan 44	Short	1/44	5/44	1/44*	1/44	1/45-	–	1/44	1/45	–
CV-19 *Hancock* Bethlehem, Quincy 15 Apr 44	Long	–	4/44	–	4/44	4/44	–	–	4/44	–
CV-14 *Ticonderoga* Newport News 8 May 44	Long	–	5/44	–	5/44	5/44	–	–	5/44	4/45
CV-20 *Bennington* New York, NY 6 Aug 44	Short	–	8/44	–	8/44	8/44	–	–	–	8/44*

Characteristics of World War II *Essex* Carriers
(continued)

Radio Masts	Port FD (A)	Bow One (B)	Two (B)	Stern One (C)	Two (C)	Island Four (D)	Three (D)	Port Spon (E)	Stbd Aft (F)	Stbd Three (G)	FD Pt Two (H)
			Quad 40mm Antiaircraft Mounts								
5	12/42	12/42	–	12/42	–	12/42	4/44	4/44	4/44	–	–
5*	2/43	2/43	–	2/43	2/43	2/43	5/45	2/43	12/43	5/45	5/45
5*	4/43	4/43	–	4/43	9/44	4/43	9/44	9/44	6/43	9/44	9/44
5*	5/43	5/43	–	5/43	1/45	5/43	1/45	1/45	5/43	1/45	1/45
4*	8/43	8/43	–	8/43	2/45	8/43	6/44	6/44	8/43	6/44	6/44
4*	11/43	11/43	–	11/43	6/45	11/43	6/45	6/45	11/43	6/45	6/45
4*	11/43	11/43	–	11/43	9/45	11/43	9/45?	9/45	11/43	9/45	9/45
4*	1/44	1/44	–	1/44	/45	1/44	1/45	1/45	1/45	1/45	1/45
4*	4/44	–	4/44	–	4/44	–	4/44	6/45	6/45	6/45	6/45
4*	5/44	–	5/44	–	5/44	–	5/44	5/44	4/45	4/45?	4/45
4	8/44	–	8/44	–	8/44	–	8/44	8/44	–	–	–

Characteristics of World War II *Essex* Carriers
(continued)

Name Builder Commissioned	Hull Type	Bridge Type		Catapults Flight Deck			SK Radar			SK-2
		Early	Late	Hangar	Stbd	Port	Mast Top	Stbd Stack	Plat Aft	
CV-38 *Shangri-La* Norfolk; NY 15 Sep 44	Long	–	9/44	–	9/44	9/44	–	–	–	9/44*
CV-15 *Randolph* Newport News 9 Oct 44	Long	–	10/44	–	10/44	10/44	–	–	–	10/44
CV-31 *Bon Homme Richard* New York, NY 26 Nov 44	Short	–	11/44	–	11/44	11/44	–	–	–	11/44
CV-36 *Antietam* Philadelphia; NY 28 Jan 45	Long	–	1/45	–	1/45	1/45	–	–	–	1/45
CV-21 *Boxer* Newport News 16 Apr 45	Long	–	4/45	–	4/45	4/45	–	–	–	4/45
CV-39 *Lake Champlain* Norfolk; NY 3 Jun 45	Long	–	6/45	–	6/45	6/45	–	–	–	6/45
CV-37 *Princeton* Philadelphia; NY 18 Nov 45	Long	–	11/45	–	11/45	11/45	–	–	–	11/45
CV-40 *Tarawa* Norfolk; NY 8 Dec 45	Long	–	12/45	–	12/45	12/45	–	–	–	12/45
CV-33 *Kearsarge* New York, NY 2 Mar 46	Long	–	3/46	–	3/46	3/46	–	–	–	3/46
CV-32 *Leyte* Newport News 11 Apr 46	Long	–	4/46	–	4/46	4/46	–	–	–	4/46
CV-47 *Philippine Sea* Bethlehem, Quincy 11 May 46	Long	–	5/46	–	5/46	5/46	–	–	–	5/46

Characteristics of World War II *Essex* Carriers
(continued)

Radio Masts	Port FD (A)	Bow One Two (B)		Stern One Two (C)		Island Four Three (D)		Port Spon (E)	Stbd Aft (F)	Stbd Three (G)	FD Pt Two (H)
				Quad 40mm Antiaircraft Mounts							
4	9/44	–	9/44	–	9/44	–	9/44	9/44	–	–	–
4	10/44	–	10/44	–	10/44	–	10/44	0/44	1/45	1/45	1/45
4	11/44	11/44	11/44	–	11/44	–	11/44	1/44	5/45	5/45	5/45
4	1/45	–	1/45	–	1/45	–	1/45	1/45	–	–	–
4	4/45	–	4/45	–	4/45	–	4/45	4/45	7/45	–	–
4	5/45	–	5/45	–	5/45	–	5/45	6/45	–	–	–
2	11/45	–	11/45	–	11/45	–	11/45	1/45	–	–	–
2	12/45	–	12/45	–	12/45	–	12/45	2/45	–	–	–
2	3/46	–	3/46	–	3/46	–	3/46	3/46	–	–	–
2	4/46	–	4/46	–	4/46	–	4/46	4/46	–	–	–
2	5/46	–	5/46	–	5/46	–	5/46	5/46	–	–	–

Characteristics of World War II *Essex* Carriers
(continued)

Name Builder Commissioned	Hull Type	Bridge Type Early	Late	Catapults Flight Deck Hangar	Stbd	Port	SK Radar Mast Top	Stbd Stack	Plat Aft	SK-2
CV-45 *Valley Forge* Philadelphia; NY 3 Nov 46	Long	–	11/46	–	11/46	11/46	–	–	–	11/46
CV-34 *Oriskany* New York, NY 25 Sep 50	N/A	N/A	N/A	N/A	N/A	N/A	N/A	N/A	N/A	N/A

*See comments in notes for individual ships.

Notes

CV-9 *Essex:* During her only wartime refit in San Francisco in Apr 44, *Essex* received the late style bridge, two 40mm quad mounts on the port side on the former hangar catapult sponson, and two 40mm quad mounts on the hangar deck level on the starboard side aft. *Essex* was the only ship of her class to retain all five radio masts during the war and the only ship to retain the single 40mm quad stern sponson. The two 40mm quad mounts added to the hangar deck on the starboard side aft were never extended outboard as on most other members of her class.

CV-16 *Lexington*: Damaged by a torpedo in Dec 43, *Lexington* was repaired at the Puget Sound Naval Shipyard, Bremerton, WA, Dec 43-Feb 44, where she was fitted with the large stern sponson and the seven "outboard" quad mounts. During her Mar-May 45 refit in Bremerton she finally received the late style bridge and three radio masts were removed, leaving only the forward two.

CV-10 *Yorktown*: During her Aug-Oct 44 refit in Bremerton, *Yorktown* received the late style bridge, the seven outboard quad mounts, three radio masts were removed, and the SK radar was moved to the port side of the smokestack.

CV-17 *Bunker Hill*: During her Nov 44-Jan 45 refit in Bremerton, *Bunker Hill* received the late style island, the seven outboard quad mounts and three radio masts were removed. Severely damaged in May 45, she was repaired in Bremerton and used for "Magic Carpet" operations after the war.

CV-11 *Intrepid*: *Intrepid* was commissioned with the two quad mounts on the starboard hangar deck aft. In Nov 43, the SK radar was moved to the starboard side of the smokestack. Torpedoed in

Feb 44, she was repaired at Hunters Point Naval Shipyard, San Francisco, CA, Mar-Jun 44, when she received the late style bridge, three quad mounts below the island, two on the port catapult sponson and two on the port flight deck aft. The SK radar was moved to the aft end of an extended masthead platform. During Jun-Aug 44 at Pearl Harbor, the forward of the two starboard side hangar deck mounts was moved outboard. Hit by kamikazes in Nov 44, she was again repaired at San Francisco Jan-Feb 45, when the enlarged stern sponson was added and the after starboard quarter quad was moved outboard. Hit by kamikaze Apr 45, she was repaired at San Francisco May-Jul 45. Radio masts were reduced to two in 45.

CV-18 *Wasp*: *Wasp* was commissioned with the two starboard quarter quad mounts. During her Apr-Jun 45 refit at Bremerton, *Wasp* received the late style bridge, the seven outboard quad mounts, the enlarged stern sponson, and the radio masts were reduced to two.

CV-12 *Hornet*: *Hornet* was commissioned with the two starboard quarter quad mounts. She retained her hangar deck catapult and early style bridge into Jun 45 when she was damaged by a typhoon off Japan. She was repaired at San Francisco Jul-Sep 45, when she received the late style bridge, the seven outboard quad mounts, the enlarged stern sponson, and the radio masts were reduced to two.

CV-13 *Franklin*: *Franklin* was completed with the two starboard quarter quad mounts. She received the late style bridge and her hangar deck catapult was removed in May 44 at Norfolk. Damaged by Kamikaze 30 Oct 44, *Franklin* received temporary repairs at Ulithi en route to Bremerton where she

Characteristics of World War II *Essex* Carriers
(continued)

Radio Masts	Port FD (A)	Bow One Two (B)	Stern One Two (C)	Island Four Three (D)	Port Spon (E)	Stbd Aft (F)	Stbd Three (G)	FD Pt Two (H)
2	11/46	– 11/46	– 11/46	– 11/46	1/46	–	–	–
N/A	N/A	N/A N/A	N/A N/A	N/A N/A	N/A	N/A	N/A	N/A

The header row spans: "Quad 40mm Antiaircraft Mounts" over Bow, Stern, Island columns.

was repaired Dec 44-Jan 45 and received a second flight deck catapult, the seven outboard quad mounts, the enlarged stern sponson, and the radio masts were reduced to two. Severely damaged in Mar 45, the three quad mounts below the island were removed for passage through the Panama Canal on her return to New York in Apr 45.

CV-19 *Hancock*: As the first "long hull" in commission, *Hancock* was completed with the late style bridge. She received her seven outboard quad mounts and two radio masts were removed during refit at Pearl Harbor Apr-Jun 45.

CV-14 *Ticonderoga*: Damaged by Kamikaze in Jan 45, *Ticonderoga* received her seven outboard quad mounts and two radio masts were removed during repairs at Bremerton Feb-Apr 45.

CV-20 *Bennington*: Although she was the first "short hull" to be completed with all the wartime improvements, *Bennington* never received the seven outboard quad mounts. As commissioned, the SK-2 radar was at the rear of an extended topmast platform. The SK-2 was moved to the starboard side of the smokestack in Jan 45.

CV-38 *Shangri-La*: *Shangri-La* was commissioned with the SK-2 radar. The positions of the SK-2 and SC-2 radars were reversed in Jan 45.

CV-15 *Randolph*: *Randolph* was commissioned with the SK-2 radar. She was refitted at Hunters Point in Jan 45 when she received the seven outboard quad mounts. These were removed after the war for passage through the Panama Canal.

CV-31 *Bon Homme Richard*: Last of the "short hull" ships to be completed, *Bon Homme Richard* received her seven outboard quad mounts during refit at Pearl Harbor in May 45.

CV-36 *Antietam*: *Antietam* was completed too late for war service (although she was present in Tokyo Bay at the end of the war) and never had the seven outboard quad mounts. Although fitted with an angled deck in 53, she was otherwise unmodernized. She was later fitted with dual funnel caps and a large pole mast similar to the SCB-27 ships.

CV-21 *Boxer*: *Boxer* was completed with four radio masts, but did not have the seven outboard quad mounts.

CV-39 *Lake Champlain*: *Lake Champlain* was the last *Essex* class to be commissioned before the end of the war. She was the only ship modernized to SCB-27 that did not receive the SCB-125 angle deck.

CV-37 *Princeton*: The first of her class to be completed postwar, the *Princeton* was completed without outboard quad mounts, but two on the port side below the island were added later, probably when she was reactivated for service in Korea. She was later fitted with dual funnel caps and a large pole mast similar to the SCB-27 ships.

CV-40 *Tarawa*: *Tarawa* was one of the first of the class to receive the SX radar, which combined the height finder and air search functions.

CV-33 *Kearsarge*: Completed postwar, the *Kearsarge* did not have the outboard quad mounts. She was the only ship of the class completed at the end of the war or afterward to be modernized.

CV-32 *Leyte*: Completed postwar, the *Leyte* did not have the outboard quad mounts. She was later fitted with dual funnel caps and a large pole mast similar to the SCB-27 ships.

CV-47 *Philippine Sea*: Completed postwar, the *Philippine Sea* did not have the outboard quad mounts. She was later fitted with dual funnel caps and a large pole mast similar to the SCB-27 ships.

CV-45 *Valley Forge*: Completed postwar, the *Valley Forge* did not have the outboard quad mounts. She was later fitted with dual funnel caps and a large pole mast similar to the SCB-27 ships.

CV-34 *Oriskany*: *Oriskany* was completed to SCB-27A standard.

Remarks

Armament: As designed, *Essex* class carriers carried 8 40mm quad mounts: 1 at the bow, 1 at the stern in a sponson offset to port, 2 on the port side at flight deck level adjacent to the single 5-inch guns fore and aft, and 4 on the island. Later, when the bridges of the early *Essex* class carriers were modified to increase the flag spaces, the forward island mount was removed, leaving only 3 mounts. Later ships were built with the revised bridge and had only 3 mounts on the island as commissioned. As the hangar deck catapults were removed on the early units, 2 mounts were added at the hangar deck level to the former catapult sponson on the port side. The "long hull" ships, which were built with the later bridge design and without the hangar deck catapult, had 2 mounts at the bow in an extended "clipper" bow and 2 at the stern in a massive sponson for a total of 11 40mm quad mounts. Beginning around mid-1943, 2 mounts were also added at the hangar deck level on the starboard side aft. These were initially fitted in recessed mountings to allow passage through the Panama Canal. On most ships these mounts were later extended outboard to give them better arcs of fire. Some ships also received 3 mounts fitted in detachable sponsons on the starboard side below the island and 2 mounts at the edge of the flight deck on the port side forward of the aft 5-inch and 40mm guns. As the older "short hull" ships received wartime refits, they were given some or all of these additional mounts (including the large stern sponson, but not the clipper bow) so that a "short hull" *Essex* could carry as many a 17 40mm quad mounts and a "long hull" as many as 18. The ships completed postwar had none of the 7 "outboard" mounts and were commissioned with 11 40mm quad mounts.

The *Essex* design called for 44 20mm single mounts, but this was soon changed to 46. The number of 20mm mounts eventually increased to 55 and by 1945, 20mm twin mounts were being introduced. (The *Wasp* and *Lexington* each carried 6 50-caliber machine gun quad mounts based on an Army antiaircraft mounting in 1945 on a trial basis.) With the end of the war, the numbers of 20mm mounts were reduced.

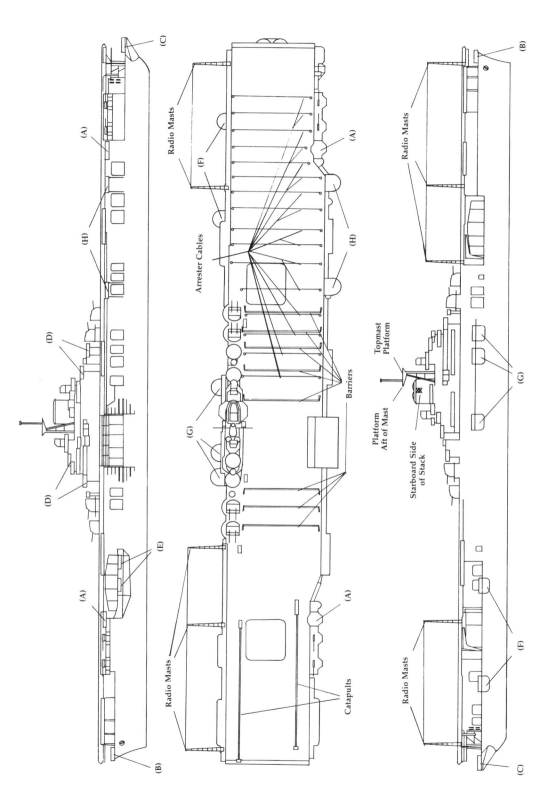

Characteristics of World War II Essex class carriers (see Appendix A table)

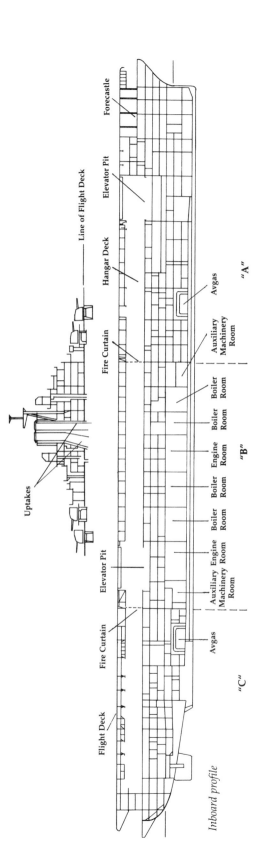

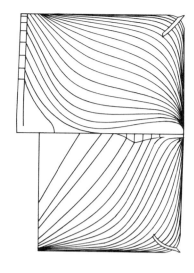

Body plan (long hull)

Uptakes

Line of Flight Deck

Forecastle

Elevator Pit

Hangar Deck

Fire Curtain

Avgas

"A"

Auxiliary
Machinery
Room

Boiler
Room

Boiler
Room

Boiler
Room

Engine
Room

Boiler
Room

Boiler
Room

"B"

Auxiliary
Machinery
Room

Engine
Room

Elevator Pit

Fire Curtain

Avgas

"C"

Flight Deck

Inboard profile

1. Main deck (hangar deck)
2. 2nd deck
3. 3rd deck
4. 4th deck
5. Transverse deck beams
6. Longitudinal deck girders
7. Stringers
8. 4-inch armor belt
9. Bilge keel
10. Outer bottom plating (overlapped and riveted)
11. Outer flat keel
12. Center vertical keel
13. Inner bottom
14. Third bottom
15. 1st backing bulkhead
16. 2nd backing bulkhead
17. 3rd backing bulkhead
18. 4th backing bulkhead
19. Frame support for flight deck foundation
20. Longitudinals (from inboard to outboard: 1st, 2nd, 3rd, 4th, 5th, 6th, and 7th)
21. "I" girder support pillar
22. "I" frame support in holding bulkhead
23. Pillar

(Lightening holes in transverse deck beams and "I" frames omitted for clarity.)

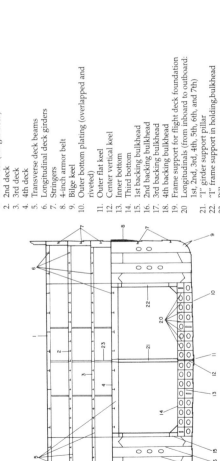

THE ESSEX CLASS CARRIERS

Individual Ships

CV-9 *Essex*

Builder: Newport News; date ordered: Feb 40; contract date: 3 Jul 40; keel laid: 28 Apr 41; launched: 31 Jul 42; commissioned: 31 Dec 42; decommissioned: 9 Jan 47; recommissioned: 1 Feb 51; SCB-27A: 1 Sep 48-1 Feb 51; redesignated CVA-9: 1 Oct 52; SCB-125: 1 Mar 55-1 Mar 56; redesignated CVS-9: 8 Mar 60; FRAM II: FY 62; decommissioned: 30 Jun 69; struck: 15 Jun 75; broken up.

World War II: Bougainville, Gilbert Islands, Kwajalein, Truk raid, Marianas, Palau, Leyte Gulf, Iwo, Pacific raids 1943-45. Hit by Kamikaze 25 Nov 44.

Korea: Three tours: Aug 51-Mar 52, Jun 52-Feb 53, Dec 53-Jul 54 (U.N. Peace Patrol). Damaged by jet crash and fire 16 Sep 51.

Remarks: Known as the "Fightin'est Ship in the Fleet" and "The Oldest and the Boldest." Participated in Lebanon and Formosa crises in 1958, Bay of Pigs invasion in 1961, and Cuban missile crisis quarantine in 1962. Collided with nuclear submarine *Nautilus* SSN-571 off North Carolina coast during ASW exercise 6 Nov 66. Prime recovery ship for Apollo 7 (Schirra, Eisele, Cunningham) 22 Oct 68. Name continued by LHD-2 *Essex* (*Wasp* class amphibious assault ship).

CV-10 *Yorktown*

Builder: Newport News; date ordered: May 40; contract date: 3 Jul 40; keel laid: 1 Dec 41; launched: 21 Jan 43; commissioned: 15 Apr 43; decommissioned: 9 Jan 47; redesignated CVA-10: 1 Oct 52; recommissioned: 2 Jan 53; SCB-27A: 15 Feb 51-2 Jan 53; SCB-125: 31 Jul 54-15 Oct 55; redesignated CVS-10: 9 Jan 57; FRAM II: FY 66; decommissioned: 27 Jun 70; struck: 1 Jun 73; museum ship, SC.

World War II: Gilbert Islands, Kwajalein, Truk raid, Hollandia, Marianas, Iwo, Pacific raids 1943-45.

Vietnam: Three tours as CVS: Feb-Apr 65, Feb-Jul 66, Mar-Jun 68.

Remarks: Laid down as the *Bon Homme Richard* and renamed 26 Sep 42. Known as "The Fighting Lady," the *Yorktown* was featured prominently in the wartime documentary film of the same name and in the 1954 film "Jet Carrier." Participated in naval forces diverted to Sea of Japan during *Pueblo* crisis in 1968. Name continued by CG-48 *Yorktown* (*Ticonderoga* class cruiser).

CV-11 *Intrepid*

Builder: Newport News; date ordered: May 40; contract date: 3 Jul 40; keel laid: 1 Dec 41; launched: 26 Apr 43; commissioned: 16 Aug 43; decommissioned: 22 Mar 47; redesignated CVA-11: 1 Oct 52; SCB-27C: 24 Sep 51-18 Jun 54; recommissioned: 18 Jun 54; SCB-125: 24 Jan 56-2 May 57; redesignated CVS-11: 31 Mar 62; FRAM II: FY 65; decommissioned: 30 Mar 74; struck; museum ship, NY.

World War II: Kwajalein, Truk raid (torpedoed 16 Feb 44), Palau, Leyte Gulf, Pacific raids 1944-45. Severely damaged by kamikazes off Luzon 25 Nov 44 and Okinawa 16 Apr 45.

Vietnam: Three tours as a "special attack" carrier (while retaining CVS designation): May-Nov 66, Jun-Dec 67, and Jul 68-Feb 69.

Remarks: Intrepid was known as the "Evil I," "Hard Luck I," and "Decrepid" for her propensity to attract enemy bombs, torpedoes and kamikazes. Ran aground 9 Dec 43 while transiting Panama Canal. Later known as "Big I" and "The Fighting I." Prime recovery ship for Aurora 7 (Carpenter) 24 May 62 and Gemini 3 (Grissom, Young) 23 Mar 65. Collided with oiler *Sabine* AO-25 on 22 Feb 66.

CV-12 *Hornet*

Builder: Newport News; date ordered: May 40; contract date: 9 Sep 40; keel laid: 3 Aug 42; launched: 29 Aug 43; commissioned: 29 Nov 43; decommissioned: 15 Jan 47; redesignated CVA-12: 1 Oct 52; SCB-27A: 14 Jun 51-1 Oct 53; recommissioned: 1 Oct 53; SCB-125: 24 Aug 55-15 Aug 56; redesignated CVS-12: 27 Jun 58; FRAM II: FY 65; decommissioned: 26 Jun 70; struck: ?

World War II: Marianas, Palau, Leyte Gulf, Iwo, Pacific raids 1944-45. Forward flight deck collapsed during typhoon 5 Jun 45.

Vietnam: Three tours as CVS: Oct 65-Jan 66, May-Oct 67, and Nov 68-Apr 69.

Remarks: Laid down as *Kearsarge* and renamed after CV-8 was lost in the Solomons in Oct 42. While searching for a downed British airliner in the South China Sea, planes from *Hornet* were attacked on 24 Jun 54 by two Chinese communist fighters, both of which were shot down. *Hornet* was also sent to the Sea of Japan in Apr 69 in response to the downing of a U.S. Navy reconnaissance aircraft. Prime recovery ship for Apollo 11 (Armstrong, Aldrin, Collins) 24 Jul 69 and Apollo 12 (Conrad, Bean, Gordon) 24 Nov 69.

CV-13 *Franklin*

Builder: Newport News; date ordered: Aug 40; contract date: 9 Sep 40; keel laid: 7 Dec 42; launched: 14 Oct 43; commissioned: 31 Jan 44; decommissioned: 17 Feb 47; redesignated CVA-13: 1 Oct 52; redesignated CVS-13: 8 Aug 53; redesignated AVT-8: 15 May 59; struck: 1 Oct 64; broken up.

World War II: Guam, Palau, Leyte, Pacific raids 1944-45. Damaged by kamikazes off Luzon 15 and 30 Oct 44. Severely damaged by bombs off Kyushu 19 Mar 45.

Remarks: Known as "Big Ben," *Franklin* was the most heavily damaged carrier to survive enemy attack and was never returned to active service.

CV-14 *Ticonderoga*

Builder: Newport News; date ordered: Aug 40; contract date: 9 Sep 40; keel laid: 1 Feb 43; launched: 7 Feb 44; commissioned: 10 Sep 44; decommissioned: 9 Jan 47; redesignated CVA-14: 1 Oct 52; recommissioned: 1 Oct 54; SCB-27C: 17 Jul 51-1 Oct 54; SCB-125: 7 Nov 55-1 Apr 57; redesignated CVS-14: 21 Oct 69; decommissioned: 1 Sep 73; struck: 16 Nov 73; broken up.

World War II: Palau, Leyte, Pacific raids 1944. Severely damaged by kamikaze off Formosa 21 Jan 45.

Vietnam: Five tours: Aug-Nov 64, Nov 65-May 66, Nov 66-Apr 67, Jan-Jul 68 and Mar-Aug 69. (First ship to complete five Vietnam tours.)

Remarks: Laid down as *Hancock* and renamed 1 May 43. Known as "Big T," "Ti," and "Tico." Prime recovery ship for Apollo 16 (Young, Mattingly, Duke) 27 Apr 72 and Apollo 17 (Cernan, Evans, Schmitt) 19 Dec 72. Name continued by CG-47 *Ticonderoga* (lead ship of a class of guided missile cruisers).

CV-15 *Randolph*

Builder: Newport News; date ordered: Aug 40; contract date: 9 Sep 40; keel laid: 10 May 43; launched: 28 Jun 44; commissioned: 9 Oct 44; decommissioned: 25 Feb 48; redesignated CVA-15: 1 Oct 52; recommissioned: 1 Jul 53; SCB-27A: 22 Jun 51- 1 Jul 53; SCB-125: 1 Mar 55-12 Feb 56; redesignated CVS-15: 31 Mar 59; FRAM II: FY 61; decommissioned: 13 Feb 69; struck: 15 Jun 73; broken up.

World War II: Iwo, Pacific raids 1945.

Hit by kamikaze while at anchor in Ulithi 11 Mar 45. Damaged by crash of Army P-38 while at anchor in Philippines Jun 45.

Remarks: Name *Randolph* requested by memo from President Roosevelt to Secretary of the Navy. Prime recovery ship for Liberty Bell 7 (Grissom) 21 Jul 61 and Friendship 7 (Glenn) 20 Feb 62. (The destroyer *Noa* DD-841 actually recovered Glenn's capsule.) Participated in Cuban missile crisis quarantine in 1962. Lost number three elevator at sea 1 Apr 64; two sailors drowned and S2F Tracker lost.

CV-16 *Lexington*

Builder: Bethlehem Quincy (Fore River); date ordered: Aug 40; contract date: 9 Sep 40; keel laid: 15 Jul 41; launched: 26 Sep 42; commissioned: 17 Mar 43; decommissioned: 23 Apr 47; redesignated CVA-16: 1 Oct 52; SCB-27C and SCB-125: 21 Jul 52-1 Sep 55; recommissioned: 1 Sep 55; redesignated CVS-16: 1 Oct 62; redesignated CVT-16: 1 Jan 69; redesignated AVT-16: 78; decommissioned: 8 Nov 91; struck: ?; museum ship, TX.

World War II: Gilbert Islands, Hollandia, Marianas, Palau, Leyte Gulf (flag), Iwo, Pacific raids 1943-45. Torpedoed off Kwajalein 4 Dec 43. Damaged by kamikaze off Luzon 5 Nov 44.

Remarks: Laid down as *Cabot* and renamed 16 Jun 42. Known as the "The Blue Ghost" during World War II because of her camouflage color and her reported sinking by Tokyo Rose. Participated in Cuban missile crisis quarantine in 1962. As the Navy's training carrier from Dec 62 until her retirement in 1991, "Lady Lex" served longer than any other carrier.

CV-17 *Bunker Hill*

Builder: Bethlehem Quincy (Fore River); date ordered: Aug 40; contract date: 9 Sep 40; keel laid: 15 Sep 41; launched: 7 Dec 42; commissioned: 24 May 43; decommissioned: 9 Jan 47; redesignated CVA-17: 1 Oct 52; redesignated CVS-17: 8 Aug 53; redesignated AVT-9: May 59; struck: 1 Nov 66; broken up.

World War II: Bougainville, Gilbert Islands, Kwajalein, Truk raid, Hollandia, Marianas, Palau, Leyte, Iwo, Pacific raids 1943-45. Severely damaged by kamikaze off Okinawa 11 Apr 45.

Remarks: Called "Holiday Express" by her crew because all her major strikes had occurred on holidays. Although repaired, *Bunker Hill* never returned to active service and was later used as a test bed for various electronic equipment. Name continued by CG-52 *Bunker Hill* (*Ticonderoga* class cruiser).

CV-18 *Wasp*

Builder: Bethlehem Quincy (Fore River); date ordered: Aug 40; contract date: 9 Sep 40; keel laid: 18 Mar 42; launched: 17 Aug 43; commissioned: 24 Nov 43; decommissioned: 17 Feb 47; SCB-27A: 1 Sep 48-28 Sep 51; recommissioned: 28 Sep 51; redesignated CVA-18: 1 Oct 52; SCB-125: 31 Jul 54-1 Dec 55; redesignated CVS-18: 1 Nov 56; FRAM II: FY 64; decommissioned: 1 Jul 72; struck: 1 Jul 72; broken up.

World War II: New Guinea, Marianas, Palau, Leyte, Iwo, Pacific raids 1944-45. Damaged by bomb off Kyushu 19 Mar 45. Forward flight deck damaged by typhoon 25 Aug 45.

Remarks: Laid down as *Oriskany* and renamed 13 Nov 42. En route to Gibralter collided with destroyer minesweeper

Hobson DMS-26 during night flight operations 26 Apr 52. (*Hobson* was split in two and sank with a loss of 176, including her commander.) Bow of *Hornet* used to repair *Wasp*. Participated in Lebanon crisis in 1958 and Cuban missile crisis quarantine in 1962. Prime recovery ship for Gemini 4 (McDivitt, White) 7 Jun 65, Gemini 6A (Schirra, Stafford) and Gemini 7 (Borman, Lovell) 16-18 Dec 65, Gemini 9 (Stafford, Cernan) 6 Jun 66, and Gemini 12 (Lovell, Aldrin) 15 Nov 66. Collided with oiler *Salamonie* AO-26 during underway replenishment (unrep) 24 Mar 67, damaging number three elevator. Minor collision with oiler *Truckee* AO-147 during unrep 12 Jun 68. Name continued by LHD-1 *Wasp* (lead ship of a new class of amphibious assault ships).

CV-19 *Hancock*

Builder: Bethlehem Quincy (Fore River); date ordered: Aug 40; contract date: 9 Sep 40; keel laid: 26 Jan 43; launched: 24 Jan 44; commissioned: 15 Apr 44; decommissioned: 9 May 47; redesignated CVA-19: 1 Oct 52; SCB-27C: 17 Jul 51-1 Mar 54; recommissioned: 1 Mar 54; SCB-125: 24 Aug 55-15 Nov 56; decommissioned: 30 Jan 76; struck: 31 Jan 76; broken up.

World War II: Philippines, Iwo, Pacific raids 1944-45. Damaged by explosion 21 Jan 45 and by kamikaze 7 Apr 45.

Vietnam: Seven tours: Nov 64-May 65, Dec 65-Jul 66, Jan-Jul 67, Aug 68-Feb 69, Sep 69-Mar 70, Nov 70-May 71, and Feb-Sep 72. *Hancock* also participated in the evacuations of Phnom Penh (Operation Eagle Pull) and Saigon (Operation Frequent Wind) in Apr 75.

Remarks: Laid down as *Ticonderoga* and renamed 1 May 43. Known as

"Hannah," she was one of the last *Essex* class carriers to operate in the attack role.

CV-20 *Bennington*

Builder: New York Naval Shipyard; date ordered: Dec 41; contract date: 15 Dec 41; keel laid: 15 Dec 42; launched: 26 Feb 44; commissioned: 6 Aug 44; decommissioned: 8 Nov 46; redesignated CVA-20: 1 Oct 52; SCB-27A: 26 Oct 50-13 Nov 52; recommissioned: 13 Nov 52; SCB-125: 31 Jul 54-15 Apr 55; redesignated CVS-20: 30 Jun 59; FRAM II: FY 63; decommissioned: 15 Jan 70; struck: ?

World War II: Iwo, Pacific raids 1945. Damaged by typhoon 5 Jun 45.

Vietnam: Three tours as CVS: May-Sep 65, Dec 66-Apr 67, and Jun-Oct 68.

Remarks: On 27 Apr 53, during shakedown following SCB-27A modernization, a boiler exploded, killing 11 and seriously injuring four. Port catapult hydraulic accumulator burst on 26 May 54, killing 103 and injuring 201.

CV-21 *Boxer*

Builder: Newport News; date ordered: Dec 41; contract date: 15 Dec 41; keel laid: 13 Sep 43; launched: 14 Dec 44; commissioned: 16 Apr 45; redesignated CVA-21: 1 Oct 52; redesignated CVS-21: 1 Feb 56; redesignated LPH-4: 30 Jan 59; FRAM II: FY 63; decommissioned: 1 Dec 69; struck: 1 Dec 69; broken up.

Korea: Three tours: Sep-Nov 50, Mar-Oct 51, Mar-Sep 52, and Apr-Nov 53. Transported aircraft to Korea Jul 50. Damaged by fire and ammunition explosions 5 Aug 52 when fuel tank on a parked aircraft exploded.

Vietnam: As LPH-4 transported helicopter units to South Vietnam for Army First Cavalry Division (Air Mobile) in Sep 65 and for First Marine Air Wing in May 66.

Remarks: Known as "Busy Bee." Participated in Cuban missile crisis quarantine in 1962 and Dominican Republic crisis in 1965. Name continued by LHD-4 *Boxer* (*Wasp* class amphibious assault ship).

CV-31 *Bon Homme Richard*

Builder: New York Naval Shipyard; date ordered: Aug 42; contract date: 7 Aug 42; keel laid: 1 Feb 43; launched: 29 Apr 43; commissioned: 26 Nov 44; decommissioned: 9 Jan 47; redesignated CVA-31: 1 Oct 52; SCB-27C and SCB-125: 21 Jul 52-1 Nov 55; recommissioned: 1 Nov 55; decommissioned: 2 Jul 71; struck: ?

World War II: Raids on Japan 1945.

Korea: Two tours: May-Nov 51 and Jun-Dec 52.

Vietnam: Six tours: Sep-Oct 64, May-Oct 65, Feb-Jul 67, Feb-Sep 68, Apr-Oct 69, and May-Oct 70. (First "ace" carrier of Vietnam war.)

Remarks: Known as "Bonnie Dick."

CV-32 *Leyte*

Builder: Newport News; date ordered: Aug 42; contract date: 23 Mar 43; keel laid: 21 Feb 44; launched: 23 Aug 45; commissioned: 11 Apr 46; redesignated CVA-32: 1 Oct 52; redesignated CVS-32: 8 Aug 53; redesignated AVT-10: 15 May 59; decommissioned: 15 May 59; struck: 1 Jan 69; broken up.

Korea: One tour: Oct 50-Jan 51.

Remarks: Laid down as *Crown Point* and renamed 8 May 45. Known as "Leading Leyte." While undergoing conversion to CVS, explosion in port catapult machinery room on 15 Oct 53 killed 32 and injured several others. (CG-55 *Leyte Gulf,* a *Ticonderoga* class cruiser, also commemorates the Battle of Leyte Gulf.)

CV-33 *Kearsarge*

Builder: New York Naval Shipyard; date ordered: Aug 42; contract date: 7 Aug 42; keel laid: 1 Mar 44; launched: 5 May 45; commissioned: 2 Mar 46; decommissioned: 16 Jun 50; recommissioned: 1 Mar 52; redesignated CVA-33: 1 Oct 52; SCB-27A: 27 Jan 50-1 Mar 52; SCB-125: 27 Jan 56-31 Jan 57; redesignated CVS-33: 1 Oct 58; FRAM II: FY 62; decommissioned: 13 Feb 70; struck: 1 May 73; broken up.

Korea: Two tours: Sep 52-Feb 53 and Jul 53-Jan 54 (armistice patrol).

Vietnam: Four tours as CVS: Aug-Dec 64, Aug-Oct 66, Jan-Apr 68, and May-Aug 69.

Remarks: Known as "Mighty K." Prime recovery ship for Sigma 7 (Schirra) 3 Oct 62 and Faith 7 (Cooper) 16 May 63. Fire broke out in aviation store room upon arrival in Sasebo, Japan, 23 Dec 67, killing three. Name continued by LHD-3 *Kearsarge* (*Wasp* class amphibious assault ship).

CV-34 *Oriskany*

Builder: New York Naval Shipyard; date ordered: Aug 42; contract date: 7 Aug 42; keel laid: 1 May 44; launched: 13 Oct 45; construction suspended 22 Aug 46 when 85 percent complete, torn back to 60 percent for completion to SCB-27A; commissioned: 25 Sep 50; redesignated CVA-34: 1 Oct 52; SCB-125A: 8 Sep 57-29 May 59; redesignated CV-34: 30 Jun 75; decommissioned: 15 May 76; struck: ?

Korea: One tour: Oct 52-Apr 53. Loose bomb from returning F4U Corsair strike aircraft exploded 6 Mar 53, killing 2 and injuring 15.

Vietnam: Seven tours: May-Dec 65, Jun-Oct 66, Jul 67-Jan 68, May-Oct 69, Jun-Nov 70, Jun-Dec 71, and Jun 72-Mar 73. Damaged by fire 26 Oct 66. Collided with ammunition ship Nitro AE-23 on 28 Jun 72, suffering minor damage.

Remarks: Known as "Big O" and "O Boat." Played the fictitious carrier "Savo" in the film version of "The Bridges at Toko Ri" in 1953 and was featured in the film "Men of the Fighting Lady" in 1954. On 2 Mar 54, an F2H Banshee crashed into the fantail, but the pilot miraculously survived. *Oriskany* was brought up to full SCB-27C standard by SCB-125A.

CV-36 *Antietam*

Builder: Philadelphia Navy Yard; date ordered: Aug 42; contract date: 7 Aug 42; keel laid: 15 Mar 43; launched: 20 Aug 44; commissioned: 28 Jan 45; redesignated CVA-36: 1 Oct 52; redesignated CVS-36: 8 Aug 53; decommissioned: 8 May 63; struck: 1 May 73; broken up.

World War II: Present in Tokyo Bay Sep 45.

Korea: One tour: Oct 51-Mar 52.

Remarks: Featured in film "Task Force" in 1951. Converted to angled deck 8 Sep-19 Dec 52, but not included in other SCB modernizations. Name continued by CG-54 *Antietam* (*Ticonderoga* class cruiser).

CV-37 *Princeton*

Builder: Philadelphia Navy Yard; date ordered: Aug 42; contract date: 7

Aug 42; keel laid: 14 Sep 43; launched: 8 Jul 45; commissioned: 18 Nov 45; decommissioned: 21 Jun 49; recommissioned: 28 Aug 50; redesignated CVA-37: 1 Oct 52; redesignated CVS-37: 1 Jan 54; redesignated LPH-5: 2 Mar 59; FRAM II: FY 62; decommissioned: 30 Jan 70; struck: 30 Jan 70; broken up.

Korea: Three tours: Dec 50-Aug 51, Apr-Oct 52, and Feb-Sep 53.

Vietnam: As LPH-5 supported ground operations Oct 64-May 65, Mar-Aug 66, Jan-Jun 67 and May-Dec 68; delivered Marine advisors and helicopters to South Vietnam in Apr 62; flood relief operations Nov 64; transported Marine air group to South Vietnam Aug 65.

Remarks: Laid down as *Valley Forge* and renamed 21 Nov 44. As LPH-5, known as "Sweet P." Appeared in episode of "The Lieutenant" television series Feb 64. Prime recovery ship for Apollo 10 (Stafford, Cernan, Watts) 26 May 69. Name continued by CG-59 *Princeton* (*Ticonderoga* class cruiser).

CV-38 *Shangri-La*

Builder: Norfolk Navy Yard; date ordered: Aug 42; contract date: 7 Aug 42; keel laid: 15 Jan 43; launched: 24 Feb 44; commissioned: 15 Sep 44; decommissioned: 7 Nov 47; redesignated CVA-38: 1 Oct 52; SCB-27C and SCB-125: 17 Jul 51-1 Feb 55; recommissioned: 1 Feb 55; redesignated CVS-38: 30 Jun 59; decommissioned: 30 Jul 71; struck: ?

World War II: Pacific raids 1945.

Vietnam: One tour: Apr-Nov 70.

Remarks: Used for series of experiments with land-based aircraft, including P-51 Mustang, Nov 44. Known as "Tokyo Express" during final operations against Japan. Participated in "Operation Crossroads" atomic tests at Bikini in 1946. Later known as "Shang."

CV-39 *Lake Champlain*

Builder: Norfolk Navy Yard; date ordered: Aug 42; contract date: 7 Aug 42; keel laid: 15 Mar 43; launched: 2 Nov 44; commissioned: 3 Jun 45; decommissioned: 17 Feb 47; recommissioned: 19 Sep 52; redesignated CVA-39: 1 Oct 52; SCB-27A: 18 Aug 50-19 Sep 52; redesignated CVS-39: 21 Aug 57; decommissioned: 2 May 66; struck: 1 Dec 69; broken up.

Korea: One tour: Jun-Oct 53.

Remarks: Wholly constructed in drydock and launched by floating. Known as "Champ." Prime recovery ship for Freedom 7 (Shepard) 5 May 61, Gemini 5 (Cooper, Conrad) 29 Aug 65, and unmanned Gemini-Titan 19 Jan 66. Participated in Cuban missile crisis quarantine in 1962. *Lake Champlain* was the only SCB-27 ship that did not get the SCB-125 angled deck and hurricane bow. Name continued by CG-57 *Lake Champlain* (*Ticonderoga* class cruiser).

CV-40 *Tarawa*

Builder: Norfolk Navy Yard; date ordered: Aug 42; contract date: 7 Aug 42; keel laid: 5 Jan 44; launched: 12 May 45; commissioned: 8 Dec 45; decommissioned: 30 Jun 49; recommissioned: 3 Feb 51; redesignated CVA-40: 1 Oct 52; redesignated CVS-40: 10 Jan 55; decommissioned: 13 May 60; redesignated AVT-12: 1 May 61; struck: 1 Jan 67; broken up.

Remarks: Name continued by LHA-1 *Tarawa* (lead ship of a class of amphibious assault ships).

CV-45 *Valley Forge*

Builder: Philadelphia Navy Yard; date ordered: Jun 43; contract date: 14 Jun 43; keel laid: 7 Sep 44; launched: 18 Nov 45; commissioned: 3 Nov 46; redesignated CVA-45: 1 Oct 52; redesignated CVS-45: 12 Nov 53; redesignated LPH-8: 1 Jul 61; FRAM II: FY 64; decommissioned: 15 Jan 70; struck: 15 Jan 70; broken up.

Korea: Four tours: Jun-Nov 50, Dec 50-Mar 51, Dec 51-Jun 52, and Jan-Jun 53. On duty with Seventh Fleet Jun 50; only carrier to complete four deployments in Korean War.

Vietnam: As LPH-8 supported ground operations Aug-Oct 64, Nov 65-Mar 66, Nov 67-Jul 68, and Mar-Sep 69.

Remarks: Known as "Happy Valley." Flight deck damaged in collision with merchant ship during heavy weather 5 Jan 59; repaired in New York Naval Yard using parts from the *Franklin.*

Name continued by CG-50 *Valley Forge* (*Ticonderoga* class cruiser).

CV-47 *Philippine Sea*

Builder: Bethlehem Quincy (Fore River); date ordered: Jun 43; contract date: 14 Jun 43; keel laid: 19 Aug 44; launched: 5 Sep 45; commissioned: 11 May 46; redesignated CVA-47: 1 Oct 52; redesignated CVS-47: 15 Nov 55; decommissioned: 28 Dec 58; redesignated AVT-11: 15 May 59; struck: 1 Dec 69; broken up.

Korea: Three tours: Aug 50-May 51, Jan-Aug 52, and Dec 52-Jul 53.

Remarks: Laid down as *Wright* and renamed to honor the Battle of the Philippine Sea. Participated in "Operation High Jump" Antarctic expedition in 1947. Known as "Phil Sea." Name continued by CG-58 *Philippine Sea* (*Ticonderoga* class cruiser).

Arrival of Essex *at Quonset Point, RI, May 1960.*

The Yorktown *has been preserved as a memorial at the Patriots Point Naval and Maritime Museum in South Carolina. Other ships on display are the experimental nuclear powered ship* Savannah *and the destroyer* Laffey *DD-459. (Courtesy Patriots Point Naval and Maritime Museum)*

Yorktown *as CVS-10, June 1962.*

Intrepid *as a museum ship in New York.*

Hornet *underway for Hawaii prior to the Apollo 11 recovery mission, July 1969.*

Franklin *as she appeared in August 1944.*

Ticonderoga *underway from San Diego for a cruise to WestPac, January 1971.*

Randolph *firing a salute to Quebec as she enters harbor, June 1960.*

The Lexington *as she looked late in her career. Nearly all of the Naval Aviators now on active service received their first carrier qualification training aboard the Lex. (Courtesy* U.S.S. Lexington Museum on the Bay)

Bunker Hill *as she looked in March 1945.*

Wasp *as CVS-18.*

Hancock entering San Francisco by the Golden Gate.

Bennington as CVS-20, May 1963.

Boxer as LPH-4 at anchor, Vieques, Puerto Rico, December 1966.

Bon Homme Richard *during a captain's full dress inspection prior to entering Hong Kong, February 1959.*

Leyte *returning to San Diego from a Korean War tour, February 1951.*

Kearsarge *as CVS-33.*

Oriskany *in San Diego Bay passing Point Loma, May 1960.*

Antietam *in her final role as training carrier.*

Princeton *as LPH-5, October 1959.*

Shangri-La *heading for Roosevelt Roads, Puerto Rico, February 1970.*

Lake Champlain late in her career with new style markings on an old style flight deck.

Tarawa underway north of the Straits of Messina, Sicily, December 1952.

Valley Forge *as LPH-8.*

HSS-1 helicopters flying formation above the Philippine Sea, May 1957.

LT James Swope taxiing his F6F for take-off from the Hornet, *February 1945.*

Aircraft from the Boxer *flown by reservists in combat over Korea, August 1951. From top to bottom: an F4U from VF-884, an F9F from VF-721, and an AD-3 from VA-702.*

Cat officer giving the launch signal to an F8 aboard the Hancock, *December 1970.*

Aircraft Technical Data*

World War II

Grumman F6F Hellcat (F6F-5)

Power Plant: One 2,000 hp Pratt & Whitney R-2800-10W.

Dimensions: Span 42 ft 10 in; length 33 ft 7 in; height 13 ft 1 in; wing area 334 sq ft.

Weights: 9,238 lbs empty; 15,413 lbs gross.

Performance: Max speed 380 mph at 23,400 ft; cruising speed 168 mph; initial climb 2,980 ft/min; service ceiling 37,300 ft; range 945 miles.

Crew: Pilot.

Armament: Six .50 cal machine guns (or two 20mm cannon and four .50 cal).

Grumman TBF Avenger (TBF-1)

Power Plant: One 1,700 hp Wright R-2600-8.

Dimensions: Span 54 ft 2 in; length 40 ft; height 16 ft 5 in; wing area 490 sq ft.

Weights: 10,080 lbs empty; 15,905 lbs gross.

Performance: Max speed 271 mph at 12,000 ft; cruising speed 145 mph; initial climb 1,430 ft/min; service ceiling 22,400 ft; range 1,215 miles.

Crew: Pilot, gunner, radio operator.

Armament: One fixed forward firing .30 cal machine gun (two .50 cal in TBF-1C); one .50 cal in dorsal turret; one ventral .30 cal. Up to 1,600 lbs in bomb bay.

Douglas SBD Dauntless (SBD-5)

Power Plant: One 1,200 hp Wright R-1820-60.

Dimensions: Span 41 ft 6 in; length 33 ft; height 12 ft 11 in; wing area 325 sq ft.

Weights: 6,675 lbs empty; 10,855 lbs gross.

Performance: Max speed 254 mph at 15,800 ft; cruising speed 144 mph; initial climb 1,190 ft/min; service ceiling 24,300 ft; range 1,100 miles.

Crew: Pilot, gunner.

Armament: Two fixed forward firing .50 cal machine guns; two flexible .30 cal. Up to 1,600 lbs under fuselage and two 325 under wings.

Curtiss SB2C Helldiver (SB2C-4)
Power Plant: One 1,900 hp Wright R-2600-20.
Dimensions: Span 49 ft 9 in; length 36 ft 8 in; height 13 ft 2 in; wing area 422 sq ft.
Weights: 10,547 lbs empty; 16,616 lbs gross.
Performance: Max speed 295 mph at 16,700 ft; cruising speed 158 mph; initial climb 1,800 ft/min; service ceiling 29,100 ft; range 1,165 miles with 1,000-lb bomb load.
Crew: Pilot, gunner.
Armament: Two fixed forward firing 20mm cannon; two flexible .30 cal. Up to 1,000 lbs internal and 1,000 lbs external.

Vought F4U Corsair (F4U-1)
Power Plant: One 2,000 hp Pratt & Whitney R-2800-8.
Dimensions: Span 41 ft; length 33 ft 4 in; height 16 ft 1 in; wing area 314 sq ft.
Weights: 8,982 lbs empty; 14,000 lbs gross.
Performance: Max speed 417 mph at 19,900 ft; cruising speed 182 mph; initial climb 2,890 ft/min; service ceiling 36,900 ft; range 1,015 miles.
Crew: Pilot.
Armament: Six .50 cal machine guns.

Postwar and Korea

Grumman F9F Panther (F9F-5)
Power Plant: One 6,250 lbs thrust Pratt & Whitney J48-P-6A.
Dimensions: Span 38 ft; length 35 ft 10 in; height 12 ft 3 in; wing area 250 sq ft.
Weights: 10,147 lbs empty; 18,721 lbs gross.
Performance: Max speed 579 mph at 5,000 ft; cruising speed 481 mph; initial

climb 5,090 ft/min; service ceiling 42,800 ft; range 1,300 miles.
Crew: Pilot.
Armament: Four 20mm cannon.

McDonnell F2H Banshee (F2H-2)
Power Plant: Two 3,250 lbs thrust Westinghouse J34-WE-34.
Dimensions: Span 44 ft 10 in; length 40 ft 2 in; height 14 ft 6 in; wing area 294 sq ft.
Weights: 11,146 lbs empty; 22,312 lbs gross.
Performance: Max speed 532 mph at 10,000 ft; cruising speed 501 mph; initial climb 3,910 ft/min; service ceiling 44,800 ft; range 1,475 miles.
Crew: Pilot.
Armament: Four 20mm cannon; provision for two 500-lb bombs.

Douglas AD Skyraider (AD-2)
Power Plant: One 2,700 hp Wright R-3350-26W.
Dimensions: Span 50 ft; length 38 ft 2 in; height 15 ft 8 in; wing area 400 sq ft.
Weights: 10,546 lbs empty; 18,263 lbs gross.
Performance: Max speed 321 mph at 18,300 ft; cruising speed 198 mph; initial climb 2,800 ft/min; service ceiling 32,700 ft; range 915 miles.
Crew: Pilot.
Armament: Two 20mm cannon; up to 8,000 lbs externally.

North American AJ Savage (AJ-2)
Power Plant: Two 2,300 hp Pratt & Whitney R-2800-44W; one 4,600 lbs thrust Allison J-33-A-19.
Dimensions: Span 75 ft; length 64 ft; wing area 836 sq ft.
Weights: 30,776 lbs empty; 48,040 lbs gross.
Performance: Max speed 443 mph at

32,000 ft; cruising speed 270 mph; initial climb 930 ft/min; service ceiling 40,000 ft; range 1,714 miles.

Crew: Not available.

Armament: Up to 12,000 lbs internally.

Grumman AF Guardian (AF-2S)

Power Plant: One 2,400 hp Pratt & Whitney R-2800-48W.

Dimensions: Span 60 ft 8 in; length 43 ft 4 in; height 16 ft 2 in; wing area 560 sq ft.

Weights: 14,580 lbs empty; 25,500 lbs gross.

Performance: Max speed 317 mph at 16,000 ft; initial climb 1,850 ft/min; service ceiling 32,500 ft; range 1,500 miles.

Crew: Two (AF-2S) or four (AF-2W)

Armament: One 2,000-lb torpedo or two 1,600-lb depth charges internally (AF-2S only).

Post Korean War and Vietnam

Grumman F9F Cougar (F9F-8)

Power Plant: One 7,250 lbs thrust Pratt & Whitney J48-P-8A.

Dimensions: Span 34 ft 6 in; length 41 ft 9 in; height 12 ft 3 in; wing area 337 sq ft.

Weights: 11,866 lbs empty; 19,738 lbs gross.

Performance: Max speed 647 mph at sea level; initial climb 5,750 ft/min; service ceiling 42,800 ft; range 1,200 miles.

Crew: Pilot.

Armament: Four 20mm cannon; four AIM-9 Sidewinder AAMs or four 500-lb bombs.

North American FJ Fury (FJ-2)

Power Plant: One 6,000 lb thrust General Electric J47-GE-22.

Dimensions: Span 37 ft 1 in; length 37 ft 7 in; height 13 ft 7 in; wing area 288 sq ft.

Weights: 11,802 lbs empty; 18,790 lbs gross.

Performance: Max speed 676 mph at sea level; cruising speed 518 mph at 40,000 ft; initial climb 7,230 ft/min; service ceiling 41,700 ft; range 990 miles.

Crew: Pilot.

Armament: Four 20mm cannon.

Vought F7U Cutlass (F7U-3)

Power Plant: Two 4,600 lb Westinghouse J46-WE-8A.

Dimensions: Span 38 ft 8 in; length 44 ft 3 in; height 14 ft 8 in; wing area 496 sq ft.

Weights: 18,210 lbs empty; 31,642 lbs gross.

Performance: Max speed 680 mph at 10,000 ft; initial climb 13,000 ft/min; service ceiling 40,000 ft; range 660 miles.

Crew: Pilot.

Armament: Four 20mm cannon; four Sparrow I AAMs.

Grumman F11F Tiger (F11F-1)

Power Plant: One 7,450 lbs thrust Wright J65-W-18.

Dimensions: Span 31 ft 8 in; length 46 ft 11 in; height 13 ft 3 in; wing area 250 sq ft.

Weights: 13,428 lbs empty; 22,160 lbs gross.

Performance: Max speed 750 mph at sea level; cruising speed 577 mph at 38,000 ft; initial climb 5,130 ft/min; service ceiling 41,900 ft; range 1,270 miles.

Crew: Pilot.

Armament: Four 20mm cannon; four AIM-9 Sidewinder AAMs.

McDonnell F3H Demon (F3H-2)

Power Plant: One 9,700 lbs thrust Allison J71-A-2E.

Dimensions: Span 35 ft 4 in; length 58 ft 11 in; height 14 ft 7 in; wing area 519 sq ft.

Weights: 22,133 lbs empty; 33,900 lbs gross.

Performance: Max speed 647 mph at 30,000 ft; initial climb 12,795 ft/min; service ceiling 42,650 ft; range 1,370 miles.

Crew: Pilot.

Armament: Four 20mm cannon; bombs or rockets.

Douglas F4D Skyray (F4D-1)

Power Plant: One 9,700 lbs thrust Pratt & Whitney J57-P-2 (or J57-P-8B with afterburner).

Dimensions: Span 33 ft 6 in; length 45 ft 8 in; height 13 ft; wing area 557 sq ft.

Weights: 16,024 lbs empty; 25,000 lbs gross.

Performance: Max speed 695 mph at 36,000 ft; initial climb 18,000 ft/min; service ceiling 55,000 ft; range 1,200 miles.

Crew: Pilot.

Armament: Four 20mm cannon; up to 4,000 lbs of bombs or rockets.

Douglas A3D Skywarrior (A3D-2)

Power Plant: Two 12,400 lbs thrust Pratt & Whitney J57-P-10.

Dimensions: Span 72 ft 6 in; length 76 ft 4 in; height 22 ft 9.5 in; wing area 812 sq ft.

Weights: 39,409 lbs empty; 82,000 lbs gross.

Performance: Max speed 610 mph at 10,000 ft; service ceiling 41,000 ft; tactical radius 1,050 miles.

Crew: Three.

Armament: Two 20mm cannon in radar-controlled rear turret; up to 12,000 lbs of bombs or other ordnance.

Douglas A4D Skyhawk (A-4M)

Power Plant: One 11,200 lbs thrust Pratt & Whitney J52-P-408A.

Dimensions: Span 27 ft 6 in; length

(excluding refueling probe) 40 ft 4 in; height 15 ft; wing area 260 sq ft.

Weights: 10,465 lbs empty; 24,500 lbs gross.

Performance: Max speed 670 mph at sea level; initial climb 8,440 ft/min; tactical radius with 4,000 lb bomb load 340 miles.

Crew: Pilot.

Armament: Two 20mm cannon; up to 9,155 lbs of bombs or rockets on five hard points.

Grumman S2F Tracker (S-2E)

Power Plant: Two 1,525 hp Wright R-1820-82WA

Dimensions: Span 72 ft 7 in; length 43 ft 6 in; height 16 ft 8 in; wing area 499 sq ft.

Weights: 19,033 lbs empty; 26,867 lbs gross.

Performance: Max speed 253 mph at 5,000 ft; cruising speed 149 mph at 1,500 ft; initial climb 1,800 ft/min; service ceiling 22,000 ft; range 1,150 miles.

Crew: Two pilots, two radar operators.

Armament: Max weapon load 4,810 lbs (fuselage weapon bay for one depth bomb or two torpedoes, six underwing pylons for depth bombs, torpedoes or rockets; up to 32 sonobuoys in nacelles).

Grumman WF Tracer (E-1B)

Power Plant: Two 1,525 hp Wright R-1820-82WA

Dimensions: Span 72 ft 7 in; length 45 ft 4 in; height 16 ft 10 in; wing area 499 sq ft.

Weights: 20,638 lbs empty; 26,600 lbs gross.

Performance: Max speed 227 mph at 4,000 ft; cruising speed 163 mph at 10,000 ft; initial climb 1,120 ft/min; service ceiling 15,800 ft; range 1,000 miles at 10,000 ft.

Crew: Pilot, copilot/tactical director, two radar operators.

Vought F8U Crusader (F-8E)
Power Plant: One 10,700 lbs thrust (18,000 lbs with afterburner) Pratt & Whitney J57-P-20.
Dimensions: Span 35 ft 8 in; length 54 ft 3 in; height 15 ft 9 in; wing area 350 sq ft.
Weights: 17,836 lbs empty; 34,100 lbs gross.
Performance: Max speed 1,133 mph at 35,000 ft; initial climb 27,200 ft/min; service ceiling 52,350 ft; combat range 1,425 miles.
Crew: Pilot.
Armament: Four 20mm cannon; four Sidewinder AAM; up to 5,000 lbs of bombs or rockets under wings.

LTV A-7 Corsair II (A-7E)
Power Plant: One 14,250 lbs thrust Allison TF41-A-2.
Dimensions: Span 38 ft 9 in; length 46 ft 2 in; height 16 ft 1 in; wing area 375 sq ft.
Weights: 19,490 lbs empty; 42,000 lbs gross.
Performance: Max speed 693 mph at sea level, clean; max speed 565 mph at 12,000 ft with 8,000 lbs of bombs; max climb 12,640 ft/min; service ceiling 43,000 ft; combat radius 490 miles with typical load, max ferry range 2,300 miles.
Crew: Pilot.
Armament: One M61-A1 multibarrel 20mm cannon; two Sidewinder AAM; up to 10,000 lbs of bombs or rockets under wings.

Helicopters

Sikorsky HO3S (HO3S-1)
Power Plant: One Pratt & Whitney R-985-AN-5
Dimensions: Rotor diameter 49 ft; length 45 ft
Weights: 5,500 lbs gross
Performance: Max speed 103 mph
Crew: Four

Piasecki HUP Retriever (HUP-2)
Power Plant: One 550 hp Continental R-975-42
Dimensions: Rotor diameter 35 ft each; length 32 ft
Weights: 5,440 lbs gross
Performance: Max speed 105 mph
Crew: Four

Sikorsky SH-3 Sea King (SH-3H)
Power Plant: Two 1,500 shp General Electric T58-GE-10
Dimensions: Rotor diameter 62 ft; length 78 ft 8 in; height 16 ft 10 in; rotor disc area 3,019 sq ft.
Weights: 13,465 lbs empty; 18,897 lbs gross ASW mission; 21,000 lbs max takeoff
Performance: Max speed 166 mph at sea level; cruising speed 136 mph; initial climb 2,200 ft/min; service ceiling 14,700 ft; range 625 miles.
Crew: Two pilots and two system operators.

---

* Source: Swanborough, Gordon and Bowers, Peter M., "United States Navy Aircraft Since 1911"

Appendix D
Camouflage

The Navy's interest in ship camouflage dates back to World War I. In the 1930s, a number of tests at sea led to the first camouflage publication being issued to the fleet in 1937. In January 1941, BuShips issued new camouflage instructions calling for different systems or "measures" to be used for various ships operating under different conditions. These "measures" were revised in September 1941 and again in June 1942. The June 1942 instructions and later supplements remained in effect during the rest of World War II and were not officially revised until 1953, although the use of camouflage was discontinued after the war ended. The "dazzle" patterns so popular during much of the war were intended to confuse the enemy as to a ship's true course and speed and reflected concern for attack by submarines. Several different designs were drawn up for the *Essex* class carriers; some designs were on more than one ship, but others were unique to a particular ship. Later in the war, as kamikazes became a threat, solid color schemes designed to reduce observation from the air became more predominant. It was not unusual for a given ship to be painted in several different schemes over the course of the war and photographs can often be dated by changes in camouflage patterns.

The colors used on the *Essex* class carriers, from the lightest to the darkest, included Pale Gray (5-P), Light Gray (5-L), Haze Gray (5-H), Ocean Gray (5-O), and Navy Blue (5-N). These colors were made by adding various amounts of a dark blue-black tinting material (5-TM) to white paint (5-U) and all had a purplish-blue cast. Dull Black (BK) was also used in some camouflage patterns. Deck Blue (20-B), as its name implies, was only used on horizontal surfaces. For use on carrier flight decks a special "blue flight deck stain (No. 21)" was issued in 1942. The relative brightness of these colors is given by their reflectance: black has a reflectance of about 2% while pure white has a reflectance of about 85%. Measure 13, overall Haze Gray (5-H) with Deck Blue

(20-B) horizontal surfaces, was not used on the wartime *Essex* class carriers, but is still in use as the most effective camouflage measure under most operating conditions. The reflectances of the camouflage colors are given below:

Pale Gray (5-P)	55%
Light Gray (5-L)	35%
Haze Gray (5-H)	27%
Ocean Gray (5-O)	18%
Navy Blue (5-N)	9%
Deck Blue (20-B)	5%

Each camouflage pattern had an identifying number such as 33/10A, that included both the measure, which indicated the color range, and the design number. The letter following the design number indicated the type of vessel the design was prepared for: A for aircraft carrier, D for destroyer, C for cruiser, etc. Designs with the same number but different letters had no relation to each other. A design could be used for more than one measure and for different types of ships. The pattern used on the *Essex*, for example, was originally drawn up for a destroyer.

In all the camouflage measures used on aircraft carriers, horizontal surfaces were solid Deck Blue (20-B). The actual color of the blue flight deck stain varied because of weathering and other factors. A darker version of this stain, matching Deck Blue (20-B) came into use in 1944. In 1943 shipyards were issued a light gray for flight deck striping, while yellow was used in the Pacific. Both were later replaced with white dashed lines. Flight deck numerals were usually dark, either black or Deck Blue (20-B). Flight deck numerals were sometimes either outlined in a light color or paint-ed a solid light color, such as white or yellow. The standard marking for aircraft elevators was an "X" across the elevators. Individual ships occasionally deviated from the "standard" markings.

Camouflage Measures

Measure 12

Measure 12 was a "graded system" that provided moderately low visibility to aerial and surface observers in all types of weather. The measure used on *Essex* carriers in 1945 was a "new" version of the original three-color measure. All vertical surfaces, from the boot topping to a line parallel to the waterline at the level of the hangar deck, were painted Navy Blue or Navy Gray (5-N). (In 1945, with blue pigment in short supply, many ships were painted in Navy Gray (5-N), which had the same reflectance and designation as Navy Blue (5-N).) Above this band, the rest of the vertical surfaces were painted Ocean Gray (5-H).

Measure 21

Measure 21 was a "solid" measure; all vertical surfaces were painted Navy Blue (5-N). It offered the lowest visibility to aerial observers, day and night. Most early *Essex* carriers were completed in Measure 21 and many later carriers converted to it in 1945.

Measure 22

Measure 22 was another graded system intended for use in areas of predominantly bright weather and fair visibility. All vertical surfaces from the boot topping to the level of the hangar deck were Navy Blue (5-N) with the rest of the ship Haze Gray (5-H).

Measure 32

Measure 32 was a "medium pattern system" considered to be the best all-around antisubmarine measure. The colors used were supposed to resolve to a medium shade with a reflectance of 20-40%. To produce the greatest deception, bold contrast between the colors was considered necessary.

Measure 33

Measure 33 was a "light pattern system" similar to Measure 32, except that the overall reflectance was approximately 40-50%. The light colors used in this measure made it highly visible to high angle aircraft observation and it was discontinued in 1945.

Camouflage Designs

Design 3A

This design was an "open measure" that did not specify any colors, only the pattern shapes. It was carried by the *Intrepid, Hornet,* and *Hancock* and was also used on the *Franklin*'s port side.

Design 6A

Design 6A was another open pattern worn by the *Franklin* and the *Bunker Hill.*

Design 6/10D

This design was the only two color, Dull Black (BK) and Light Gray (5-L), pattern prepared for *Essex* class carriers and was used only on the *Essex* herself. The full designation was Measure 32/6-10D

Design 10A

This design was considered the most graceful of all the carrier camou-flage patterns and was carried on four carriers: the *Wasp, Yorktown, Ticonderoga,* and *Shangri-La.*

Design 17A

This design is unusual because it included two versions with the same design number. (The original was revised based on observations made in the Pacific.) The patterns in the two designs are similar in shape, but the colors used were considerably different. The original version, which called for six colors, was used on the *Randolph* and *Bennington.* The revised design was applied to the *Bennington, Bon Homme Richard,* and *Antietam.*

Individual Ship Camouflage

CV-9: As completed, the *Essex* carried Measure 21 up to the time of her only wartime refit at San Francisco in April 1944, when Measure 32/6-10D was applied. Standard blue stain was used on the flight deck and both numerals and dash lines were painted dull black. The elevators were outlined in yellow. She carried this measure until at least 25 November 1944 when she was hit by a kamikaze. She may have been repainted in Measure 21 while undergoing flight deck repair at Ulithi.

CV-10: Yorktown was commissioned in Measure 21 and sometime prior to May 1944 was repainted in Measure 33/10A, either at Pearl Harbor or Majuro. The design called for Navy Blue (5-N), Ocean Gray (5-O), and Light Gray (5-L), but Pale Gray (5-P) may have been used in place of the Light Gray. The *Yorktown* retained her camouflage pattern when she was refitted at Puget Sound in September 1944. Her deck markings were standard except for the position and length of the dash lines.

CV-11: The *Intrepid* was commissioned in Measure 21, but repainted in Measure 32/3A using Light Gray (5-L), Ocean Gray (5-O), and Dull Black (BK) while being refitted at Hunters Point in April 1944. She carried Measure 32/3A from June to December 1944, when she was redone in Measure 12. Her flight deck had dull black numerals with white dash lines. The numerals and elevators were outlined in yellow and several fake yellow "X"s were painted off the elevators in an attempt to confuse enemy pilots, which often used the vulnerable elevators as aiming points.

CV-12: The *Hornet* was the first fleet carrier to wear a "dazzle" pattern as commissioned in November 1943. She wore Measure 33/3A with Pale Gray (5-P), Haze Gray (5-H), and Navy Blue (5-N). *Hornet* was also one of the last to have her pattern painted out, when she was repainted in Measure 22 in July 1945. *Hornet's* flight deck had dull black numerals with yellow dashes and at least one photo shows her forward numeral reading from the bow. Later photos show her with both numerals reading from the stern, the standard practice. The thin dash line, normally centered on the ship's centerline, was offset to starboard to line up with the center of the forward elevator.

CV-13: The *Franklin* was commissioned in Measure 32/6A using Light Gray (5-L), Ocean Gray (5-O), and Dull Black (BK) in January 1944, but by the time she left for the Pacific three months later, her port side was repainted in a different pattern, Design 3A. She was the only carrier to carry two different camouflage patterns and during the period from May to November 1944, her camouflage was designated Measure 32/6A-3A. *Franklin* was repainted in Measure 21 in January 1945. *Franklin's* numerals were in dull black with yellow outlines. The dash lines were reported to be white with yellow elevator outlines and "X"s.

CV-14: The *Ticonderoga* was completed in Measure 33/10A with Light Gray (5-L), Ocean Gray (5-O), and Navy Blue (5-N). By the spring of 1945, she was redone in Measure 21 and her white dashes were changed to black.

CV-15: The *Randolph* was commissioned in the original version of Measure 32/17A in October 1944. This complex pattern used six colors: Pale Gray (5-P), Light Gray (5-L), Haze Gray (5-H), Ocean Gray (5-O), Navy Blue (5-N), and Dull Black (BK). Her flight deck was stained with the darker Deck Blue (20-B) stain, making her dull black numerals hard to see. These were repainted over in white, making her the first wartime carrier with white flight deck numerals. During her January 1945 refit at Hunters Point, she was repainted in Measure 21.

CV-16: The *Lexington* was the only *Essex* class carrier that never had a "dazzle" pattern. She went through the entire war in Measure 21 until her final wartime refit at Puget Sound early in 1945, when she was repainted in Measure 12. Because of her color, she was nicknamed "The Blue Ghost."

CV-17: The *Bunker Hill* was painted in Measure 32/6A using Light Gray (5-L), Ocean Gray (5-O), and Dull Black (BK) in January 1944, although she was probably commissioned in Measure 21. During her refit at Puget Sound in January 1945, she was again painted in Measure 21. Her flight deck numerals were outlined in yellow and her dash lines may also have been yellow.

CV-18: The *Wasp* was completed in November 1943 in Measure 21, but was repainted in Measure 33/10A using Pale Gray (5-P), Haze Gray (5-H), and Navy Blue (5-N) in March 1944 in Boston. During her refit at Puget Sound in June 1945, she was repainted in Measure 21. The *Wasp's* flight deck markings were standard except for her numerals. In June 1944, both read from the stern; in January 1945, both were outlined in yellow; in June 1945, the forward numeral was turned around to read from the bow and the outlines removed; and in November 1945, both numerals again read from the stern and the outlines returned.

CV-19: The *Hancock* was painted in Measure 32/3A using Light Gray (5-L), Ocean Gray (5-O), and Dull Black (BK) in April 1944. She was repainted in Measure 12 while refitting at Pearl Harbor from April to June 1945.

CV-20: As completed in August 1944, the *Bennington* wore the original version of Measure 32/17A. This complex pattern used six colors: Pale Gray (5-P), Light Gray (5-L), Haze Gray (5-H), Ocean Gray (5-O), Navy Blue (5-N), and Dull Black (BK). When this pattern was simplified (but with the same designation) she was repainted in the new design using Haze Gray (5-H), Ocean Gray (5-O), and Navy Blue (5-N) in December 1944. She was repainted in Measure 21 in July 1945. Her flight deck had black numerals and dash lines, but no centerline dash or elevator outlines.

CV-31: The *Bon Homme Richard* was completed in November 1944 with the revised Measure 32/17A using Haze Gray (5-H), Ocean Gray (5-O), and Navy Blue (5-N). She was repainted in Measure 12 in March 1945. Her flight deck markings were the standard black

numerals, white dash lines and yellow elevator outlines and "X"s.

CV-36: The *Antietam* was completed in January 1945 in the revised Measure 32/17A using Haze Gray (5-H), Ocean Gray (5-O), and Navy Blue (5-N). She was repainted in Measure 21 in May 1945. Her flight deck markings appear to have been the standard black numerals and white dash lines. The *Antietam* did not operate in combat, but was present in Tokyo Bay in September 1945.

CV-38: When completed in September 1944, the *Shangri-La* wore Measure 33/10A with Light Gray (5-L), Ocean Gray (5-O), and Navy Blue (5-N), but was repainted in Measure 21 early in 1945. Although specific information is hard to come by, the *Shangri-La* at some point, perhaps after the war, carried the letter "Z" on her flight deck instead of the usual numerals. This may be related to the assignment of code letters for air groups ordered by Admiral John S. McCain as Commander Task Force 38 late in July 1945. The letter assigned to *Shangri-La's* air group was "Z."

Note: The *Boxer* (CV-21), *Lake Champlain* (CV-39), and *Leyte* (CV-32) were commissioned before the end of the war but too late to serve in combat. The *Lake Champlain* was commissioned in June 1945 in Measure 21, which she continued to wear into 1946. The *Kearsarge* (CV-33), *Oriskany* (CV-34), *Princeton* (CV-37), *Tarawa* (CV-40), *Valley Forge* (CV-45), and *Philippine Sea* (CV-47) were all commissioned postwar.

Credit: Drawings reproduced by permission of Tom Walkowiak from United States Navy Camouflage of the WW2 Era - 2. Catalogue available from The Floating Drydock, c/o General Delivery, Kresgeville, PA 18333.

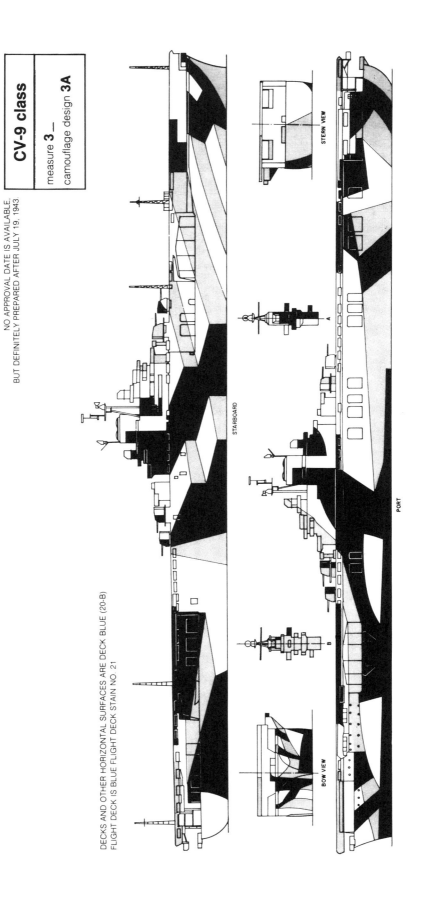

CV-9 class

measure **3** —
camouflage design **3A**

NO APPROVAL DATE IS AVAILABLE,
BUT DEFINITELY PREPARED AFTER JULY 19, 1943

DECKS AND OTHER HORIZONTAL SURFACES ARE DECK BLUE (20-B)
FLIGHT DECK IS BLUE FLIGHT DECK STAIN NO 21

STARBOARD

PORT

STERN VIEW

BOW VIEW

A

B

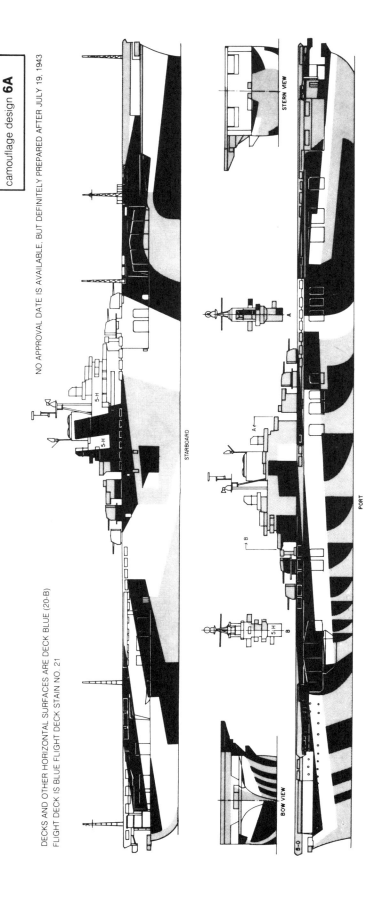

CV-9 class

measure **3** —
camouflage design **6A**

NO APPROVAL DATE IS AVAILABLE, BUT DEFINITELY PREPARED AFTER JULY 19. 1943

DECKS AND OTHER HORIZONTAL SURFACES ARE DECK BLUE (20-B)
FLIGHT DECK IS BLUE FLIGHT DECK STAIN NO. 21

STARBOARD

PORT

STERN VIEW

BOW VIEW

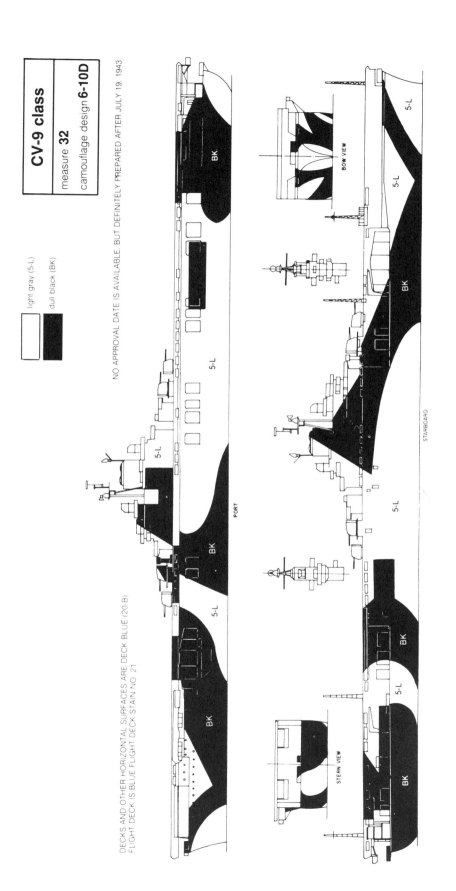

CV-9 class

measure **32**

camouflage design **6-10D**

light gray (5-L)

dull black (BK)

NO APPROVAL DATE IS AVAILABLE, BUT DEFINITELY PREPARED AFTER JULY 19, 1943

DECKS AND OTHER HORIZONTAL SURFACES ARE DECK BLUE (20-B).
FLIGHT DECK IS BLUE FLIGHT DECK STAIN NO 21

PORT

STARBOARD

BOW VIEW

STERN VIEW

BK

5-L

5-L

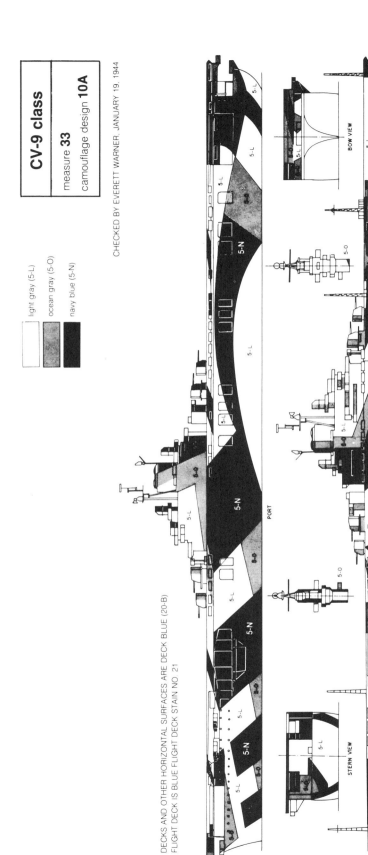

CV-9 class

measure **33**

camouflage design **10A**

CHECKED BY EVERETT WARNER, JANUARY 19, 1944

light gray (5-L)

ocean gray (5-O)

navy blue (5-N)

DECKS AND OTHER HORIZONTAL SURFACES ARE DECK BLUE (20-B)
FLIGHT DECK IS BLUE FLIGHT DECK STAIN NO. 21

PORT

STARBOARD

BOW VIEW

STERN VIEW

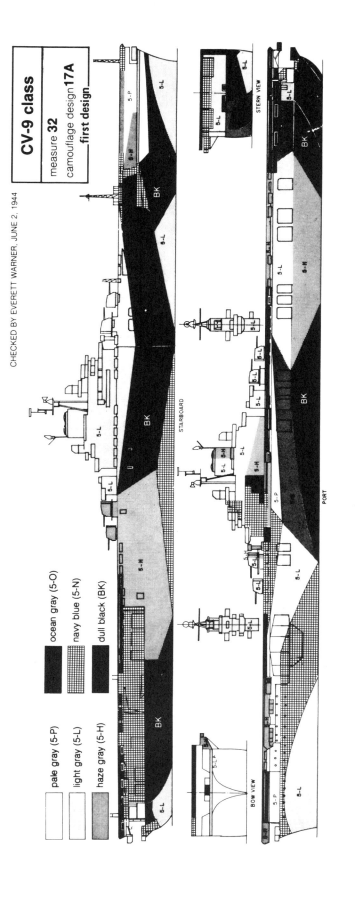

CHECKED BY EVERETT WARNER, JUNE 2, 1944

CV-9 class

measure **32**

camouflage design **17A**

first design

pale gray (5-P)

light gray (5-L)

haze gray (5-H)

ocean gray (5-O)

navy blue (5-N)

dull black (BK)

STARBOARD

PORT

STERN VIEW

BOW VIEW

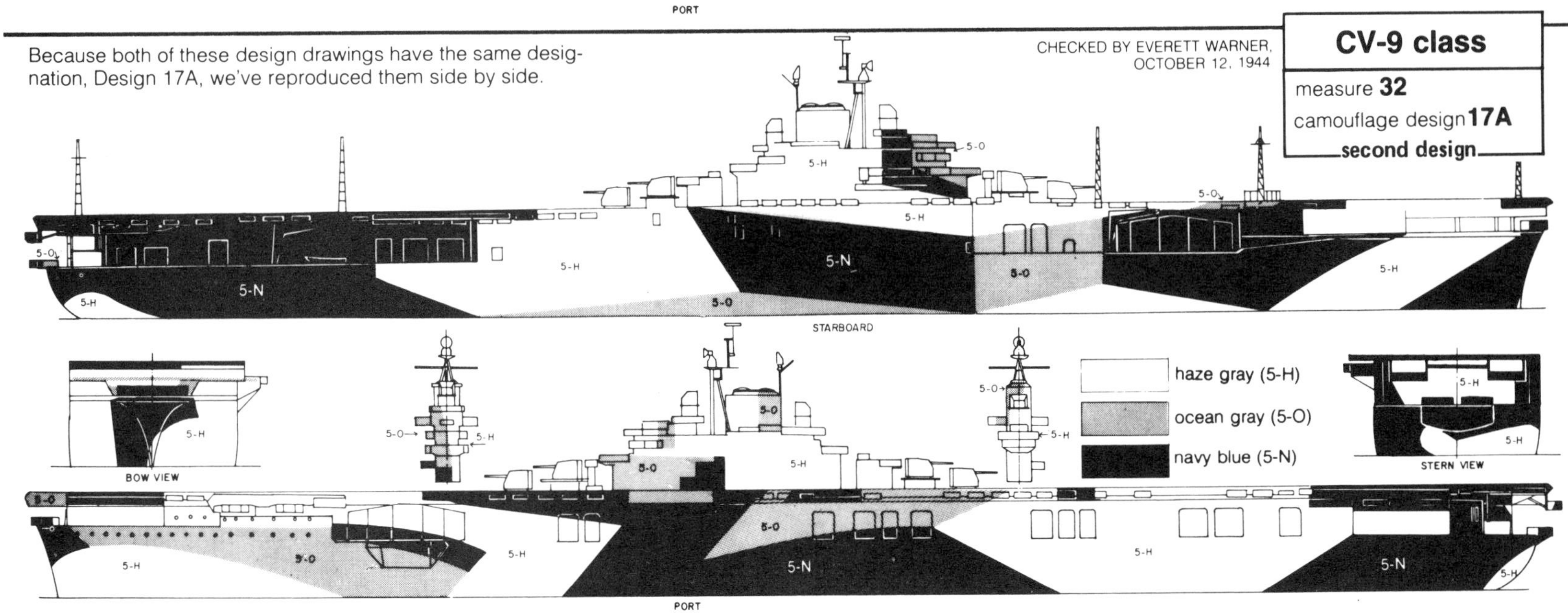

CV-9 class

measure **32**
camouflage design **17A**
second design

CHECKED BY EVERETT WARNER,
OCTOBER 12, 1944

Because both of these design drawings have the same designation, Design 17A, we've reproduced them side by side.

PORT
5-O
5-H
5-N
5-H
5-O
5-H
5-N
5-O
5-O
5-H
5-O
5-H
STARBOARD
BOW VIEW
5-H
5-O
5-H
5-O
5-H
5-O
5-H
5-O
5-H
5-N
5-O
5-H
5-N
5-H
5-O
5-H
STERN VIEW
5-H
5-H
haze gray (5-H)
ocean gray (5-O)
navy blue (5-N)
PORT

Notes

Introduction

1. *Lexington* was laid down on 8 January 1922 as a battle cruiser, CC-2. Launched on 3 October 1925, she was commissioned as an aircraft carrier, CV-2, on 14 December 1927. *Lexington* was sunk on 8 May 1942 at Coral Sea and stricken from the Navy List on 24 June 1942. *Saratoga* was laid down on 25 September 1920 as CC-3, launched on 7 April 1925, and commissioned on 16 November 1927 as CV-3. *Saratoga* survived the war only to be sunk on 25 July 1946 after being used as a target during the postwar Bikini atomic tests. She was stricken from the Navy List on 15 August 1946.

2. In 1927 Coolidge had urged the chairman of the House of Representatives committee on naval affairs, Representative Thomas S. Butler, to introduce legislation to bring the U.S. to parity with the British. Chairman Butler submitted a program for 71 new ships, including 5 carriers and 25 cruisers. This was cut back to 15 cruisers and one carrier, but was rejected by the Senate. The "cruiser bill" was re-introduced in 1928 and passed.

3. *Ranger* was ordered under the FY 30 program. Laid down on 26 September

1931, she was launched on 25 February 1933 and commissioned on 4 June 1934. Withdrawn from service on 18 October 1946, she was stricken from the Navy List on 29 October 1946 and scrapped in 1947.

4. The Kellogg-Briand Pact, also known as the Pact of Paris, was an agreement reached in 1928 by 15 nations (and eventually ratified by 62 nations) that renounced war as an instrument of national policy and called for the peaceful settlement of all conflicts. The pact had no means of enforcement, however, and ultimately proved meaningless. The treaty was named for its sponsors, the U.S. Secretary of State Frank Billings Kellogg and the French Foreign Minister Aristide Briand.

5. The London Naval Conference of 1930 was an outgrowth of the failed 1927 Geneva conference. It continued the capital ship building holiday until 1936 and tried to deal with the classes of ships, not originally covered, i.e., cruisers and submarines. It did, however, include an "escalator clause" which allowed any signatory to scuttle the limitations if attacked by a non-signatory or if one of the other signatories violated the limits.

6. The League of Nations Disarmament Conference of 1932-34 ended in failure. The treaties from the London Naval Conference of 1930 were to run until 1936. In December 1935, in accordance with the 1930 treaty, another naval conference met in London. Japan withdrew and the treaty, signed in March 1936, provided for little more than consultation. Although the United States and Great Britain adhered to the restrictions for a time, in 1938 they invoked the escape provisions in response to Japan's resumption of large scale warship construction.

7. Representative Carl Vinson of Georgia was appointed chairman of the House Naval Affairs Committee in 1931. He became one of the best supporters in Congress that the Navy ever had. Not everyone agreed with the build-up in naval strength. In 1934 the Nye Report, named after a committee chaired by Senator Gerald Nye, "proved" that the bankers and munitions makers, "merchants of death," had gotten America into World War I. Public sentiment against war and involvement in foreign "entanglements" ran high and Congress passed a series of neutrality acts in 1935, 1936, 1937, and 1939.

8. The *Yorktown* and *Enterprise* were ordered under the FY 33 program. Yorktown was laid down on 21 May 1934, launched on 4 April 1934, and commissioned as CV-5 on 30 September 1937. The *Yorktown* was sunk at Midway on 7 June 1942 and stricken from the Navy List on 2 October 1942. The *Enterprise* was laid down on 16 July 1934, launched on 3 October 1936, and commissioned as CV-6 on 12 May 1938. The *Enterprise* survived the war, having participated in nearly every major naval engagement and suffering damage on many occasions. She was withdrawn from service on 16 February 1947. Despite attempts to have her preserved as a memorial, she was stricken from the Navy List on 2 October 1956 and scrapped in 1958.

9. The *Wasp* was ordered under the FY 35 program. She was laid down on 1 April 1936, launched 4 April 1939, and commissioned as CV-7 on 25 April 1940. She was sunk on 15 September 1942 by Japanese submarine I-19 off Guadalcanal and stricken from the Navy List on 2 November 1942.

10. The *Hornet* was ordered under the FY 39 program. She was laid down on 25 September 1939, launched on 14 December 1940, and commissioned as CV-8 on 20 October 1941. The *Hornet* is best known as the carrier from which LTC Jimmy Doolittle launched the "Tokyo Raid" with sixteen Army B-25 bombers in April 1942. She was sunk on 26 October 1942 after having been crippled during the Battle of the Santa Cruz Islands. She was stricken from the Navy List on 13 January 1943.

11. The British also converted another light cruiser with a flying-off deck forward. Completed in 1918 as the *Vindictive,* she was reconverted to a cruiser after the war.

12. Of the other carriers built before the *Ark Royal,* only the *Furious* and *Argus* survived the war.

13. Although too small for fleet use, the *Hosho* was still in service in 1941 and survived the war.

14. Originally, the 40,000 ton battle cruiser hulls of the *Akagi* and *Amagi* were to be converted, but the *Amagi* was severely damaged by an earthquake in 1923 and the hull of the slightly smaller *Kaga* was substituted.

Chapter 1

1. Quoted from Pawlowski, Gareth L., *Flat-Tops and Fledglings: A History of American Aircraft Carriers*, pp. 80-81.

2. The Bureau system was established by Congress in 1842 to provide professional advice to the Secretary of the Navy for the administration of the Navy Department, each bureau chief reporting directly to the

Secretary. Except for an increase in the number of bureaus, no changes were made in this system until 1915, when the post of Chief of Naval Operations was established. The Bureau system was abolished in 1966.

3. The General Board was created in 1900 to make both war plans and recommendations to the Secretary of the Navy regarding the operations of the fleet. It was primarily an advisory body composed largely of senior officers in their final tour. The General Board was more powerful than the newer position of CNO well into the late 1930s.

4. Construction, Repair, and Engineering were merged to form the Bureau of Ships (BuShips) in 1940.

5. During World War II, Admiral King combined the offices of CNO and the Commander-in-Chief U.S. Fleet (CominCh) in his own person. He also created the position of Deputy Chief of Naval Operations for Air, Op-05 (DCNO (Air)) in 1943, which brought more operational influence into carrier design.

6. This contrasted with British doctrine, which called for all aircraft to be struck below to the hangar decks when under air attack.

7. Forward arresting gear on U.S. carriers was not removed until 1944.

8. The later *Midway* class carriers, which did incorporate an armored flight deck, were considerably larger at 45,000 tons.

9. By the time of the contract award in August 1940, 230,000 gallons of aviation fuel were specified.

10. This change was approved on 20 December 1940.

11. Quoted from Russell, James S. "Design for Combat" p. 96. The primary BuShips design officer was Commander Kniskern, who responded, "Well, okay, we can do this, but it's going to be difficult, and we won't be able to support properly, from the standpoint of the structure, those two

forward corners of the flight deck. If you get in very heavy weather, they'll fail." Russell came back with, "Well, until we get the ship into very heavy weather, we've had a proper flying field. How about it?" Kniskern agreed. Both the *Hornet* and *Bennington* were damaged during a typhoon in June 1945. The *Wasp* was damaged by another typhoon in August 1945 shortly after hostilities had ceased.

Chapter 2

1. The flight deck is at the O4 level in more modern carriers.

2. Reilly, John C., Jr., *United States Navy Destroyers of World War II*, p. 76.

3. The SK was developed from the earlier SC radar and was produced from January 1943. The *Essex* was the first ship in the Navy to be fitted with the SK radar.

4. The SC had a 15-foot by 4-foot 6-inch mattress antenna with an IFF antenna along the top. It had a range of up to 80 nautical miles. As ships were refitted in 1945, it was often replaced with the newer SR radar.

5. The SP radar was a lightweight replacement for the SM introduced early in 1945. It had an 8-foot dish antenna and had a maximum range of 80 nautical miles.

6. Naval guns are described by the diameter of the bore and the length of the barrel, stated in "calibers." A 5"/38 has a bore diameter of 5 inches and a barrel length (from breech to muzzle) of 38 calibers. The actual length of the barrel is found by multiplying the bore dimension by the number of calibers, or 190 inches in the case of the 5"/38.

7. The High Capacity projectile weighed 54 pounds.

8. The Mark 14 allowed a gunner to manually set the target range and then aim directly at the target, the necessary lead being computed by the sight itself. It was sometimes difficult to persuade gunners to trust the sight and not lead their targets by eye.

9. The Navy also experimented late in the war with Army type quad .50 caliber machine gun mounts. These took up the same deck area as a twin 20mm. Six were fitted to the *Lexington* and *Wasp* in the spring of 1945.

10. Although the masts were sometimes described as antennas, the actual antennas were the long wires strung between the masts.

11. On ships with arresting gear on the bow, there were an additional 13 cross deck pendants and 3 Davis barriers.

Chapter 3

1. Friedman, Norman, *U.S. Aircraft Carriers*, p. 134.

2. The *Independence* class light carriers included: *Independence* (CVL-22), *Princeton* (CVL-23), *Belleau Wood* (CVL-24), *Cowpens* (CVL-25), *Monterey* (CVL-26), *Langley* (CVL-27), *Cabot* (CVL-28), *Bataan* (CVL-29), and *San Jacinto* (CVL-30). *Langley* was named after the original CV-1 which had been converted to a seaplane tender, AV-3, in 1937 and sunk off Java in February 1942.

3. *Leyte* was originally named *Crown Point,* but was renamed in honor of the Battle of Leyte Gulf.

4. The *Philippine Sea* was laid down as the *Wright,* but was renamed to commemorate the Battle of the Philippine Sea.

5. The *Reprisal* was used as a hulk for explosive tests beginning in 1948 in Chesapeake Bay. She was sold in August 1949 and broken up.

6. The *Princeton* had originally been named *Valley Forge,* but was renamed in November 1944 to honor the original light carrier lost in the Battle of Leyte Gulf the month before.

Chapter 4

1. When the original Naval Aviation Cadet Act of 1935 was revised in 1939, the V-5 program, as the Naval Aviation Cadet program was called, was opened to third- and fourth-year college students who were allowed to complete their current school year before reporting to active duty. The V-5 program was eventually opened to high school seniors and graduates. The V-1 program was for first- and second-year collegians who might transfer to V-5 status at the end of their sophomore year or transfer to the V-7 program, permitting two more years of college with the ulti- mate goal of training as a deck officer. At the end of 1942, when President Roosevelt ended voluntary enlistment for men subject to the draft and the draft age was lowered to 18, the Navy combined the V-1 and V-7 programs and accepted 17-year- olds into the new V-12 college program. As apprentice seamen, they could be sent to college and have their way paid by the government until they transferred to the cadet program. There was also the "Tar- mac" program where enrollees were called to active duty and worked on the flight line until openings were available for further training.

2. The Navy Flight Preparatory School used colleges under contract to provide cadets with 15 weeks of ground training to prepare them more fully for the later training stages. The Civilian Pilot Training program, established in 1939 to train young pilots and support the nation's commercial flying schools, was absorbed by the armed forces as the War Training Service at the end of 1942.

3. Before 1941, operational training had been conducted in squadrons attached to the fleet. After the war began, the Operational Training Command was established at Jacksonville, Florida.

4. As the basic unit of naval aviation, the squadron exercised both operational and administrative control over its members.

5. Naval aircraft used a designation system which indicated both the role and the

manufacturer. In the example of the F6F-3 Hellcat, the first "F" indicated a fighter, the "6" and the second "F" the sixth fighter design by Grumman, and the "-3" the third modification of the basic design. Other role designations were "SB" for scout bombers, as in SDB and SB2C, and "TB" for torpedo bombers. Other manufacturer's designations included "D" for Douglas, "C" for Curtiss, "J" for North American, and "M" for the Eastern Aircraft Division of General Motors, which produced the Wildcat and Avenger during World War II.

6. Existing earlier air groups continued to be known by their names until reformed or disbanded. Only two, the Ranger Air Group and the Saratoga Air Group, were reformed; the rest were disbanded.

7. *Sangamon* class escort carrier air groups were CVEG and air groups for the large carriers (CVB) of the *Midway* class were CVBG. The small escort carriers were assigned composite squadrons, designated VC.

8. Oddly enough, the *Essex* class trial displacement calculations of November 1940 were based on Grumman F5F-1 fighters, Brewster SB2A-1 bombers, and Vought TBU-1 torpedo bombers. None of these aircraft entered operational service. Friedman, Norman, *U.S. Aircraft Carriers*, p. 138.

9. The Hellcat was originally ordered not only as a potential replacement for the Wildcat, but as a back-up for the Corsair, which experienced teething troubles during the early stages of its development.

10. Reynolds, Clark G., *The Carrier War*, p. 137

11. The Dauntless was the only aircraft to participate in all five engagements fought exclusively between carriers.

Chapter 5

1. In the 1920s, legislation was passed requiring that commanding officers of aircraft carriers be commanded by aviation quali-

fied officers. Many senior officers who could not qualify as pilots were given "Naval Aviation Observer" wings, others, like Ernie King and Bill Halsey, actually qualified as pilots. By the time the *Essex* class carriers were built, many early Naval Aviators were senior enough to command them.

2. Blackburn, Tom, *The Jolly Rogers*, p. 65.

3. Buchanan, A.R., *The Navy's Air War*, pp. 316-17.

4. The *Essex* preliminary design provided for a complement of 215 officers (98 ship, 22 flag, and 95 aviation) and 2,171 enlisted men (1,528 ship, 106 flag, 537 aviation), but even on her trials the *Essex* carried 226 officers and 2,880 enlisted men. Friedman, Norman, *U.S. Aircraft Carriers*, pp. 155-156.

5. Buell, Harold L., *Dauntless Helldivers*, p. 136.

6. Buell, Harold L., *Dauntless Helldivers*, p. 137.

7. The description of carrier flight operations was compiled from three primary sources: *Dauntless Helldivers* by Harold L. Buell, *The Jolly Rogers* by Tom Blackburn, and *Feet Wet* by Paul T. Gillcrist.

8. Blackburn, Tom, *The Jolly Rogers*, p. 73.

9. Buchanan, A.R., *The Navy's Air War*, pp. 20-25.

Chapter 6

1. The Japanese also lost a number of midget submarines, but these inflicted no losses on the American fleet.

2. The *Saratoga* had been torpedoed by a Japanese submarine in January 1942 while operating 500 miles southwest of Oahu. After limping into Pearl Harbor, she proceeded to Bremerton, Washington, where she was out of the war for five months.

3. An early 1942 decision by the Joint Chiefs of Staff divided the Pacific into the Southwest Pacific Area under MacArthur and the Pacific Ocean Areas under Nimitz.

4. A compromise was worked out in early July whereby the Navy would command the initial landings. As the American forces advanced up the Solomons chain, the transition to Army control could be made as advanced airfields became available.

5. Under the command of the battleship admiral Willis A. "Ching" Lee, *Princeton* and *Belleau Wood* participated in their own learning strikes against Baker Island on 1 September as part of Task Force 11.

6. Although SBDs continued in their scouting role, new fighters and torpedo bombers equipped with radar were being assigned to this function. SBDs last served in the scouting role during the Gilberts invasion.

7. Admiral Mineichi Koga succeeded Admiral Yamamoto, who was killed in April 1943 while on an inspection trip of the forward areas. Allied intelligence had cracked the Japanese communications codes and learned of the planned trip. Yamamoto's transport aircraft was ambushed over the northern Solomons by Army P-38 Lightning fighters from Guadalcanal.

8. When Rear Admiral Radford arrived in Hawaii with the repaired "Big E," the new air group was deficient in night training, so Captain Matt Gardner asked Rear Admiral Jack Towers, ComAirPac, for the veteran Air Group 6, commanded by Commander Butch O'Hare. When Rear Admiral Radford hoisted his flag as Commander, Task Group 50.2, he immediately formed a three-plane night fighter team led by O'Hare.

9. Rear Admiral Radford was sent back to Pearl Harbor, where he became Tower's chief of staff, with *Saratoga* and *Princeton*.

10. Oddly enough, Spruance ordered Rear Admiral Lee to attack the airfield with a surface bombardment. Air cover was provided by Task Group 50.8 under Rear Admiral Sherman with *Bunker Hill* and *Monterey*. The shelling was carried out 8 December 1943.

Chapter 7

1. In December 1942 Mitscher commanded Fleet Air in the Guadalcanal campaign, taking over command of all Allied air in the Solomons in April 1943. In August 1943, he took over Fleet Air West Coast until returning to the Pacific.

2. The battleships remained part of the screen on the 29th, but detached to begin shelling on the 30th. They were relieved by Vice Admiral Turner's amphibious forces, seven old battleships (OBBs) and eight CVEs under the command of Rear Admirals VanRagsdale and Davison, on 31 January.

3. As part of Operation Flintlock, the 4th Marine Division landed on Roi-Namur, in the northern part of the Kwajalein atoll, 31 January; Roi was secured on 1 February and Namur on 2 February. The Majuro atoll, southeast of Kwajalein, was to be used as a fleet anchorage and was occupied 31 January. The landings on Kwajalein Island were carried out by the 7th Infantry Division on 1 February and the island was secured on 5 February. Ebeye was taken next. Kwajalein atoll was secured by 7 February. The Japanese flew a long-range bomber strike against American forces on Roi-Namur 12 February. The attack was carried out by Saipan-based aircraft staged out of Ponape, in the eastern end of the Carolines. Seventh Air Force B-24s hit Ponape between 15 and 26 February to prevent any further attacks.

4. Task Group 58.4 hit Eniwetok 11 and 13 February and returned on 17 February with the escort carriers. The islets were taken 17-22 February and the carriers departed 28 February.

5. Mitscher later admitted that "All I knew about Truk was what I'd read in the National Geographic."

6. Pawlowski, Gareth L., *Flat-tops and Fledgelings*, p. 99.

7. In December 1943, following the Gilberts operations, Rear Admiral Radford became Chief of Staff to ComAirPac. He began to

formulate a nightfighter policy and issued a training syllabus to each carrier captain. Each *Essex* class carrier would form at least two "bat teams" of either one TBF and two Hellcats, or two TBFs and two Hellcats. Every task group would conduct experiments to figure out the best combinations and develop night doctrine. Using the ship's fighter directors and radars, the planes would maintain visual contact with each other to avoid shooting each other down, as had probably happened to Commander O'Hare. On 8 January 1944, each *Essex* class carrier was assigned a bat team of one TBF and two Hellcats. These teams were later strengthened by the arrival of four-plane night Corsair teams, although *Yorktown* and *Bunker Hill* got teams of four night Hellcats each.

8. Operation Catchpole, the Eniwetok landings, were carried out by the 22nd Marine Regiment who landed on Engebi, at the northern end of Eniwetok atoll, on 17 February; Engebi was secured the next day. The 106th Infantry Regiment (part of the 27th Infantry Division) landed on Eniwetok Island at the southern end of atoll, but the island was not secured until 21 February. Landings on Parry Island, north of Eniwetok Island, began on 22 February and the island was secured that day.

9. Mitscher had earlier been only the senior carrier division commander.

10. Buell, Harold L., *Dauntless Helldivers,* p. 217.

11. Buell, Harold L., *Dauntless Helldivers,* pp. 238-240.

12. Admiral Koga, who had replaced Yamamoto as Commander in Chief of the Combined Fleet in April 1943, was lost in April 1944 on an aircraft flight that never reached its destination in the Philippines, probably because of bad weather. Admiral Soemu Toyoda, Koga's replacement, was a much more aggressive commander.

13. Ozawa's aircraft included 145 Zero fighters (Zeke model 52), 80 Zero fighter-bombers (Zeke model 32), 99 Judy dive bombers (90 Judy model 33s and 9 Judy model 11s), 87 Jill torpedo bombers (33 Jill model 11s and 54 Jill model 12s), and 12 Kate torpedo bombers. He was also counting on the support of nearly five 500 land-based aircraft from Admiral Kurita's First Air Fleet. These aircraft, however, were dispersed by Kurita between Yap and the Palaus.

14. The *Puffer* sank two of the precious tankers. The *Harder* later added to the score by sinking three of the destroyers between 3 and 8 June. The Japanese submarines, on the other hand, did not play a significant part in the coming battle. Deployed along the "NA" line running northeast from Manus in the Admiralty Islands, they did not sink any American ships, but became victims of American antisubmarine hunter-killer groups, which sank 17 of them in the last days of May.

15. The Aslito airfield on Saipan was later renamed Isley Field in honor of Lieutenant Commander Isly, but the spelling was never corrected.

Chapter 8

1. Just after the *Taiho* launched her aircraft, she was struck by a torpedo from the submarine *Albacore,* but the damage was not immediately regarded as serious.

2. Task Group 58.1 was assigned the *Monterey* and *Cabot,* giving Clark six carriers in one formation, something that hadn't been done since the Wake strikes of the previous October.

3. The Tinian landings on 24 July did not need the fast carriers and close air support was provided by artillery and land-based air from Saipan. Organized resistance on Tinian ended on 1 August.

4. The new F4U-4 model Corsair would join Navy squadrons in October 1944.

5. In June 1944, Task Force 58 abandoned Majuro and Kwajalein for Eniwetok in the

western Marshalls, Manus in the Admiralties, and Saipan. Manus was abandoned by the carriers in October 1944 and Saipan in November 1944 in favor of Eniwetok and closer anchorages such as Ulithi.

Chapter 9

1. On 18 August, Vice Admiral McCain relieved Clark as commander of Task Group 58.1.
2. Within the dual command structure, the Fast Carrier Force Pacific became the First Fast Carrier Force Pacific under Mitscher and the Second Fast Carrier Force Pacific under McCain.
3. Nimitz did not cancel the 15 September Pelelieu landings because the forces were already at sea and he felt that a base in the Palaus was necessary to support the upcoming Leyte invasion. The casualties suffered in taking Pelelieu and nearby Anguar, however, far outweighed their limited usefulness in later Philippine operations. Organized resistance on Pelelieu did not end until the night of 24-25 November. Anguar was secured by 23 October. The fierce Japanese resistance was a prelude to later landings at Iwo Jima and Okinawa.
4. Servron 10 moved to Ulithi in October. While Servron 2 operated all repair, salvage, and hospital ships in the combat zone, Servron 8 supplied a ship pool of service vessels at Pearl Harbor and Servron 12 was building harbor facilities at Guam and Saipan.
5. The Visayan Islands form the central part of the Philippines and include Bohol, Cebu, Leyte, Masbate, Negros, Panay, Samar, Romblon, and their adjacent islets.
6. Pawlowski, Gareth L., *Flat-tops and Fledgelings*, p. 120.
7. Pawlowski, Gareth L., *Flat-tops and Fledgelings*, p. 83. Task Force 38 was west of the International Date Line, hence the reference to Columbus Day.

8. The designations "northern," "center," and "southern" were chosen by American historians. The actual Japanese organization for the Sho-I ("victory") plan was as follows: CinC Combined Fleet, Admiral Toyoda at Tokyo; the Advance Force (with 16 submarines) under Vice Admiral Miwa in the Inland Sea; Mobile Force under Vice Admiral Ozawa; and the Southwest Area Force under Vice Admiral Mikawa in Manila. The Southwest Area Force included the Fifth Base Air Force under Vice Admiral Teraoka in Manila, the Sixth Base Air Force and Second Air Fleet under Vice Admiral Fukudome on Formosa and the Ryukyus, and the Second Striking Force under Vice Admiral Shima in the Inland Sea. The Southwest Area Guard Force transport unit under Vice Admiral Sakonju was also under Vice Admiral Shima's Second Striking Force. Ozawa's Mobile Force was made up of the Main Body with the aircraft carriers, i.e., the "northern force" and the First Striking Force under Vice Admiral Kurita at Lingga Roads in Singapore. Kurita's First Striking Force included Force "A" under Kurita, i.e., the "center force" and Force "C" under Vice Admiral Nishimura, i.e., the van of the "southern force." Although Nishimura's and Shima's units both made up the "southern force" they never operated together tactically, having come from different directions to the Surigao Strait.

Chapter 10

1. The submarines *Darter* and *Dace* performed brilliantly, sinking two heavy cruisers and putting a third out of action, although *Darter* ran aground and had to be abandoned, her crew taken off by *Dace*.
2. The *Ise* and *Hyuga* were battleships whose aft superstructures had been removed and replaced with a short flight deck. During this battle neither ship carried aircraft; they had been included in the decoy force mainly because of their fourteen-inch guns.

3. McCampbell would eventually become the Navy's highest scoring ace, with 36 kills.
4. There were 16 escort carriers available, two had departed for Morotai the day before.
5. The text of the original message read: "Turkey trots to water. From CINCPAC. Where is, repeat, where is Task Force 34. The world wonders."
6. Unknown to Kurita, the American held airfields on Leyte were still operating on an emergency basis only.
7. The official histories of the Battle for Leyte Gulf list four separate actions: the strike on Kurita's center force in the Sibuyan Sea, the battle of the Surigao Strait, the battle off Samar between the center force and Sprague's escort carriers, and the battle off Cape Engano, which is sometimes called the Second Battle of the Philippine Sea. The primary sources for this chapter were Clark Reynolds's *The Fast Carriers*, pp. 253-278 and Samuel Eliot Morison's *The Two-Ocean War*, pp. 421-475.

Chapter 11

1. Reynolds, *Clark, The Carrier War*, p. 156.
2. Pawlowski, Gareth L., *Flat-tops and Fledgelings*, p. 121.
3. Rear Admiral Arthur Radford was on standby for a task group command, while Rear Admiral Clark cut his leave short to be available if needed.
4. Pawlowski, Gareth L., *Flat-tops and Fledgelings*, p. 83.
5. The *Lexington* returned to Ulithi for repair and sailed to rejoin the task force on 11 December.
6. The *Intrepid* departed Ulithi 2 December and stayed briefly at Pearl Harbor before proceeding to Hunters Point Naval Shipyard for seven weeks of repairs. The *Intrepid* returned to Hawaii in early March 1945, and arrived at Ulithi 13 March.

7. A second airfield was now in operation with P-38s and P-40s, but Kenney's fliers were kept busy repelling Japanese air attacks. The P-61 Black Widow night fighters proved to be too slow for the Japanese night raiders and a squadron of Marine night Hellcats had to be brought in from the new air base at Palau.
8. Pawlowski, Gareth L., *Flat-tops and Fledgelings*, p. 111.
9. During January 1945 only, air groups of 91 fighters and 15 torpedo bombers were used aboard the *Essex* and *Wasp*.
10. Rear Admiral Montgomery returned to Hawaii to command the training CarDiv 11. Another training unit at Pearl Harbor, CarDiv 12, was under Rear Admiral Ralph Jennings, recent skipper of the *Yorktown*.
11. The new Escort Carrier Force Pacific Fleet was commanded by Rear Admiral Cal Durgin, who came from the Mediterranean. Felix Stump was in tactical command of the escort carriers at Mindoro.
12. The day after Christmas, Montgomery got caught between a motor launch and the hull of an escort carrier that he was visiting and suffered several cracked ribs.
13. During the first month the Marines lost seven pilots and 13 aircraft to operational accidents.
14. The attack on neutral Portuguese port of Macao led to a Court of Inquiry and a formal apology to Portugal.
15. Altogether 143 were killed and 202 wounded, including her captain and executive officer.
16. The primary source for this chapter was Clark Reynolds's *The Fast Carriers*, pp. 278-300.

Chapter 12

1. Servron 6 was created as the general logistics support group in December 1944. Servron 10 fuel storage and service ships remained at Ulithi, but ship's stores and repair base facilities were later transferred

to the naval base being constructed at Leyte-Samar. Servron 6 and Servron 10 stopped using Saipan, Guam and Kossol Passage to concentrate at Ulithi. When the Leyte-Samar base was finished in April, the headquarters of the service force moved there, but the fast carriers continued to use Eniwetok, Guam and Ulithi until June.

2. Other new *Essex* class carriers in 1945 included: *Antietam*, commissioned in January, *Boxer* in April, and *Lake Champlain* in June. The *Kearsarge* and *Tarawa* were launched in May. The large carrier *Midway* was launched in March followed by the *Franklin D. Roosevelt* in April. With the war winding down, six more *Essex* class and two *Midway* class carriers were cancelled.

3. Rear Admiral Tommy Sprague, ComarDiv 3, had reported in "makee learn" training status and Rear Admiral Gerry Bogan, ComCarDiv 4, went home on a month's leave. Also, in January 1945, the Carrier Training Squadron Pacific was formed with Training CarDivs 11 and 12 commanded by Rear Admiral Ralph Jennings in the spring and Rear Admiral Freddy McMahon during the summer.

4. Because the Seventh Fleet was occupied in regaining the rest of the Philippines, the Central Pacific forces would provide cover for both the Iwo Jima and Okinawa landings. Iwo was to precede the landings on Okinawa because it was thought to be the easier of the two.

5. *Saratoga* limped back to Eniwetok and then proceeded to the West Coast for major repairs. She would be out of the war for good.

6. The crew member had worked for the Otis elevator company and used his experience to repair the arresting gear machinery.

7. Lieutenant Commander O'Callahan was presented with the Congressional Medal of Honor by President Harry S. Truman on 23 January 1946, the first military chaplain to be so honored. Since then only two other chaplains, one of them Navy, have been awarded the Medal of Honor. The destroyer escort DE-1051 was named in his honor.

8. Primary sources for the story of the *Franklin* include Pawlowski, Gareth L., *Flat-tops and Fledgelings*, pp. 119-126 and Wheeler, Keith, *The Road to Tokyo*, pp. 84-85.

9. Japanese records show 163 aircraft lost out of 193 aircraft launched, with an undetermined number destroyed on the ground.

10. The British hit Miyako Island on 26 and 27 March and withdrew to refuel the next day. The escort carriers covered the gap until Task Force 57 returned and the Sakishima strikes were resumed 31 March. Task Force 57 experienced its first kamikaze attack when one crashed the *Indefatigable* at the base of her island, but her armored flight deck allowed her to promptly resume flight operations. The British remained on station until 3 April, when Task Group 58.1 relieved them, after which they retired for replenishment.

11. The floating chrysanthemum was the emblem on the banner of Masahige Kusanoki, a great Japanese military hero who sacrificed his forces for the sake of his lord.

12. The commander of the gunfire force, Rear Admiral M.L. Deyo, made plans for a line of 6 battleships, 7 cruisers and 21 destroyers to form a barrier between the advancing Japanese and the American transports.

13. On 20 April the *Intrepid* entered Ulithi. Inspection revealed previously undetected damage to her elevators, requiring her to return to Hunters Point for repair. The shipyard workers began to regard the *Intrepid* as "their" carrier.

14. Reynolds, Clark, *The Carrier War*, p.170.

15. Wheeler, Keith, *The Road to Tokyo*, p. 166.

16. Few realized just how beat up Mitscher was; his medical officer, Captain Ray Hege, had been killed on the *Bunker Hill*.

17. Davison had been relieved because he missed an important airplane flight.

18. Rear Admiral Matt Gardner, without a night

carrier, detached ComCarDiv 7 on 7 April.

19. At the Court of Inquiry held on Guam on 15 June, the blame was placed firmly on Halsey and McCain. For morale reasons, Halsey was not relieved of command, but would not get his fifth star during the war.

20. On 20 June, Task Group 12.4 under Rear Admiral Ralph Jennings attacked by-passed Wake Island. *Lexington, Hancock* and *Cowpens* participated.

21. The primary source for this chapter was Clark Reynolds's *The Fast Carriers*, pp. 324-350.

Chapter 13

1. A similar, smaller, attack had been made unsuccessfully on Okinawa, but the planned target for this attack was actually the B-29 bases in the Marianas.

2. Near the end of the war a number of carriers en route to the Western Pacific conducted training strikes against bypassed Wake Island. The *Wasp* hit Wake on 18 July, followed by *Cabot* on 1 August and *Intrepid* five days later. The new *Boxer* departed San Diego for Hawaii on 1 August. The new *Antietam* departed Pearl Harbor 12 August and was to hit Wake on 16 August, but cancelled her strikes when word of the surrender was received.

3. Towers was to have relieved McCain on 14 August, but took his time in gathering an excellent staff.

4. Reynolds, Clark, *The Carrier War*, p. 170.

Chapter 14

1. Many of the troops from Europe were sent home by ships operated by the War Shipping Administration, which had planned to redeploy them from the European Theater to the Pacific. The end of the war in the Pacific caught many planners off guard and the Navy did not participate in the return of troops until after the Japanese surrender.

2. The *Franklin* was too badly damaged during the war and was never returned to active service. The *Leyte, Kearsarge, Oriskany, Princeton, Tarawa, Valley Forge,* and *Philippine Sea* were all commissioned postwar and did participate in Magic Carpet operations.

3. The *Lake Champlain*'s Atlantic crossing record stood until beaten in 1952 by the passenger liner *United States*.

4. Oddly enough, the British did not favor the Nene, but the Russians used it in their famous MiG-15 design.

5. Jet engines are rated in pounds of thrust instead of horsepower.

6. Another aircraft designed to the same specification was the Martin AM Mauler, which saw service in limited numbers.

7. As an interim measure, the Navy also modified the large twin-engine P2V Neptune long-range patrol bomber as an atomic bomb carrier. These aircraft nor-mally operated from the shore, but could be craned aboard the large *Midway* class carriers for launching.

8. The Ship Characteristics Board (SCB) was created within the office of the Chief of Naval Operations in 1945. The SCB tried to impose greater operational influence on ship design, but lacked the prestige enjoyed by the General Board. The position of Deputy Chief of Naval Operations (Air), created by King in 1943, became more influential in carrier design. Until 1945 ships were designed according to characteristics formulated by the General Board. The General Board was dissolved early in 1951. The last carrier design studies by the General Board were for the *Forrestal* class.

9. Friedman, Norman, *U.S. Aircraft Carriers*, pp. 289-291.

10. Admiral Sherman died in office in July 1951, a victim of overwork.

Chapter 15

1. At the outbreak of hostilities in Korea in June 1950 only four *Essex* class carriers were on active duty: *Valley Forge, Philippine Sea, Boxer,* and *Leyte.* They were immediately sent to Korea and were joined that fall by the recommissioned *Princeton,* and in 1951 by the *Bon Homme Richard* and *Antietam.* The last three served in much the same configuration as at the end of World War II. The seven unmodernized vessels were joined by three newly modernized carriers: *Essex, Kearsarge, Oriskany,* and *Lake Champlain* during 1951-1953, making a total of 11 that served in Korea. The other carriers operational at the beginning of the Korean War were the large carriers *Midway, Coral Sea,* and *Franklin D. Roosevelt,* the light carriers *Bataan, Cabot, Saipan,* and *Wright,* and the escort carriers *Mindoro, Palau, Badoeng Strait,* and *Sicily.*

2. The special mission aircraft included three F4U-5N night fighters, two F4U-5P photo aircraft, two AD-3N night attack aircraft, three AD-5W early warning aircraft and three AD-4Q and one AD-3Q radar countermeasures aircraft.

3. Formosa was the Japanese name for Taiwan after it was ceded to them in 1895. Even though it reverted to Chinese control in 1945, the old name continued in common use in the west.

4. The world's first jet-versus-jet combat had occurred the day before, 8 November 1950, when an Air Force F-80 shot down a MiG-15.

5. The *Princeton* was ordered activated on 25 July 1950 and recommissioned a month later, manned largely by reservists. The *Princeton* departed Pearl Harbor for Korea late in November.

6. Hudner was present when a new destroyer escort, the *Jesse L. Brown* DE-1089, was commissioned in 1973.

7. The *Bon Homme Richard* was recommissioned in mid-January 1951.

8. The belt was to run from 38 degrees 15 minutes north latitude to 39 degrees 15 minutes north.

9. Rashin was the Japanese name for the port; the Korean name for the city is "Wojin."

10. Hallion, Richard P., *The Naval Air War in Korea,* pp. 137-141.

11. The primary sources for this chapter were Richard P. Hallion's *The Naval Air War in Korea* and Norman Polmar's *Aircraft Carriers,* pp. 519-561.

Chapter 16

1. In 1962 the Navy changed its aircraft designations to conform to a joint system based on the one used by the Air Force. Aircraft still in operational service were redesignated in this system. Some of the more common ones were as follows: the AD, A3D, and A4D became the A-1, A-3 and A-4; the F8U became the F-8; the S2F became the S-2. Other aircraft were also redesignated, but since they were near the end of their service lives, the new designations were never widely known.

2. Early jets used high octane aviation gasoline (avgas), but later HEAF (high energy aircraft fuel) was developed, which is more like kerosene. The Air Force normally uses JP-4 (jet propellant-4) while the Navy uses JP-5 which is safer in a carrier environment. Avgas continued to be required until the last piston-engine aircraft retired from the fleet. Current propeller aircraft, such as the E-2 Hawkeye, are powered by turbo-prop engines, which operate on jet fuel.

3. A decision in favor of steam catapults had already been made in April 1952, after British tests.

4. The first five C-11 catapults were purchased from the British. One was used at the Naval Air Engineering Center in Philadelphia, the other four were installed in the *Hancock* and *Ticonderoga.* All subsequent C-11 catapults were built in the U.S. using higher steam pressures and longer runs. Gillcrist, Paul T., *Feet Wet,* p. 162.

5. Gillcrist, Paul T., *Feet Wet,* pp. 158-162.
6. These consisted of painting the landing stripes at an eight degree angle to the centerline. All but six of the cross deck pendants were removed, as were the barriers.
7. Gillcrist, Paul T., *Feet Wet,* pp. 156-158.
8. Gillcrist, Paul T., *Feet Wet,* pp. 162-164.
9. Pawlowski, Gareth L., *Flat-tops and Fledgelings,* pp. 291-292.
10. Pawlowski, Gareth L., *Flat-tops and Fledgelings,* pp. 116-177.
11. The Nationalists were supplied with the heat-seeking Sidewinder air-to-air missile, which marked its first use in combat against Chinese MiGs.

Chapter 17

1. With the fall of Dienbienphu in 1954, the French government was forced to seek peace with the Vietminh. The Geneva Agreements of 1954 partitioned Vietnam into North and South Vietnam with a Demilitarized Zone (DMZ) along the 17th parallel. The Communists, however, continued their guerrilla warfare in the south and began infiltrating neighboring Laos to aid the Pathet Lao forces seeking the overthrow of Prince Souvanna Phouma in Laos and Prince Norodom Sihanouk in Cambodia. In February 1961 the situation in Laos became critical, but a coalition government representing both royalist and Pathet Lao interests was formed which allowed a breathing space for a time.
2. South Vietnam had been under the repressive rule of Ngo Dinh Diem since 1954 and the country was ripe for increased activity by the Viet Cong (as the Communist guerrillas in the south were now known). Diem was killed in a coup on 1 November 1963, three weeks before President Kennedy was assassinated. Diem was replaced by General Duong Van Minh, who in turn was replaced by General Nguyen Khanh on 30 January 1964. To

counter calls from disgruntled Buddhists for a greater role in the government, Khanh called for more aggressive action against the Communists and wanted to invade North Vietnam. The contingency planning was intended to placate Khanh.
3. The *Maddox* was passing off the coast of Hon Me Island, 30 miles south of the North Vietnamese torpedo boat base at Loc Chao, which South Vietnamese commandoes had raided the night before.
4. The area of the attacks ranged from a small base at Quang Khe, 50 miles north of the DMZ, to the large base at Hon Gai in the north.
5. Lieutenant (j.g.) Everett Alvarez, flying an A-4 from the *Constellation,* was shot down during these strikes, becoming the first American POW of the war. He was released eight and a half years later in 1973.
6. The *Kearsarge* was to protect the task force from possible submarine activity by Communist China.
7. The South Vietnamese contingent, led by the air force commander, General Nguyen Kao Ky, in his personal A-1 Skyraider, did manage to hit a secondary target at Vinh.
8. The northeast monsoon is born with the surface winds which spread inland from the South China Sea from November through April. Warmer air meets cooler polar air coming down from China and Siberia, setting up a clockwise weather system that produces northeasterly surface winds reaching from the South China Sea to continental Asia. The mountainous terrain of North Vietnam contributes to this system of rain and clouds, known as the "Crachin" to the Vietnamese and sailors of the South China Sea. The mountains block other air masses and funnel cold air against warmer air from the sea, enlarging and strengthening the monsoon.
9. The reconnaissance aircraft suffered particularly from the restrictions imposed. Many aircraft and crews were lost because

the Communist defenses were looking for the photo aircraft they knew would follow the strike force.

10. Yankee Station was created originally for operations against North Vietnam. Dixie Station was created at the request of General Westmoreland, Commander of the U.S. Military Assistance Command, Vietnam, because he was impressed with the quality of Navy close air support to ground operations.

11. Because of restrictions against bombing villages, the Viet Cong parked their trucks in the open during the day where they could be clearly seen and therefore safe from air attack.

12. The first site was detected on 5 April 1965 by an RF-8A from the *Coral Sea.* A second site was found a month later. The first Navy losses were A-4s from the *Midway* in August.

13. The first MiG kills were by two F-4s from the *Midway* on 17 June 1965. The third was by an A-1 on 20 June 1965. The *Midway* also scored the last MiG kill of the war in 1973.

14. According to some reports the sailors were "playing catch" with the flares when the incident happened.

15. Navy fighters claimed five more MiGs in 1967, bringing the total for the year to 17.

16. The mining was done at night by A-6 Intruders flying off the big deck carriers. The river traffic was known as WBLC (Waterborne Logistic Craft, pronounced "wiblick"). The important ports of Haiphong, Hon Gai, and Cam Pha remained off limits to mining.

17. In May 1972 an unusual "kill" occurred when a MiG pilot ejected before two F-8s from the *Hancock* could get within firing range. Under Navy rules, no credit was given for downing the MiG.

18. The last operational attack squadron, VA-25 from the *Coral Sea,* was decommissioned in April. Special mission electronic

variants of the Spad continued to operate for another year.

19. The *Enterprise* was repaired at Pearl Harbor and left Hawaii in June, arriving on Yankee Station in October after stopovers in the Philippines and the Indian Ocean.

20. There were occasional MiG kills in the first months of 1972; a MiG-21 was shot down by an F-4 from the *Constellation* in January and a MiG-17 by an F-4 from the *Coral Sea* in March. The MiGs were not really active until May, when 16 were downed by the F-4s from the big deck carriers.

21. With the retirement of the *Essex* class ASW carriers, the big deck carriers began to receive specialized jet antisubmarine aircraft, the S-3 Vikings, and ASW variants of the H-3 Sea King helicopter. The CVAs were redesignated CVs as these changes were made.

22. The primary reference for this chapter was Peter B. Mersky and Norman Polmar's *The Naval Air War in Vietnam.*

Chapter 18

1. The *Lexington* was redesignated CVS-16 on 1 October 1962, but briefly resumed the role of attack carrier during the Cuban missile crisis. She was reclassified CVT-16 on 1 January 1969 and AVT-16 in 1978.

2. Older ships used asbestos as a fireproofing and insulating material. The cost of removing this material can be prohibitive.

3. The *Bon Homme Richard* is being scrapped at Terminal Island, California, in the Long Beach area, at the time of writing.

4. Also present were: Vice Admiral John Fetterman, Chief of Naval Education and Training; the Honorable Earl Hutto, Congressman from Panama City, Florida; Jerry L. Maygarden, Mayor of Pensacola; and Rear Admiral William R. McGowan, Chief of Naval Air Training. *Naval Aviation News,* January-February 1992, p. 15.

Bibliography

Sources

The information in this book was compiled from several sources. Norman Friedman's *U.S. Aircraft Carriers, An Illustrated Design History* provided most of the information about the *Essex* class design and technical characteristics. Clark G. Reynolds's *The Fast Carriers: The Forging of an Air Navy* was a very valuable source for the chapters dealing with World War II carrier operations. Other major sources for World War II included Norman Polmar's *Aircraft Carriers: A Graphic History of Carrier Aviation and Its Influence on World Events* and Samuel Eliot Morison's multi-volumed *History of United States Naval Operations in World War II*, along with his one volume summary *The Two Ocean War*. Polmar also provided information for the chapter on the Korean War along with Richard P. Hallion's *The Naval Air War in Korea*. *The Naval Air War in Vietnam* by Peter B. Mersky and Norman Polmar was the principle source for the Vietnam chapter. Information on individual ships came from Gareth Pawlowski's *Flat-Tops and Fledglings: A History of American Aircraft Carriers*, the *Dictionary of American Naval Fighting Ships*, and the files on individual ships located in the Ships History Branch of the Naval Historical Center.

Bibliography

Belote, James H. and William M. Belote, *Titans of the Sea*, New York, NY: Harper & Row, 1975.

Blackburn, Tom, *The Jolly Rogers*, New York, NY: Orion Books, 1989.

Brown, Eric M., CAPT, RN, *Duels in the Sky: World War II Naval Aircraft in Combat,* Annapolis, MD: Naval Institute Press, 1988.

Buchanan, A.R., LT, USNR, *The Navy's Air War, Aviation History* Unit OP-519B, DCNO (Air), New York, NY: Harper & Brothers.

Buell, Harold L., *Dauntless Helldivers*, New York, NY: Orion Books, 1991.

Dictionary of American Naval Fighting Ships, U.S. Government Printing Office, Washington, D.C.: Naval Historical Center, Department of the Navy.
   Volume I, Part A, Historical Sketches - Letter A, 1991.
   Volume I, Historical Sketches - A and B, 1961.
   Volume II, Historical Sketches - C through F, 1963.

Volume III, Historical Sketches - G through K, 1968.

Volume IV, Historical Sketches - L and M, 1969.

Volume V, Historical Sketches - N through Q, 1970.

Volume VI, Historical Sketches - R and S, 1976.

Volume VII, Historical Sketches - T through V, 1981.

Volume VIII, Historical Sketches - W through Z, 1981.

Friedman, Norman, *U.S. Aircraft Carriers, An Illustrated Design History,* Annapolis, MD: Naval Institute Press, 1983.

Gillcrist, Paul T., RADM USN (Ret.), *Feet Wet,* Novato, CA: Presidio Press, 1990.

Gow, Ian, *Okinawa 1945: Gateway to Japan,* Garden City, NY: Doubleday & Company Inc., 1985.

Hallion, Richard P., *The Naval Air War in Korea,* Baltimore, MD: The Nautical & Aviation Publishing Company, 1986.

Hammel, Eric, *Aces Against Japan, The American Aces Speak, Volume 1,* Novato, CA: Presidio Press, 1992.

Hines, E.G., *The Fighting Hannah: A War History of the* USS Hancock *(CV19),* Nashville, TN: The Battery Press, Inc., 1989.

Hoyt, Edwin P., *Closing the Circle,* New York, NY: Van Nostrand Reinhold Company, 1982.

___. *Storm Over the Gilberts, War in the Central Pacific: 1943,* New York, NY: Van Nostrand Reinhold Limited, 1978.

___. *The Battle of Leyte Gulf,* Chicago, IL: Playboy Press, 1972.

___. *To The Marianas, War in the Central Pacific: 1944,* New York, Cincinnati, Toronto, London, Melbourne: Van Nostrand Reinhold Company, 1980.

Humble, Richard, *United States Fleet Carriers of World War II,* Poole, Dorset, U.K.: Blandford Press, 1984.

Keegan, John, editor, *Who Was Who In World War II,* New York, NY: Thomas Y. Crowell Publishers, 1978.

Mason, John T., Jr., editor, *The Pacific War Remembered: An Oral History Collection,* Annapolis, MD: Naval Institute Press, 1986.

Moore, Carl J., RADM, "Command Decisions During the Battle of the Philippine Sea," pp. 209-215.

Strean, Bernard M., VADM, "A High Score and a Close Call," pp. 216-220.

Mayer, S.L., editor, *The Rise and Fall of Imperial Japan 1894-1945,* The Military Press, 1984.

Preston, Antony, "Chapter 4, The Imperial Japanese Navy," pp. 72-91.

Kirk, John Grayson, "Chapter 6, Japanese Air Power," pp. 118-147.

Koenig, William J., "Chapter 8, The Long Retreat," pp. 166-189.

Heiferman, Ronald, "Chapter 9, Kamikaze," pp. 190-211.

Mersky, Peter B. and Norman Polmar, *The Naval Air War in Vietnam,* Second Edition, Baltimore, MD: The Nautical & Aviation Publishing Company, 1986.

Miller, Nathan, *The Naval Air War 1939-1945,* Baltimore, MD: The Nautical & Aviation Publishing Company, 1980.

___. *The U.S. Navy, An Illustrated History,* New York, NY: American Heritage Publishing Co., Inc., 1977.

Morison, Samuel Eliot. *History of United States Naval Operations in World War II,* Boston, MA: Little, Brown and Company.

Volume VI, Breaking the Bismarks Barrier, 22 July 1942-1 May 1944, 1950.

Volume VII, Aleutians, Gilberts and Marshalls, June 1942-April 1944, 1951.

Volume VIII, New Guinea and the Marianas, March 1944-August 1944, 1953.

Volume XII, Leyte, June 1944-January 1945, 1958.

Volume XIII, The Liberation of the Philippines: Luzon, Mindanao, the Visayas 1944-45, 1959.

Volume XIV, Victory in the Pacific, 1945, 1960.

Volume XV, Supplement and General Index, 1962.

___. *The Two Ocean War,* Boston, Toronto: Little, Brown and Company, 1963.

Morris, James M., *History of the U.S. Navy,* New York, NY: Exeter Books (Simon & Shuster), 1984.

Pawlowski, Gareth L., *Flat-Tops and Fledglings, A History of American Aircraft Carriers,* Cranburg, NJ: A.S. Barnes and Co., Inc., 1971.

Phillips, Christopher., *Steichen at War,* New York, NY: Henry N. Adams, Inc., 1987.

Polmar, Norman, *Aircraft Carriers: A Graphic History of Carrier Aviation and Its Influence on World Events,* Garden City, New York: Doubleday & Company, Inc., 1969.

Raven, Alan, Essex-*Class Carriers*, Annapolis, MD: Naval Institute Press, 1988.

Reilly, John C., Jr., *United States Navy Destroyers of World War II*, Poole, Dorset: Blanford Press, 1983.

Reynolds, Clark G., *The Carrier War*, Alexandria, VA: Time-Life Books, Inc., 1982.

___. *Famous American Admirals*, New York, NY: Van Nostrand Reinhold Company, 1978.

___. *The Fast Carriers: The Forging of an Air Navy*, Huntington, NY: Robert E. Krieger Publishing Company, 1978 (original edition 1968).

Roberts, John, *The Aircraft Carrier* Intrepid, London: Conway Maritime Press, 1982.

Silverio, Stephen R., Cdr, "Farewell, Lady Lex," *Naval Aviation News*, Vol. 74, No. 2, January-February 1992, p. 15.

Silverstone, Paul H., *U.S. Warships of World War II*, Garden City, NY: Doubleday & Company, Inc., 1968.

Sowinski, Larry and Tom Walkowiak, *United States Navy Camouflage 1 of the World War II Era*, Philadelphia, PA: The Floating Drydock, 1976.

___. *United States Navy Camouflage of the WW2 Era, 2*, Phildelphia, PA: The Floating Drydock, 1977.

Steichen, Edward, *The Blue Ghost*, New York, NY: Harcourt, Brace and Company, 1947.

Steinberg, Raphael, *Island Fighting*, Alexandria, VA: Time-Life Books, Inc., 1978.

___. *Return to the Philippines*, Alexandria, VA: Time-Life Books, Inc., 1979.

Swanborough, Gordon and Peter M. Bowers, *United States Naval Aircraft Since 1911* (3rd ed.), Annapolis, MD: Naval Institute Press, 1990.

Terzibaschitsch, Stefan, *Aircraft Carriers of the U.S. Navy*, Annapolis, MD: Naval Institute Press, 1989.

United States Naval Aviation 1910-1990, U.S. Government Printing Office, Washington, D.C.: NAVAIR 00-80P-1, 1991.

Wheeler, Keith, *The Road to Tokyo*, Alexandria, VA: Time-Life Books, Inc., 1979.

Wooldridge, E.T., editor, *Carrier Warfare in the Pacific: An Oral History Collection*, Washington, DC: Smithsonian Institution Press, 1993.

　　Russell, James S., ADM, "Design for Combat," pp. 91-99.

　　Lee, Fitzhugh, VADM, "First Cruise of the *Essex*," pp. 106-114.

Picture Credits

Unless otherwise noted all photographs are Official United States Navy.

Acknowledgments

I wish to express my appreciation to the following individuals and organizations, who have given generously of their time and advice, for their assistance and encouragement in writing this book:

Dr. Dean Allard, Director of Naval History; Bob Cressman and Ray Mann of the Naval Historical Center (NHC); Ed Finian of the NHC Photographic Branch; Commander Steve Silverio, Director of the NHC Naval Aviation History and Publication Division; Lieutenant Commander Dick Burgess and the staff of Naval Aviation News; Charlie Cart of the Naval Sea Systems Command; Dr. Steve Ewing, Senior Curator of the Patriots Point Museum; Stasi Tsirkas, Director of Public Relations for the *Intrepid* Sea-Air-Space Museum; Tom Ewart, curator of the *Lexington* museum, and Dana Stephens of the Corpus Christi Area Convention & Visitors Bureau; Roy Bruce, who provided insights into the wartime experiences of the *Randolph*; the research staff of the National Archives Still Picture Branch; the librarians of the U.S. Army Materiel Command Technical Library and the Central Rappahannock Regional Library; my editor, Pam Gilbert; and the staff of The Nautical & Aviation Publishing Co. Finally, I would like to thank my wife Sherryl and my sons James, Chris, and Dave who have put up with me while I struggled with this book.

Glossary

AAA—Antiaircraft artillery.

ACI—Air Combat Intelligence officer

Air boss—Nickname for the air officer; head of the air department.

Air group—The complement of aircraft aboard a carrier. Attack carrier air groups became air wings.

Air wing—The complement of aircraft aboard an attack carrier. (Term used after 1962.)

Alpha strike—Term from the Vietnam war for a carrier strike on a pinpoint target simultaneously by multiple aircraft.

Angels—Fighter direction brevity code for altitude in thousands of feet, e.g. "angels twenty" is 20,000 feet.

ASW—Antisubmarine warfare.

Balanced formation—Three or more aircraft in formation with equal numbers on either side of the flight leader.

BARCAP—Barrier combat air patrol.

BDA—Bomb damage assessment.

Betty—Japanese Mitsubishi G4M long-range, land-based, twin-engine bomber frequently used as a torpedo bomber.

Bingo—Term to describe a flight from the carrier to a shore base, usually because of an emergency that prevents recovery aboard the carrier.

Black Shoes—Non-aviation Naval officers.

Bogey—Fighter direction brevity code for an unknown aircraft.

Bolter—A missed carrier arrested landing attempt.

Break—The position in the landing pattern directly over the point of intended touchdown where individual members of a formation break out of formation and turn to the downwind leg for separate landing approaches.

Brown Shoes—Naval aviation officers.

Bulkhead—Nautical term for a wall; also a vertical panel in an aircraft.

Buster—A fighter direction brevity code used during intercept telling the pilot to use full military power.

CAG—Commander of the air group. The commander of an air wing is still called CAG.

Caliber—In smaller weapons, caliber refers to the diameter or the bore in hundredths of an inch, i.e., a "fifty caliber" machine gun has a bore diameter of .50 inches. In larger naval weapons, caliber refers to the length of the barrel, i.e., a 5"/38 gun has a barrel length of 190 inches (the bore in inches times the calibers).

CAP—Combat air patrol.

CarDiv—Carrier Division. A Carrier Division was an administrative or "type" command, not an operational "task" command. During World War II, a CarDiv was commanded by a Rear Admiral, with three to four carriers assigned. CarDivs were renamed Carrier Groups ("CarGru") in 1973. One or two carriers belong to a group.

CarQual—Carrier qualifications; landings and takeoffs under controlled conditions to prepare for normal operations.

Chandelle—A steep climbing turn, usually started at high speed.

Charlie—Radio transmission meaning "return to the ship for recovery." (The signal flag for the letter "C" is flown when flight operations are being conducted.)

CIC—Combat Information Center

COD—Carrier onboard delivery. Fixed wing aircraft used to transport personnel and supplies to and from the carrier.

Displacement—The weight of a ship is equal to the weight of the water it displaces, hence the term used to indicate the size of a warship. Merchant ship "tonnage" refers to a ship's volume, from the ancient word "tun," a cask used to store cargo.

Dixie Station—The carrier operating area in the Gulf of Tonkin off South Vietnam. Carriers in Dixie Station provided close air support and interdiction in the south.

DMZ—Demilitarized zone.

Echelon—Two or more aircraft in a formation lined up with equal spacing in a line from the flight leader.

FDC—Fighter Direction Center

Feet wet—Fighter direction brevity code to indicate that the aircraft had left land and was now over water. (Feet dry indicated crossing the shore from the sea.)

"G"—Unit of force of gravity.

GP bombs—General purpose explosive bombs.

High-side run—A fighter attack pattern using a dive from the side.

Jill—Japanese Nakajima B6N Tenzan torpedo bomber.

Judy—Japanese Yokosuka D4Y Suisei dive bomber.

Kate—Japanese Nakajima B5N torpedo and level bomber.

Link trainer—Instrument training device with a simulated cockpit used to practice instrument flight procedures.

LSO—Landing Signals Officer

Mainmount—One of the main landing gear wheels on an aircraft.

Maru—Japanese term for "ship."

Overhead—A steep diving attack run from directly above a target; aboard ship, the ceiling.

Porpoise—Broach of a torpedo when dropped from an aircraft.

PriFly—Primary Flight Control; station located on the island from where the air boss controls flight operations.

Revetment—Horseshoe-shaped embankment around an aircraft parking spot for protection from horizontal blast.

Saddle position—Astern of another aircraft in position for attack.

Scramble—Launch aircraft as fast as possible.

Scuttlebutt—Rumor, gossip.

Slipstream—Turbulent air caused by an aircraft propeller.

Split-S—A violent half-roll to an inverted position, followed by a vertical dive.

Sponson—A projecting structure from a ship hull, often used to mount weapons.

Standard rate turn—A gentle turn of approximately 3 degrees per second.

Tojo—Japanese army Nakajima Ki-44 radial-engine fighter.

Tony—Japanese army Kawasaki Ki-61 in-line engine fighter.

Torpecker—Slang term for torpedo plane.

Unrep—Underway replenishment. Refueling and resupply at sea where the receiving ship steams alongside the supply ship. During most of World War II, only refueling underway from oilers was possible, but by 1945, ammunition and other stores were being transferred.

Val—Japanese Aichi D3A dive bomber.

Vertrep—Vertical replenishment. The development of the helicopter allowed another means of transferring supplies from one ship to another at sea. Vertreps are usually accomplished during an unrep.

Vultures Row—Area of the carrier's island where those not on watch can observe flight operations.

Wave-off—Direction to discontinue a landing approach and go around.

Yankee Station—A station off the coast of North Vietnam for carriers striking the north.

Zeke—Japanese Mitsubishi A6M Zero fighter.

Zoom—A steep climb started from high speed for maximum altitude gain.

Index

ACI (Air Combat Intelligence) officers, 38
Aircraft, American:
 Beech SNB, 33
 Boeing B-29 Superfortress, 64, 78, 95, 98, 102,
  120, 123, 125-8
 Boeing B-52 Stratofortress, 150-1
 Consolidated B-24 Liberator, 62, 109
 Consolidated B-36 Peacemaker, 118
 Consolidated PBY Catalina, 33, 84-5
 Curtiss SB2C Helldiver, 34, 35-36, 51-2, 64,
  71, 73, 103, 114
 Douglas AD (A-1) Skyraider, 114, 119-20,
  122-3, 125-7, 129-30, 132, 142, 145
 Douglas A3D (A-3) Skywarrior, 132
 Douglas A4D (A-4) Skyhawk, 132, 137, 139,
  142, 145-7, 149-50, 153
 Douglas F3D Skyknight, 113
 Douglas F4D Skyray, 132
 Douglas R4D (C-47) Skytrain, 113
 Douglas SBD Dauntless, 34-5, 49, 71, 73, 95
 General Dynamics F-111, 151
 Grumman A-6 Intruder, 147, 150-1, 153
 Grumman AF Guardian, 114, 132
 Grumman E-2 Hawkeye, 153
 Grumman F4F Wildcat, 34, 81, 155
 Grumman F6F Hellcat, 34-5, 49-51, 54, 58, 64,
  69-71, 73, 81, 83, 87, 91, 110, 114, 128
 Grumman F7F Tigercat, 114

The following abbreviations are used in
the index:

Naval ranks:
 FADM, Fleet Admiral
 ADM, Admiral
 VADM, Vice Admiral
 RADM, Rear Admiral
 COMO, Commodore
 CAPT, Captain
 CDR, Commander
 LCDR, Lieutenant Commander
 LT, Lieutenant
 LTJG, Lieutenant Junior Grade
 ENS, Ensign

Other abbreviations:
 USAAF, United States Army Air Forces
 USA, United States Army
 IJN, Imperial Japanese Navy
 RN, Royal Navy

Geographic references: for islands and
atolls of the Pacific, the island group
follows in parentheses, e.g., Saipan
(Marianas) indicates that Saipan is in the
Marianas Islands.

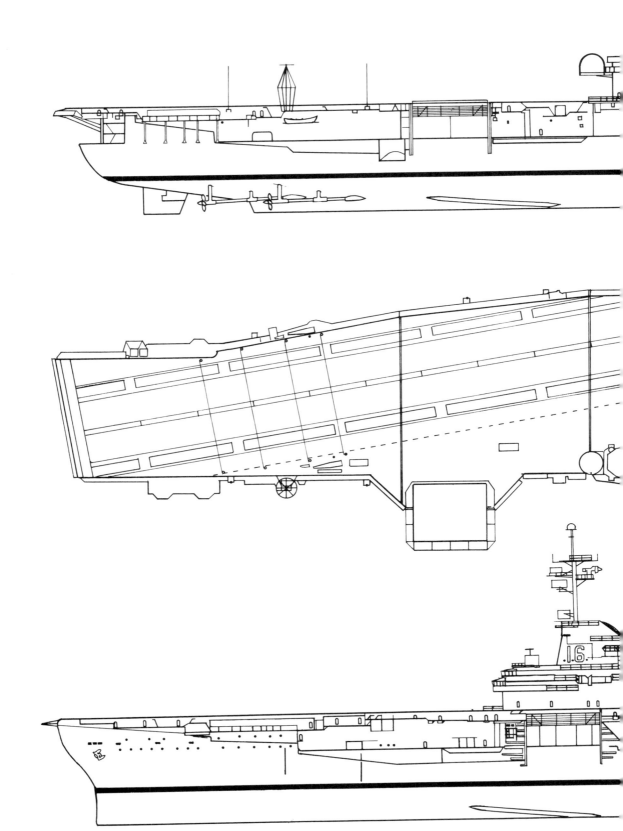